ANCHOR YOUR VISION

NAVIGATIONAL TOOLS AND **STRATEGIES** FOR EVERY STAGE IN A **PLC AT WORK®**

SHAWN **CRESWELL**   EMILY **MCCLAIN**   KATY SUE **TRAICOFF**

Solution Tree | Press

Copyright © 2025 by Solution Tree Press

Materials appearing here are copyrighted. With one exception, all rights are reserved. Readers may reproduce only those pages marked "Reproducible." Otherwise, no part of this book may be reproduced or transmitted in any form or by any means (electronic, photocopying, recording, or otherwise) without prior written permission of the publisher.

555 North Morton Street
Bloomington, IN 47404
800.733.6786 (toll free) / 812.336.7700
FAX: 812.336.7790

email: info@SolutionTree.com
SolutionTree.com

Visit **go.SolutionTree.com/PLCbooks/AYV** to download the free reproducibles in this book. To access the exclusive reproducibles in this book, enter the unique access code found on the inside front cover.

Printed in the United States of America

Library of Congress Cataloging-in-Publication Data

Names: Creswell, Shawn, author. | McClain, Emily (Teacher), author. | Traicoff, Katy Sue, author.

Title: Anchor your vision : navigational tools and strategies for every stage in a PLC at Work® / Shawn Creswell, Emily McClain, Katy Sue Traicoff.

Description: Bloomington, IN : Solution Tree Press, 2025. | Includes bibliographical references and index.

Identifiers: LCCN 2024027090 (print) | LCCN 2024027091 (ebook) | ISBN 9781960574688 (paperback) | ISBN 9781960574695 (ebook)

Subjects: LCSH: Professional learning communities. | Teachers--Professional relationships. | Educational leadership.

Classification: LCC LB1731 .C6948 2024 (print) | LCC LB1731 (ebook) | DDC 371.1--dc23/eng/20240702

LC record available at https://lccn.loc.gov/2024027090

LC ebook record available at https://lccn.loc.gov/2024027091

Solution Tree
Jeffrey C. Jones, CEO
Edmund M. Ackerman, President

Solution Tree Press
President and Publisher: Douglas M. Rife
Associate Publishers: Todd Brakke and Kendra Slayton
Editorial Director: Laurel Hecker
Art Director: Rian Anderson
Copy Chief: Jessi Finn
Production Editor: Kate St. Ives
Text and Cover Designer: Kelsey Hoover
Acquisitions Editors: Carol Collins and Hilary Goff
Assistant Acquisitions Editor: Elijah Oates
Content Development Specialist: Amy Rubenstein
Associate Editor: Sarah Ludwig
Editorial Assistant: Anne Marie Watkins

In loving memory of my parents, Richard and Hedy, who anchored me in faith and instilled in me the importance of making a positive difference in the world.

—Shawn

To my family, you are both the reason I do what I do and the reason I can do it! Thank you for your inspiration, continual encouragement, and support.

—Emily

To my beloved family for whom I am profoundly grateful. Dave, your unwavering love and encouragement have been my guiding light, and you make me feel like anything is attainable. Taylor, Thomas, and Bailey, you are my everything. Your love and support inspire me to do my best and keeps me anchored in what truly matters. I pray this book inspires you to live your life filled with purpose toward a vision that brings you joy.

—Katy Sue

To the memory of the visionary leader, Dr. Rick DuFour, for positively impacting our educational journey and life's work while illuminating the path to ensuring learning for all.

—Shawn, Emily, and Katy Sue

ACKNOWLEDGMENTS

I would like to thank the educational superstars who paved my path to becoming an author. I am forever grateful to each of them for their impact on my life. First, Linda Ross, for believing in me, placing me in leadership roles and encouraging me to become a principal. Paula Klapesky, for hiring me in my first administrator role, you taught me so much while being my cheerleader every step of the way. Debbie Phillips, the most amazing assistant superintendent who has been a transformational leader, mentor, and friend. My best friend and rock star superintendent, Lori Motsch, who inspires me every single day! To my co-authors and incredible friends, Emily McClain and Katy Sue Traicoff, who have always supported my ideas, influenced my thinking, and are the first people to say, yes we can, to creating incredible schools dedicated to ensuring learning for all. I continue to be blessed to collaborate and work with so many spectacular educators along my journey. Thank you for your commitment and dedication to all students and our profession. Finally, this book would not have been possible without the ongoing love and support from my husband Steve and children Billy, Sarah, Grace, and Jack, our daughter-in-law Morgan, and the most precious grandchildren, Tory and Wesley. You all are my everything.

—Shawn Creswell

Both the journey that led to this book and the book itself would not have been possible without the love and support of so many people in my life. I want to acknowledge all the amazing educators I've been blessed to collaborate with over the years. I am continually inspired by your relentless pursuit of high levels of learning for all—both students and the staff who teach them. I also want to express my thankfulness and gratitude to my co-authors, Shawn Creswell and Katy Sue Traicoff. Shawn, you awe and amaze me. Thank you for being my mentor, cheerleader, and dear friend. You dream big, and help me (and occasionally push me) to dream big too. None of this would be possible without you. Katy Sue, you inspire and encourage me. I am so thankful for your friendship and for the generous way you share your wisdom and give your support. I wouldn't have been able to do this without you. Last, but most important, I am overwhelmed with thankfulness for my family—my mom, Charlotte Hawkins; my husband, Gordon; and our amazing kiddos, Grace and Ella. Thank you for believing in me, listening to me, and encouraging me, as well as for the patience you showed and sacrifices you made so that I could live out my love of learning and share that love with others. You are my greatest blessings. I love you all with all my heart.

—Emily McClain

I am incredibly thankful to the many educators I have been honored and blessed to work with and learn alongside throughout my career. I am grateful to my collaborative teammates with whom I journeyed to become a Model PLC campus. A special thank you to my co-author, Shawn Creswell, for encouraging me to grow outside my comfort zone and beyond my own vision for myself. You have a special way of inspiring me to believe I can do great things—and then taking the time and effort to help me achieve those great things! To Emily McClain, thank you for your support and camaraderie as we took on new work and adventures. Many thanks to my incredible parents who always modeled the value of being a lifelong learner. You set the stage for our family to never stop exploring, learning, and growing. To my siblings, for whom I have always had the utmost respect for all you each have accomplished. I am thankful for your friendship and support throughout this process. Most important, to my incredible family for helping make this book possible due to your patience, love, and support. I am beyond blessed.

—Katy Sue Traicoff

Together we, Shawn, Emily, and Katy Sue, would like to thank the numerous people who made this book possible. First and foremost, to Jeff Jones, who created a company dedicated to transforming education worldwide, and our dear friend, Douglas Rife, who said, "Everyone has a story inside them that needs to be shared"—thank you both for believing in us. We also thank our acquisitions editor, Hilary Goff, who was our very first support and editor in this process; Amy Rubenstein, our incredible content editor, who made our book come to life with her thoughts and ideas; and Kate St. Ives, our production editor, who refined our writing to ensure every word was filled with intention and clarity for our readers. We are so grateful to every person at Solution Tree Press who enhanced our work. In addition, we would like to thank the hundreds of positive educators we have worked with both in schools and throughout the United States. This book is for you.

Solution Tree Press would like to thank the following reviewers:

Gina Cherkowski
Education Researcher
Headwater Learning, Calgary Academy
Calgary, Alberta, Canada

Colleen Fleming
Literacy Specialist
Calgary Academy
Calgary, Alberta, Canada

Johanna Josaphat
Teacher Leader
Urban Assembly Unison School
Brooklyn, New York

Teresa Kinley
Secondary School Humanities Teacher
Calgary, Alberta, Canada

Ian Landy
District Principal of Technology
School District 47
Powell River, British Columbia, Canada

Visit **go.SolutionTree.com/PLCbooks/AYV** to download the free reproducibles in this book.

To access the exclusive reproducibles in this book, enter the unique access code found on the inside front cover.

TABLE OF CONTENTS

Reproducibles are in italics.

ABOUT THE AUTHORS XVII

FOREWORD XXI

INTRODUCTION 1

    Who This Book Is For 2

    What You'll Find in This Book 3

    How to Navigate This Book 5

    Foundational First Steps 6

    Tool: Key Vocabulary Sort 9

1   THE WHY 13

    Our Why 13

    The Universal Why 14

    Why We Can't Skip This Step 15

    The Ultimate Why 16

    Anchors Away! 16

2   MISSION 19

    Navigating the Mission 20

    Examining Evidence of a Successful Mission 22

    Taking a Deep Dive Into the Research for
    Developing a Mission 23

    Sailing Into Action for Each Stage of
    Developing a Shared Mission 24

    Staying Afloat Through Common Challenges
    to Developing a Mission 30

Knowing the Ropes for Mission Development 31
Celebrating the Mission 31
Stay the Course 32
Anchors Away! 32
Mission Continuum (District) 34
Mission Continuum (School) 35
What's My Why? 37
The Power of a Mission Statement (District) 38
The Power of a Mission Statement (School) 41
Mission Sort 44
Investigate and Create the Mission Statement 45
Guiding Coalition Mission Formalization 47
Mission Proposal and Adoption (Step 1) 48
Mission Proposal and Adoption (Step 2) 49
Celebration Planning 50
Mission in Action and Parent Celebration Certificates . . . 51
Mission Survey (District) 54
Mission Survey (School) 56
Mission Survey Analysis (District) 58
Mission Survey Analysis (School) 59
Staff Reflections—Implementing Stage (District) 60
Staff Reflections—Implementing Stage (School) 61
Guiding Coalition Analysis—Implementing Stage 62
School Action Plan—Implementing Stage 64
Staff Reflections—Developing Stage (District) 65
Staff Reflections—Developing Stage (School) 66
Guiding Coalition Analysis—Developing Stage 67
School Action Plan—Developing Stage 69
Staff Reflections—Sustaining Stage (District) 70
Staff Reflections—Sustaining Stage (School) 72
Guiding Coalition Analysis—Sustaining Stage 74
School Action Plan—Sustaining Stage 76

3 VISION 79

Navigating the Vision 80
Examining Evidence of a Successful Vision 81
Taking a Deep Dive Into the Research for
Developing a Vision 82

Sailing Into Action for Each Stage of
Developing a Shared Vision 84
Staying Afloat Through Common Challenges to
Developing a Shared Vision 90
Knowing the Ropes for Vision Development 91
Celebrating the Vision 92
Stay the Course 92
Anchors Away! 92
Vision Continuum 94
Vision Sort 95
The Power of a Shared Vision (District) 96
The Power of a Shared Vision (School) 98
Trending Stories (District) 100
Trending Stories (School) 102
Trending Stories Analysis 104
Proposal and Adoption (Step 1) 107
Proposal and Adoption (Step 2) 108
Plan to Celebrate! 109
Vision Survey (District) 111
Vision Survey (School) 113
Vision Survey Analysis (District) 115
Vision Survey Analysis (School) 116
Evidence of Impact (District) 117
Evidence of Impact (School) 118

4 COLLECTIVE COMMITMENTS 121

Navigating the Collective Commitments 122
Examining the Evidence of Successful
Collective Commitments 123
Taking a Deep Dive Into the Research for
Developing Collective Commitments 126
Sailing Into Action for Each Stage of
Developing Collective Commitments 127
Staying Afloat Through Common Challenges
to Developing Collective Commitments 132
Knowing the Ropes for Collective
Commitments Development 133
Celebrating the Collective Commitments 133
Stay the Course 134

Anchors Away! 134
Collective Commitments Continuum 137
The Power of Collective Commitments (District) 138
The Power of Collective Commitments (School) 140
My Dreams for You 142
Collective Commitments Wishlist (District) 144
Collective Commitments Wishlist (School) 145
Beliefs and Collective Commitments Sort 146
Beliefs to Commitments (District) 147
Beliefs to Commitments (School) 148
Example Beliefs to Commitments 149
Drafting Collective Commitments 150
Ratification Survey 153
Collective Commitments Violations 156
Celebration Planning 157
Recognition Nomination 158
Staff Feedback (District) 159
Staff Feedback (School) 160
Taking Ownership 161
Evidence of Action 163
Fulfilling Our Collective Commitments (District) 164
Fulfilling Our Collective Commitments (School) 165
Status Survey (District) 166
Status Survey (School) 168
Acknowledgment Survey 170
Celebration Jot 171

5 GOALS **173**

Navigating the Goals 174
Examining the Evidence of Successful Goals 176
Taking a Deep Dive Into the Research for Developing Goals 176
Sailing Into Action for Each Stage of Developing Goals 177
Staying Afloat Through Common Challenges to Developing Goals 182
Knowing the Ropes for Goal Development 182
Celebrating the Goals 183
Stay the Course 184

Anchors Away! 184
Goals Continuum (District) 186
Goals Continuum (School) 187
Goals to Impact Student Learning (District) 188
Goals to Impact Student Learning (School) 190
A Data Picture of Our District 192
A Data Picture of Our School 194
Using Our Data Part 1: Studying Our Data (District) 196
Using Our Data Part 1: Studying Our Data (School) 197
Using Our Data Part 2: Setting Our Goals (District) 198
Using Our Data Part 2: Setting Our Goals (School) 199
Using Our Data Part 3: Goals Action Plan (District) 200
Using Our Data Part 3: Goals Action Plan (School) 201
Goals Survey (District) 202
Goals Survey (School) 204
Creating Rituals and Celebrations 206
Plan to Celebrate! 207
Data Analysis to Identify Department Goals 208
Data Analysis to Identify Team Goals 209
Data Analysis to Identify Teacher Goals 210
Teacher SMART Goal 211
Student SMART Goal 213
Team Accountability Partners 215
Setting Our District Department or School Team Goals . 216

6 MOTTO 219

Navigating the Motto 220
Examining the Evidence of a Successful Motto 220
Taking a Deep Dive Into the Research for
Developing a Motto 221
Sailing Into Action for Each Stage of
Developing a Motto 221
Staying Afloat Through Common Challenges
to Developing a Motto 224
Knowing the Ropes for Motto Development 225
Celebrating the Motto 225
Stay the Course 226
Anchors Away! 226
Motto Continuum 228

Motto Sort 229
The Power of a Motto (District) 230
The Power of a Motto (School) 231
Analyze the Power of a Motto (District) 232
Analyze the Power of a Motto (School) 233
One Word 234
Synthesizing the "One Word" 235
Celebrations Survey 236
Celebration Planning 237
The Power of a Motto (Parent) 238
Analyze the Power of a Motto (Parent) 239

7 HIRING, CONNECTING, AND MAINTAINING 241

Navigating Hiring, Connecting, and Maintaining
the Work 243

Examining the Evidence of Successful Hiring,
Connecting, and Maintaining the Work 244

Taking a Deep Dive Into the Research for
Hiring, Connecting, and Maintaining the Work 245

Sailing Into Action for Each Stage of Hiring
and Connecting the Work 246

Sailing Into Action for Each Stage of Maintaining
the Work 249

Staying Afloat Through Common Challenges to
Hiring, Connecting, and Maintaining the Work 251

Knowing the Ropes for Hiring, Connecting,
and Maintaining the Work 252

Celebrating Hiring, Connecting, and Maintaining
the Work 253

Stay the Course 254
Anchors Away! 255
Hiring and Connecting New Staff Continuum (District) . 257
Hiring and Connecting New Staff Continuum (School) . 258
Hiring Committee Application 259
Hiring Committee Professional Commitments
and Norms 260
New Hire Onboarding 261
Screening Criteria for a Vacancy 263
Criteria-Based Interview Questions 264
Applicant Interview Rubric 266

Reference Question Examples (District) 267
　　Reference Question Examples (School) 268
　　The Foundation of Our District or School—Example 269
　　The Foundation of _____ District 270
　　The Foundation of _____ School 271
　　Maintaining the Work Continuum (District) 272
　　Maintaining the Work Continuum (School) 273
　　Maintaining the Work Planning Sheet (District) 274
　　Maintaining the Work Planning Sheet (School) 275
　　Guiding Coalition Synthesis 276
　　Action Plan for Our Next Steps 277

EPILOGUE **279**

REFERENCES AND RESOURCES **281**

INDEX **287**

ABOUT THE AUTHORS

Shawn Creswell, an author, PLC coach, consultant, and national presenter, works with educators throughout the country to implement Professional Learning Communities at Work. She is also certified in RTI at Work and Yes We Can. With over twenty-five years of experience in education, she has served as a classroom teacher, middle school assistant principal, and principal of a K–6 school; opened a new preK–6 school; and was the district director of curriculum, instruction, and assessment for a large school district. She serves as a school board member in the community where she resides to support educators, students, and their families in continuous school improvement efforts.

Shawn is an experienced administrator who is passionate about exceptional learning and growth for all students. She is committed to adding value to every student and believes educators can accomplish this in all schools. Shawn has worked in both urban and suburban settings and has the knowledge and expertise to help transform schools.

Under Shawn's leadership as principal, Coulson Tough K–6 School in Texas received certification as a High Reliability School at level 1 in 2019 and at level 2 in 2020. Through the implementation of the PLC at Work process, Coulson Tough had dramatic and sustained student growth during the six years Shawn was school principal. In the spring of 2020, Coulson Tough was recognized as a Model PLC at Work school through Solution Tree. In addition, Coulson Tough was the second school in the United States to receive distinctions as both a High Reliability School and a Model PLC at Work school.

Shawn earned a bachelor's degree in elementary education from Illinois State University and a master's degree in educational administration from Sam Houston State University.

Emily McClain lived and led the work of professional learning communities as an elementary school teacher, school and district instructional coach, and district literacy specialist. She continues her passion for ensuring high levels of learning for all by supporting districts and schools across the nation as a PLC coach, presenter, and author.

Emily is deeply committed to the work of PLCs to ensure exceptional learning and growth for all students and staff. She utilizes a variety of coaching models to support teachers and school leadership in becoming highly effective collaborative teams. Emily brings with her a depth of knowledge and expertise in content, collaboration, and assessment practices, and her goal is to support the implementation and refinement of the PLC at Work process to guarantee learning at high levels.

Emily's first success in the work of PLCs was achieved at Coulson Tough K–6 School, which received certification as a High Reliability School at level 1 in 2019 and at level 2 in 2020. Through the implementation of the PLC at Work process, Coulson Tough had dramatic and sustained student growth during the six years Emily served as a classroom teacher, guiding coalition member, and school instructional coach. In the spring of 2020, Coulson Tough was recognized as a Model PLC at Work school through Solution Tree. In addition, Coulson Tough was the second school in the United States to receive distinctions as both a High Reliability School and a Model PLC at Work school.

Emily holds a bachelor's degree in elementary education from Sam Houston State University and is completing her master's degree in curriculum and instruction and reading.

Katy Sue Traicoff is an experienced educator with a passion for fostering collaborative learning environments and supporting the professional development of educators. Katy Sue has proven success in leading school improvement initiatives leveraging over eighteen years in education from the classroom, to district instructional coaching, to serving on a school administration team, to serving as a professional learning community presenter, coach, and author. Her experience with both high-performing and Title I schools provides a perspective of how the PLC process benefits both student and educator learning and growth and, more importantly, a deep belief in how collaboration can help educators manage the intense pressures and demands of today's educational challenges.

Katy Sue possesses a deep understanding of the value of collaborative decision making within professional learning communities. As a teacher leader for eight years, she collaboratively helped guide her school to achieve Model PLC at Work recognition through Solution

Tree, demonstrating her commitment to fostering a shared vision, mission, and collective responsibility for student and adult learning.

Katy Sue earned her bachelor's degree in business communication from the University of Wisconsin–River Falls and her master's degree in administration from Lamar University in Beaumont, Texas.

To book Shawn Creswell, Emily McClain, or Katy Sue Traicoff for professional development, contact pd@SolutionTree.com.

FOREWORD

By Jeanne Spiller

Welcome aboard! Whether you're setting sail on your first professional learning community (PLC) voyage or you're a seasoned traveler, this book is your guide. It's designed to help you navigate through the essential process of creating and sustaining the foundational pillars of a PLC.

Shawn, Emily, and Katy Sue engage the reader (you!) in this voyage by beginning with exploring the why behind the work—understanding, and helping others understand, that the purpose that drives the PLC process is *crucial*. Subsequent chapters guide you through developing your mission, vision, collective commitments, goals, and motto, providing you with clear steps and practical tools at each stage. A PLC needs a robust foundation built on a clear mission, vision, and collective commitments. Without these, it's like trying to sail a boat with holes in the hull—it simply won't float.

The beauty of *Anchor Your Vision* lies in its practicality. It doesn't just tell you what to do; it shows you how to do it. The tools provided are not only effective but also incredibly accessible. Everything you need is right here in these pages, ready to be implemented, adapted, and celebrated. Imagine having a toolkit that's not just full of useful instruments but also simple to use. That's what you'll find here. Each tool is presented in a way that's clear and engaging, making the process of building your PLC foundation feel less like a chore and more like an exciting yet navigable adventure. You'll be equipped with templates, checklists, continuums, and practical advice to help you navigate each step with confidence and ease. This book recognizes that no two schools are exactly alike, that each has its own unique challenges and strengths, and it guides you in recognizing these differences and targeting your work to address them. Whether you're just setting sail or looking to strengthen your existing culture, you'll find strategies and insights that resonate with your specific context. The emphasis is on creating a foundation that is not only strong but also flexible—able to grow and evolve with your team.

One of the standout features of this book is its emphasis on collective commitments. These are the promises that team members make to each other and to their students. They are the glue that holds the PLC together, fostering a sense of accountability and shared responsibility. The tools provided to develop and sustain these commitments are nothing short of brilliant. They encourage open communication, mutual respect, and a shared belief in the potential of every student.

As you read *Anchor Your Vision*, not only will you find practical advice, useful tools, and actionable steps, but you will find plenty of inspiration. The stories, reflections, and insights from Shawn, Emily, and Katy Sue will resonate with your experiences and aspirations. Their commitment to the PLC process and belief in every student's potential to achieve high levels of learning will inspire you to take bold steps in your educational journey.

I've had the privilege of working in an environment with a strong foundation in place. In this environment, every educator is not just a teacher but a passionate advocate for student success. The mission isn't just a statement on the wall; it's a guiding star, steering us through both calm seas and stormy waters. The vision isn't just a distant dream; it's a clear pathway we're all committed to walking together. And the collective commitments aren't just words; they're promises we make to each other and to our students. This strong foundation has been the bedrock of ensuring high levels of learning for all students, and it can be for you too.

As you embark on your voyage, remember to keep the tone light and the spirits high. Building a professional learning community is serious work, but it doesn't have to be drudgery. Embrace the process with a sense of curiosity and playfulness. Celebrate the small victories along the way and don't be afraid to laugh at the occasional missteps. After all, learning is a lifelong adventure, and the best adventures are the ones where we enjoy the ride.

I commend you for taking this important step toward creating a thriving professional learning community. The journey you're about to undertake will transform not only your professional practice but also the lives of your students. With the solid foundation this book helps you build, you'll be well on your way to ensuring high levels of learning for all. So, hoist the sails, grab your toolkit, and let's get started. Here's to navigating toward and anchoring in a brighter future together!

With over thirty-four years in K–12 education, Jeanne Spiller is a seasoned educational leader and consultant specializing in implementation of the PLC process, curriculum development, instructional coaching, and professional development. As a co-author of influential education books and an associate for Solution Tree, she is dedicated to fostering high-quality, equitable education and driving innovation in school districts.

INTRODUCTION

*The fundamental purpose of a school
is learning, not teaching.*
—RICHARD DuFOUR

The three of us vividly remember our very first Professional Learning Community (PLC) at Work® institute together in San Antonio, Texas, in June, 2015. We had just finished our first year working in the same school—Shawn a first-year principal, Emily a first-year teacher, and Katy Sue a veteran teacher. We sat in the sold-out auditorium alongside the other members of our leadership team, intently listening to Richard DuFour as he presented his keynote speech. We nodded and took detailed notes on all the ideas we wanted to consider for the upcoming school year. As we continued listening, DuFour discussed the foundational pillars of a PLC at Work, pausing in his presentation to ask us to "turn and tell your shoulder partner your school's vision." The groups around us burst into chatter. *School vision?* We looked at one another and then dropped our voices to a whisper: "What *is* our school vision?" Like participants in a game of telephone, we sent the question down the row to the other members of our leadership team. While the shrugs we got in response provided us a small sense of relief—we were all in the same predicament—they told the truth: none of us knew our school's vision. As DuFour continued with his keynote, we learned the importance of not only knowing but attaining a meaningful shared school vision. This simple yet impactful prompt reaffirmed our true purpose as educators and incited in us a determination to embark on the foundational work we needed to accomplish in our school.

The work that began at our first PLC institute led to improved learning and growth for all students and staff and eventual recognition as a Model PLC school. While we actively sought to grow and learn as a PLC through book studies, attending additional PLC and response to intervention (RTI) institutes and workshops, and truly learning by doing, we know without a doubt that the success of our work was possible only because of the way our entire staff was committed to continually working together to initiate, implement, develop, and sustain our foundational pillars. With the shared foundational pillars in place, collaborative team meetings were focused on teachers learning from one another to share instructional practices, powerful resources, and specific interventions resulting in high levels of learning for students. The staff became hungry for evidence of student growth and eager to respond to data with urgency and specificity. This strong foundation allowed the guiding coalition to support teams in creating thoughtful learning cycles around essential standards, move into the powerful work of meaningful assessment with intentional data conversations, and establish a structure for the RTI practices.

As we expanded our work to districts and schools across the United States, we quickly realized the need to reiterate and rally those undertaking the work of PLCs to the charge we felt Rick DuFour called us to at our first PLC institute. We see too many schools and districts wonder why their efforts are not resulting in success, why all the numerous costly resources are not making a difference, and why not all students are learning at high levels. We are confident that until teams are working collaboratively to ensure clarity and commitment toward the shared mission, vision, collective commitments, and goals (the four foundational pillars), as well as a motto, they will not bring about the greatest possible impact on student learning. Yet, too often districts and schools lack solid foundational pillars. Sometimes, their leaders and staff don't understand the critical need for the foundational pillars in the work of a PLC; sometimes the pillars are set but not sustained; or, in many places, educators recognize the pillars' value but aren't clear on *how* to set and sustain the pillars.

Addressing these enduring dilemmas represents our why for writing this book. In the following chapters, we'll help districts and schools translate ideas into actions by providing steps, tools, and resources as a guide to the work of setting and sustaining the foundational pillars of a PLC—work that is essential in achieving our fundamental purpose as educators: ensuring high levels of learning for all. First, we want to talk about who this book is for, what you'll find in it, how to make the most of this resource, and some key pieces you'll need to put in place at the outset of your work.

Who This Book Is For

This book is written for educators who have a strong desire to lead the type of change in districts and schools that impacts learning for both students and the adults who serve them. What does it mean to lead? First and perhaps most important is the reminder from author Simon Sinek (2009) in his suggestion that the trait to lead isn't necessarily innate—we can all learn to lead. He also reminds us that, at their core, "leaders are the ones who have the courage to go first and open a path for others to follow" (Sinek, 2017, p. 32). In this regard, a person in any position can be an inspirational leader—whether they are a teacher, counselor, paraprofessional, instructional coach, interventionist, coordinator, or school- or district-level administrator. Because anyone can be a leader and because we believe it takes everyone working together to sustain change, it is vital that everyone in an organization be part of creating the foundational pillars. In many districts and schools, the perceived leader, often the school principal or the district superintendent, is the only one doing this type of work. Sometimes, those with job titles that imply leadership positions find that staff rely on them because they are in defined positions of power to not only develop the mission and vision, but also single-handedly take on that work. Although most such administrators could likely craft those statements and post them on a website or wall, the reality is that such an approach would be unlikely to connect members of the organization to the mission and vision in a way that maximizes the organization's growth and success. Therefore, this book is a how-to for school- and district-level collaborative leadership teams, who must work with staff to imagine what's possible, *together* creating a vision around which people can unite and transform individual thoughts into collective actions to anchor that vision and make it a reality.

What You'll Find in This Book

Though a how-to resource, *Anchor Your Vision* is much more than a to-do list for leading your district or school in creating your foundational pillars and motto. Rather than providing a checklist of activities, it's meant to support educators throughout the process of carefully and collectively constructing and sustaining these critical components that impact the work of all staff. Accordingly, in addition to the motto, the individual pillars have their own dedicated chapters, opening with relevant stories from other districts and schools and featuring definitions and descriptions of what the work entails, evidence of the pillars and research that supports their significance, detailed action steps, common challenges, tips and key points, means to monitor progress, suggestions for celebrations, and of course, practical tools. To help you and your organization take the foundational pillars from theory to action, we capture within these chapters' action steps the five continuum stages your district or school may navigate when attending to the mission, vision, collective commitments, and goals, as well as motto: (1) preinitiating, paired with a spyglass image in each chapter to emphasize taking a look at the way forward, (2) initiating, paired with a propeller image to emphasize starting up the journey, (3) implementing, paired with a throttle to highlight gaining momentum on the journey, (4) developing, paired with an image of a boat's navigation system as a reminder of the navigating you'll be doing in your journey, and (5) sustaining, paired with an image of a radar system to emphasize keeping your eye on progress and scanning for obstacles as you go forward. In this way, we offer all schools and districts a clear path forward regardless of where they find themselves in the process of creating and living out a given pillar, and the end-of-chapter reproducibles constitute the respective tools you'll make use of along your journey. Following the pillar and motto chapters, we give you a window into what it takes to ensure your pillars' strength and longevity—namely, intentionally aligned hiring practices and considerations.

With regard to the reproducibles in this book, they are all available online as well as featured in the book. Check this book's inside front cover to find a unique access code to enter at **go.SolutionTree.com/PLCbooks/AYV** to digitally access all reproducibles. The code on the inside front cover is unique to your book and can only be used once. After entering your code, the exclusive reproducibles will be added to your customer dashboard on the Solution Tree website, allowing you access to the reproducibles at any time. Each reproducible indicates if it is free to access or requires a code.

While the nature of the discrete pillars and the aforementioned five stages of pillar establishment lend themselves to a Choose Your Own Adventure–style utilization of this book, we nevertheless encourage you to start by reading chapter 1, "The Why" (page 13), as the information in this chapter provides the necessary background for navigating the remaining chapters. That is, before we can dedicate ourselves to any work, it's essential to understand the why, and this chapter supports the why behind the work of developing the foundational pillars with which to create a high-functioning PLC. After reading this chapter, you'll be better equipped to then decide which chapter best fits where you are in the establishment of the foundational pillars. Most leaders will find themselves reading the book as it's written from cover to cover, completing each chapter before moving on to the next one. In districts or at schools that have some or all of the pillars in place, leaders may focus on just those chapters that meet their current needs. But if you know you're at the beginning of the process, move right into chapter 2 as we recommend a particular order for creating and building your foundation.

Beginning the pillar chapters, chapter 2, "Mission" (page 19), addresses the concise statement that clarifies an organization's purpose. A clear mission statement is critical to setting a strong foundation on which to build a community of both student and adult learners focused on a common purpose. A failure to establish a mission is often the reason why schools tend not to have the success they desire. Too frequently, we work with districts and schools that don't have a mission statement, or don't have one that's meaningfully used throughout the organization. We observe educators who are passionate about the work they do for students and the desire to see success in student learning; however, they aren't aiming their efforts toward a shared mission. Here we provide the what, why, and how for collaborating to determine the mission for your school or district.

The subject of chapter 3, "Vision" (page 79), answers the question, What must our district or school become to accomplish our purpose? The vision is closely linked to the shared mission and together with the mission provides not only a purpose but a target that can be achieved through that shared purpose. This chapter walks your district or school through a process of analyzing what you collectively hope your organization can become. We all have hopes and dreams for bigger and better results, but for a community, it is critical that there is a shared vision driving everyone's energy in the same direction.

Chapter 4, "Collective Commitments" (page 121), captures the actions and behaviors that support the mission. Once the mission and vision have been created, adopted, and celebrated, collective commitments (sometimes called *values*) are the agreed-on behaviors specific to the mission that ensure the individuals of the community are living out the actions required to fulfill the mission.

"Goals," chapter 5 (page 173), is about ensuring the district or school is focused on learning growth, which includes setting attainable goals aligned to district and school goals. Long- and short-term goals, along with timelines to measure and attain these goals, are included in the chapter. Goals provide a way to show how the district and schools are laser focused on student learning and growth.

Chapter 6, "Motto" (page 219), marks the transition from the four pillars to a phrase that will inform many stakeholders' first impressions of your district or school. It communicates succinctly what your district or school is about and what you believe. The motto is often a battle cry for the community that rallies everyone around what the organization values. This is purposeful but also a unique way to involve not only staff but also students, parents, and the community in a call to action connected to the fundamental purpose of the educational community.

Chapter 7, "Connecting, Hiring, and Maintaining" (page 241), is all about guaranteeing that your hard work of adopting the shared mission, vision, collective commitments, goals, and motto has a successful launch and, just as important, longevity. Strong foundational pillars take time and attention, and this chapter provides tools to focus on intentionally making the pillars a priority. As part of the maintenance work, this chapter addresses recruiting, hiring, orienting, and retaining staff. When leaders intentionally align their hiring practices with the organization's core beliefs, values, and aspirations, new staff are able to quickly assimilate into the culture of the school and easily become part of the PLC.

At the end of each chapter you will find a section called Anchors Away! Please use the writing space provided in this section to review your thoughts on the chapter's content and to prepare for your next steps as you move forward.

Wherever you are in the PLC journey, from starting with the mission to having all the foundational pillars in place, you'll be able to utilize the tools within this book to assist you in your forward momentum toward a district or school focused on ensuring learning for all.

How to Navigate This Book

As educators who understand both the power of a PLC and the challenges and peculiarities unique to each organization, we encourage you to make this book work for your specific needs. Leadership teams or entire organizations are of course free to use this book as a guidebook or part of a book study. But in the same way that you may find certain pillar-focused chapters more relevant to your school or district than others, within each chapter, you may or may not need to use all the tips, steps, and tools we've provided. Instead, you should determine which stage your district or school is in by utilizing the supplied continuum reproducible for that pillar, proceeding to the section indicated for that stage, and selecting the steps and tools based on your organization. For instance, some tools are specific to districts and others to schools. We designed this book to be an ongoing resource as you will want to seek staff input on a yearly basis using the provided continuums. Each chapter in this book can be a stand-alone for the area you want to address in your district or school. Also, you may find that a tool we share inspires you to create one of your own that's more specific to your needs—that's fantastic! It's all part of the ingenuity and collaborative spirit that drive a high-functioning PLC.

Please note that the timetable for the various stages, steps, and tools depends on where you are on the continuum, the time available for your staff to meet collaboratively, and the experience of working within a PLC. If you are brand new to exploring the journey of a PLC, this work may take a bit more time, but we encourage you to continue moving forward through the steps with dedication and intention to make progress in a timely way. Most schools and districts will be able to create a mission, vision, collective commitments, and goals within a year or two when they spend some time each month to meet and discuss this work together. Our leadership team met twice a month for an hour and utilized tools such as surveys to gather input from the staff in between meeting together. For districts and schools that might be in what Rick DuFour and Douglas Reeves (2016) would call the "PLC lite" phase, you may be able to move much more fluidly through the steps and tools. PLC lite occurs when districts or schools operate on the surface of a PLC rather than deeply embracing all of the processes of a high-performing PLC. They have a basic understanding of pieces of the PLC process, allowing these schools to move more quickly through the foundational pillar process. Districts and schools that find themselves missing only one or two of the foundational pillars will be able to complete this work within the school year if staff are meeting together at least monthly. We've worked with districts and schools that set aside days in the summer months to work with leadership teams to create a plan for implementation for the year ahead. Being intentional in structuring time together is key. It is important to remember these are the foundational pillars on which your PLC will be built. Therefore, be thoughtful in dedicating time to doing this work correctly while having urgency to get the foundation built in a timely manner. We urge districts and schools that find themselves at the preinitiating or initiating stage to work quickly to set their pillars, typically within the school year. Those who find themselves in the implementing or developing stage will find it important to set timelines for their action plans to move the work forward. Once districts or schools are in the sustaining stage, the work to maintain this stage lasts for the life of the district or school.

Make decisions for how and with whom to use this book by keeping in mind that the goal is for each district or school to have a solid foundation on which to build their work as a PLC. When districts and schools have created and connected their staff to the foundational pillars and motto, they provide the compass that dictates the direction in which they will go. When there is clarity, districts and schools are much more likely to achieve their desired outcomes.

Foundational First Steps

Before you dive into the work outlined in this book, it's important to have a few key pieces, processes, teams, and understandings in place. Let's spend some time reviewing the role of your guiding coalition, common language, loose and tight structures, and celebrations.

Creating Your Guiding Coalition

It will be essential to have a guiding coalition in place throughout this work. A guiding coalition is a leadership team designed to lead the district or school in creating a high-functioning PLC. The guiding coalition of the district or school will play an important role in supporting the creation, adoption, and maintenance of the foundational pillars. Author and educator Bill Hall (2022) states, "It is the guiding coalition that sets the tone for the collaborative work done throughout the school" (p. 4). John Kotter, author and business and management thought leader, emphasizes the importance of this collective rather than solitary effort:

> No one person, no matter how competent, is capable of single-handedly developing the right vision, communicating it to vast numbers of people, eliminating

all the key obstacles, generating short-term wins, leading and managing dozens of change projects, and anchoring new approaches deep in an organization's culture . . . Putting together the right coalition of people to lead a change initiative is critical to success" (Kotter, 2010, p. 52).

The team is essential in gathering and synthesizing staff input, along with promoting, celebrating, and sustaining the work. "An effective leadership team must be comprised of people who possess strong positional power, broad expertise, and high credibility with their peers" (Buffum, Mattos, & Malone, 2018, p. 39). We need to have the right people leading our district or school in order to be successful in our efforts. "Team members must model the purpose and beliefs of the leadership team both formally and informally" (Buffum et al., 2018, p. 40).

Developing Common Language

Creating a common language across the district or school around key vocabulary terms of PLCs will be essential to the success of this work. We have found that there is often a wide interpretation of the language utilized in education in general and PLCs specifically. Most districts and schools have staff who have held similar positions at other organizations. Terms in one district or school may have different meanings than in another. Centering everyone on common vocabulary is crucial to nurturing a deep, shared understanding of concepts and supports the needed clarity in conversations among staff. We have included a reproducible "Tool: Key Vocabulary Sort" (page 9) resource at the end of this introduction to lead your staff through clarifying and aligning a common language of the PLC. Make this activity work for you and the needs of your staff in a way that maximizes the opportunity for discussion. If you're at the beginning of your PLC journey, you may want to consider chunks of time to explore smaller sets of words to allow for meaningful conversations, which will encourage a deeper understanding of the terms. If your staff have more experience operating as a PLC, you may want to be intentional in selecting words to use in the sort as a review or recentering activity to support discussions for clarification. We have found as we use the sort with districts and schools that it not only encourages dialogue around knowing the terminology of the PLC but, more importantly, promotes collaboration and common understanding of the work. At your school, add these vocabulary terms and definitions to your staff binder so everyone can refer to them as needed. This also supports new staff who might be joining your school midyear.

Clarifying Loose and Tight Structures

By establishing the foundational pillars of a PLC through collaboration, discussion, and consensus, each district or school creates a common and clear understanding of its shared purpose, commitments, and goals that guide the work of every member of the organization. Richard DuFour, Rebecca DuFour, Robert Eaker, Mike Mattos, and Anthony Muhammad (2021) contend that leaders must articulate what the tight expectations in the organization are and what is to be loose. "Tight" expectations are "elements of the PLC process that are . . . nondiscretionary and everyone in the school is required to adhere to"

(DuFour, DuFour, Eaker, Many, & Mattos, 2016, p. 13), whereas "loose" expectations are decisions made with teacher autonomy. Without clarity around your why, it can become very murky to decipher the tight and loose expectations. Creating shared foundational pillars helps define and clarify for staff the tight and loose expectations, and once the shared vision, mission, collective commitments, and goals are in place, an outline evolves of what must be held tight and what should remain loose.

Committing to Celebrate

One critical piece that does not have its own chapter, although it is so important, is celebration! As our colleague Timothy Kanold shares in his book *Heart!* (2017), "I have never heard of any team of educators complain that their work, effort, behavior, or results were celebrated too much" (p. 141). In each chapter and stage, we intentionally suggest opportunities for celebrations as a critical practice in building the foundational pillars of the district or school. We firmly believe in the power of celebration—not only because we appreciate any opportunity for a good celebration but because we have witnessed the tremendous impact celebration has on moving the work forward. Acknowledging staff for their efforts to support the collective work of the district or school builds a strong culture and promotes employee well-being. Reporting on a workplace survey, Kristin Ryba (2023) writes that "53% of employees feel culture most strongly through recognition and celebrations." When organizations take time and effort to recognize or honor work toward goals, employees feel more connected, are more eager to perform at higher levels, and are more likely to continue working at the organization. In fact, reporting on employee engagement trends, Natalie Wickham (2023) states, "Organizations with formal employee recognition programs have 31% less voluntary turnover than organizations that don't have any program at all." Whether the celebration is on a large scale involving many individuals or a more personal celebration of an individual educator, celebration creates a community of connectedness, fosters a culture of trust, and communicates the value of the individual. Ideas and tools are embedded within chapters to guide and inspire your efforts in celebrating the work of creating, growing, and living your shared motto, vision, mission, collective commitments, and goals. Meaningful and intentional recognition and celebration are simple ways to keep staff invested in the organization while focusing on the journey to creating a strong collective foundation of the PLC.

Let's set sail! The introduction sets the groundwork for how to successfully use this book to lead your district or school to becoming a high-performing PLC. We encourage you to be transparent with your staff as you move through the processes. Gather input, have conversations, listen, and have clarity about why you value this work. As you will see in chapter 1 (page 13), understanding our why creates community, urgency, and a commitment to making change. We know your work will impact students in your district or school, and we can't wait to hear about your successes. Now, it's time to take action and "seas" the day!

Tool: Key Vocabulary Sort

Instructions: Cut apart the key vocabulary terms and definitions and place them in bags for table teams. Provide teams with ten minutes to match terms with definitions. It is helpful to have them first alphabetize the terms and then match them with the corresponding definitions. (The way they're shown here is correct.) Collectively discuss the correct matches, creating a common understanding of the vocabulary. Ensure all staff have a copy of this key vocabulary sheet to reference throughout the year.

COLLABORATION	"A systematic process in which [people] work together, interdependently, to analyze and impact their professional practice in order to improve individual and collective results" (DuFour et al., 2016, p. 60).
COLLECTIVE COMMITMENTS	Actionable promises made among and between all stakeholders that answer the question, What must we do to become the organization we have agreed we hope to become?
COMMUNITY	A group of people linked by common interests and collective responsibility and who have a sense of belonging.
CONSENSUS	When all points of view have been solicited and heard; the will of the group is evident.
CULTURE	"The assumptions, beliefs, expectations, and habits that constitute the norm for a school and guide the work of the educators within it" (DuFour et al., 2016, p. 22).
ESSENTIAL LEARNING	The small subset of agreed-on critical skills, knowledge, and dispositions all students must acquire in each course, grade level, and unit of instruction.
FOUNDATIONAL PILLARS	Professional learning communities rest on a shared mission of high levels of learning for all students. In order to achieve that mission, educators create a common vision of the school they must create, develop collective commitments or values regarding what they will do to create such a school, and use goals as measurable milestones to monitor their progress.

GOALS	Measurable milestones that are used to assess progress in advancing toward a vision and that establish targets and timelines to answer the question, What results do we seek, and how will we know we are making progress?
GUARANTEED AND VIABLE CURRICULUM	The agreed-on knowledge and skills taught by all teachers in a specific grade, course, or content area in the time provided.
GUIDING COALITION	A leadership team that champions the work of the professional learning community process and whose shared goals unite the members in leading collaborative work within the organization.
INTERVENTION	Targeted instruction focused on essential learnings that a student has not yet mastered.
LEARNING	The acquisition of new knowledge or skills.
MISSION STATEMENT	The fundamental purpose of an organization; answers the question, Why do we exist?
MOTTO	A slogan, chant, or catchphrase that embodies the organization's purpose.
PROFESSIONAL	An individual with expertise and advanced training in a specialized field who is expected to remain current in research-based best practices.
PROFESSIONAL LEARNING	Focused training that may be attained in a variety of settings, such as conferences, institutes, collaborative practices, virtual, or job embedded (that is, coaching, instructional rounds, and so on).

PROFESSIONAL LEARNING COMMUNITY	"An ongoing process in which educators work collaboratively in recurring cycles of collective inquiry and action research to achieve better results for the students they serve" (DuFour et al., 2016, p. 10).
TEAM	"A group of people working interdependently *to achieve a common goal* for which members are held mutually accountable" (DuFour et al., 2016, p. 91).
VALUES	The specific attitudes, behaviors, and collective commitments that must be demonstrated in order to advance the organization's vision.
VISION STATEMENT	The future for the organization of what it can achieve. It answers the question, What do we hope to become at some point in the future?

Reference

DuFour, R., DuFour, R., Eaker, R., Many, T. W., & Mattos, M. (2016). *Learning by doing: A handbook for Professional Learning Communities at Work* (3rd ed.). Bloomington, IN: Solution Tree Press.

CHAPTER 1
THE WHY

When we know WHY we do what we do, everything falls into place.
When we don't, we have to push things into place.
—SIMON SINEK

If you've ever been around a young child, you've probably experienced—or perhaps even been bombarded by—their favorite question: "Why?" It is a question that helps children make meaning, connections, and evaluations of the world around them. As educators, we, too, find it necessary to ask why in order to become passionately driven toward change implementation. So what is the answer to why establishing, embracing, and reaffirming the foundational pillars is essential to every district and school? Through the work on our own schools and those with whom we consult as well as in conferring with colleagues across the United States, we have experienced that the effectiveness and sustainability of a high-performing PLC comes down to a shared understanding of the why behind the work we are asked to do combined with a deep understanding and connection to each individual's why. In the following pages, we'll begin by describing how together we began to grasp the why as we dug into the work of a PLC. Then, we'll take the time to connect the universal why of learning for all to the pillars themselves—and how staff's collaborative construction of and engagement with the pillars ensures their individual and organizational efforts support this why.

Our Why

On the four-hour drive home from our first PLC institute in San Antonio, our leadership team realized we had a lot of work to do. The fact that we didn't know our own school's vision was just the start. We further recognized that the other foundational pillars we had learned about at the conference were also not evident in our school. We didn't have collective commitments or schoolwide goals—at least not ones that were collectively agreed on and communicated throughout our school. We did have a school mission and motto. We even had a school shirt that was a couple of years old with the motto printed across the front. However, the leadership team felt a revision might be needed as it didn't create a call to action, nor did it resonate with all staff.

Once back at school, we took the first step in our work by applying another key takeaway from the PLC institute: the importance of appropriate representation of the school on the guiding coalition. We knew that the work of constructing our foundational pillars would require the collaboration and leadership of the right team. So in the fall of that year, with a larger and stronger guiding coalition in place, we intentionally focused on our own learning first. We studied and utilized *Learning by Doing* (DuFour et al., 2024) to develop professional learning for the staff that focused on engaging in collaborative practices, building high-functioning teams, and shifting from a focus on teaching to a focus on learning.

With this learning in place, we realized that it wasn't going to be good enough to just come together and agree on the order of a few adjectives to describe the school we aspired to become. So we intentionally worked through collaborative processes that engaged all staff and sought feedback from our school families to find out what the school community valued. First, we surveyed the entire staff to gather feedback on the current motto. We found the vast majority of staff did not feel connected to the current motto (as we had anticipated). This feedback ignited a flame in our leadership team and kicked off our work of revising the motto. Then, we moved forward revisiting, refining, and creating our foundational pillars. The reason we started with the motto is because we wanted to rally our staff and center our purpose on learning and growth. For us, the motto became the springboard to delve into our vision and mission. In chapter 6 (page 219), you will learn more about the motto and its intended purpose. Through our experiences working with districts and schools that did not have the foundational pillars in place, we highly recommend beginning with the mission and vision.

As we worked together, we continually reminded one another to keep focused and ensure we spent our time, effort, and resources to establish our mission, vision, and goals. We filtered everything we did through the lens of learning, and we saw the resulting changes in how we collaborated and what we collaborated on. We saw shifts in all aspects of our work, from our data analysis for monitoring all students' growth to the way we talked about students to our hiring practices. Along the way, we became more intentional about celebrating student—and staff—growth. Through this process of providing clarity for the learning community, we saw the results of great change—learning and growth for *all*, which eventually led us to become a Model PLC school.

The Universal Why

Learning for all, however, is not the reality in many K–12 schools, including those in the United States. The reality in education after the COVID-19 pandemic, according to researchers John Schmitt and Katherine deCourcy (2022) of the Economic Policy Institute, is that U.S. districts and schools are finding more and more students below mastery of essential academic skills, potentially by multiple years. This has created a frenzied search for the "right" resource—one that meets all the state standards and fills all the potential gaps in student learning. At the same time, says *Education Week*'s Liana Loewus (2021), educators in all positions, at both district and school levels, are struggling to see the impact of their efforts on student growth, and teachers are exiting the profession in record numbers—all while there is a current lack of college graduates to fill the voids. These compounding issues create a state of disorientation in leaders as they ask, "Where should we focus our efforts? How can we ensure our efforts have an impact? What should we use to guide our decision making?" The answers to these questions lie in the foundational pillars of a PLC. The vision, mission, collective commitments, and goals must be created and established and done in such a way that they live and breathe within the organization.

It is through the collaborative practices of a high-performing learning community, not another new resource or the next training, that educators will be able to fill gaps in foundational skills and grow students to achieve grade-level mastery and beyond. When stakeholders feel tied to a shared purpose, the education sector will find itself equipped with a workforce of educators recommitted to their chosen profession, achieving tremendous success for all students. And it is the clarity of collaboratively created foundational pillars that provides educators with the focus to prioritize their actions and affirm their decisions. When an organization is brought together, it achieves what the individual members never thought possible. In *8 Steps to Accelerate Change in Your Organization*, change management consulting firm Kotter International (2018) states, "Large-scale change can only occur when very significant numbers of employees amass under a common opportunity and drive in the same direction" (p. 19). In addition, in the book *Taking Action* (2018), authors Austin Buffum and colleagues state "educators rarely embrace and effectively implement new practices when they don't understand why they are doing them" (p. 10). Therefore, change can only exist when both the why and the will work together. Establishing shared foundational pillars can turn the tide in education and ensure learning for all students.

Why We Can't Skip This Step

We have seen numerous districts and schools that are tempted to skip revisiting, revising, or creating the foundational blocks of a PLC, or rush this process by assigning the work to one or only a few members of the organization. Robert J. Marzano, Philip B. Warrick, Cameron L. Rains, and Richard DuFour (2018) share their observations based on the numerous schools they worked with across the United States:

> Schools often prefer to avoid these foundational questions [asked in the foundational pillars] and get right to the nuts and bolts of the PLC process. Doing so is a mistake. A school will struggle in its PLC implementation efforts if a faculty persists in believing that its job is to teach rather than to help all students learn, and if staff members have no idea where the school wants to go in its improvement efforts. (p. 4)

This highlights the realization that even when districts and schools do the work of creating the foundational pillars, they frequently do little if anything to engage the staff with them. Instead, it becomes a checkbox task to complete and has no real impact on student learning.

Educators frequently ask us how working on foundational pillars helps improve learning for students, or how it makes a difference for staff. As the author Simon Sinek (2009) says, "People don't buy what you do, they buy *why* you do it" (p. 41). Sinek discusses the

Golden Circle as a model for leaders to communicate from the inside out to garner connection, inspiration, and commitment from all. In his book *Start With Why*, Sinek (2009) shares how "the Golden Circle provides compelling evidence of how much more we can achieve if we remind ourselves to start everything we do by first asking why" (p. 38). In the Golden Circle, the why is the inner circle, which is where we must start; the how is the middle circle; and the what is the outer circle. Based on Sinek's research, the key for a business, for example, to become a runaway success is communicating a purpose that unites and inspires its staff—"make more money" won't do the trick.

Similarly, in education, "teach more" won't do the trick either. Although staff may know what they were hired to do—teach—do they know the why behind their work and have a vision of where they're going? Are they connected and committed to helping the district and school achieve their goals together? Is there clarity on the fundamental purpose behind what they do? The why is likely the most important message that both districts and schools should communicate with all staff. The why connects staff to the organization and inspires them to take action in fulfilling the mission and vision. As leaders of our districts and schools, we can bring our mission, vision, collective commitments, and goals to fruition by connecting our staff to the why.

The Ultimate Why

Until teams are working collaboratively to have clarity and commitment on their shared mission, vision, collective commitments, goals, and motto, they will not bring about the greatest possible impact on student learning. When we say student learning, we reflect upon the words of our colleagues Heather Friziellie, Julie Schmidt, and Jeanne Spiller (2016), who suggest our educational philosophy must have two critical core beliefs about learning: "(1) all students can learn at high levels, and (2) teams must take collective responsibility for the learning of *all* students" (p. 14). Why did we write this book? Because turning a vision into reality is the way to ensure learning and growth for all students. After all, ensuring student learning should be the fundamental purpose of every school, and it is our moral obligation to make this a reality. Plans, tips, and suggestions to help your district or school become a high-performing PLC will be shared in greater detail in the chapters ahead because, as author Jon Gordon (2018) explains, "when you know your why, and you know the way, you won't let obstacles get in the way" (p. 25).

Our hope is for this book to help your district or school navigate the process of establishing your foundation in an efficient and meaningful way. We find that a solid foundation makes a valuable impact on moving districts and schools to become powerful PLCs.

Anchors Away!

Rarely does a change take place without knowing the why. It's heard from the early stages of learning to talk in school classrooms around the world and in most meetings. "Why?" people ask. What's the reason for what we are going to do or change? We cannot stress enough the importance of communicating, or perhaps even overcommunicating, the why when you are implementing a mission, a vision, a collective commitment, and goals—or changes to any of these.

As you consider your next chapter to read, we encourage you to ponder, if you are not planning to read it from cover to cover, the why behind your next step. Perhaps you do not yet have one of the foundational pillars in place, so that is your why for jumping into a different chapter. Maybe you or your leadership team feel it is time to update the vision for where you want to go. Wherever you choose to go for your next step, we encourage you to consider first having your staff members complete the continuums found in the chapters to help guide your work. There have been times when we thought our school was at a stage on a continuum that was actually not accurate according to the staff survey results. Therefore, there is great value in administering continuums with the entire staff on a yearly basis or even more frequently as a check-in for your next steps. Whichever path you choose, we hope that you will recognize that this book is an ongoing resource to come back and use throughout your journey as a PLC.

Use the space provided to anchor your thoughts and chart your course for your next steps.

CHAPTER 2
MISSION

In a learning-centered school ensuring that all students learn must be at the heart of its mission.

—RICHARD DuFOUR, REBECCA DuFOUR, ROBERT EAKER, THOMAS W. MANY, AND MIKE MATTOS

After our first fateful PLC at Work institute together, we were compelled to apply our new knowledge and reignited passion for ensuring high levels of learning in a way that would move our school from PLC lite to PLC right. While we knew there was much to do, we also realized that the key to our journey to becoming a highly effective PLC centered on clarifying and laying or *relaying* the groundwork. We knew that a shared mission would be key to connecting all stakeholders and aligning the why of our work—from decisions about the school master schedule to instructional practices in individual classrooms.

We reflected on the current reality of our students' learning: Were all our students learning at high levels? Were we all in—meaning did all staff feel connected to our why and passionate in making decisions and aligning actions based on that why? In looking at our data, we realized that although many of our students were successful by our state's standards, this wasn't true for *all* students. And in fact, this was more true for certain populations—even certain grade levels or classrooms—than others. We simply couldn't allow this to continue. We felt a moral imperative to dig in and uncover the roots of these discrepancies. In this process, we discovered that a mentality of *mine* versus *yours*—these are *my* students, those are *your* students—though unobtrusive, had become pervasive in educators' thoughts and actions. For example, we often came to the table with a "This is what we've always done" mindset rather than considering best practices, we made excuses for data rather than analyzing them to maximize our impact, and we often worked in silos rather than leveraging the skills of each educator. To begin to shift this culture, we created a survey and invited staff to share what they valued and believed about students and our responsibilities as educators. As our guiding coalition reflected on the survey responses, we came to an understanding: in our ongoing efforts, we needed to keep at the forefront of our minds our collective belief that every school's fundamental responsibility is to ensure exceptional learning and growth for all students. We felt compelled to have a mission statement that clearly articulated the reason our school existed and what we would guarantee for the students we were blessed to serve.

With that purpose in mind, we began the process of creating a mission statement that would undergird our decision making, guide our work within collaborative teams, and launch a culture of collaboration and trust to ensure high levels of learning for all students and staff. We solicited the voices of our staff and engaged our guiding coalition in analyzing the feedback we received. We then began to craft our mission statement, routinely reminding ourselves of our fundamental purpose as a school—learning, not teaching—and of our desire that our mission statement inspire and drive our work and further clarify our why. Ultimately, our guiding coalition created the mission statement "Guaranteed exceptional learning and growth for all students." It was an exciting day when the new mission was adopted and celebrated by the school community.

As we implemented our new mission statement, we constantly connected all decision making within the school system back to our mission, using it as a sieve to filter out ideas that would not move us forward, and we saw the results in the daily actions of all staff—from how they collaborated and what they collaborated on to what was happening in classrooms. As we became a school truly focused on all learners, embracing *we* and *our* rather than *me* and *mine*, the continual improvements we witnessed in our students' outcomes reflected the impact of our redirected efforts. Our mission was apparent throughout our school, not only in our collaborative team meetings but in our instructional programming, data-driven discussions, student and teacher relationships, parent conversations, professional learning, and initiative priorities. This change positively affected our staff and our students, and we were able to live out the mission by guaranteeing exceptional learning and growth for all students.

In this chapter, we intend to ignite in you and your colleagues a passion for creating a shared mission and to guide your organization to ensure that your mission clarifies your purpose in such a way as to establish priorities and shape decisions. First, we clarify what a shared mission is and is not and utilize research from across the fields of business and education to highlight the elements needed for success. Next, we lay out possible steps that district and school teams can use to take on the work of creating, assessing, adopting or readopting, monitoring, and celebrating their shared mission. Finally, we provide tools to support each step and facilitate your successful creation and establishment of your district's or school's mission.

Navigating the Mission

The district's or school's mission statement answers the question, Why do we exist? (DuFour et al., 2024, p. 47). Answering this question clarifies the priorities and sharpens the focus of the daily actions of all stakeholders in their collective effort to reach the vision of what the school or district is intent on becoming. The greatest impact on moving a district or school forward occurs when this shared purpose is clearly captured in the mission, and all staff members deeply understand it.

There are several key components of a successful mission statement. First, the shared mission must be more than lofty aspirations or current educational verbiage. In the book *Learning by Doing* (DuFour et al., 2024), the authors share the importance of being thoughtful about the words used in the mission statement and being wary of simply "offering" learning to students. There is a temptation to use words like "provide," "help," "guide," and "administer." Though these words are common vocabulary in education and perhaps convey a sense of kindness or support—because we all want to provide what is best for students—caution must be taken against the employment of these words as they set a tone that misses the essential intention of *guaranteed* learning. Choose words that boldly state your mission, for example, "guarantee," "ensure," and "commit." Districts and schools exist to do more than just provide and impart their knowledge to students. Please see page 45 for examples of mission statements.

Another key component for a successful mission statement is that it includes a focus on learning for *all* students, as this chapter's opening epigraph quote from DuFour and colleagues indicates. It is important to define what is meant by *all* as it relates to the mission to methodically guard against omitting certain student groups, such as those who receive additional educational supports in special education, students receiving language support, or students who have a different socioeconomic background. *All* means *every single student*. No qualifiers needed. Consider if you were to ask parents why they send their children to school what their responses might be. Most would share they want to be sure their children are learning. Therefore, consider using words to capture the mission statement such as parental expectations.

The goal in creating a mission statement is not merely to create a catchy phrase but for all staff to commit to *guaranteeing or ensuring* learning for *all* students. Collectively acting and collaborating in a way that guarantees high levels of learning for all students takes intentional alignment of decisions on practices within the school. Without a clear mission, teachers are left to make decisions based on individual experiences and perspectives, many of which are based on good intentions, but when a wide variety of differing opinions and practices are brought to an organization, it is nearly impossible to collectively move forward with maximum impact. Therefore, it is critical to create a shared mission and align the efforts of the educational community to this common purpose. The mission statement of the district or school is evidenced in the actions of its members. We are frequently asked if a school should create its own foundational pillars. We believe the answer is yes. Schools have differences even in the same district. For example, high school goals and visions will often center around graduation, college, and career readiness, and so on, whereas elementary, intermediate, junior high, and other school students' goals may focus more on their schoolwork. Some districts have schools tailored to unique learning programs such as dual language; science, technology, engineering, and mathematics (STEM); science, technology, engineering, the arts, and mathematics (STEAM); and so on and would want to add those to their foundational pillars in some way.

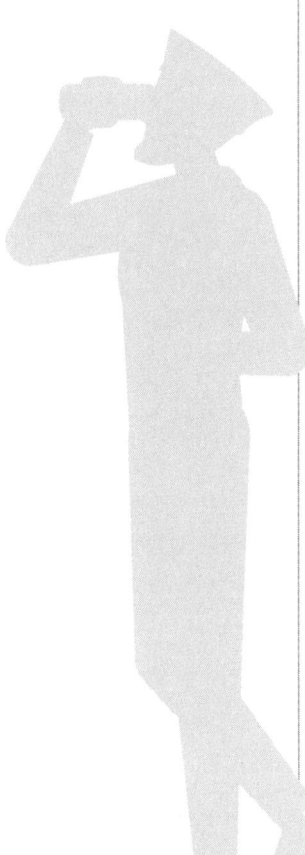

Examining Evidence of a Successful Mission

When families are looking for a place to live, they often visit schools in the area to get a sense of what school might be a good fit for their children. When Shawn moved from Mexico to Texas, a place she had never lived before, she visited schools in the area where her family thought they might purchase a home. She had narrowed her options down to two different schools in close proximity to one another. When she visited the first school, she spoke with the receptionist and asked a few questions, but the receptionist told her most things could be found and read on the school's website. Shawn left feeling discouraged, having many unanswered questions, and not feeling welcome. At the next school, she was greeted by evidence of the school celebrating both student and staff success through brightly colored bulletin boards spotlighting academic and character achievement. Shawn visited with the receptionist, who not only was so pleasant to speak with but also took a genuine interest in learning about Shawn's children and what they were looking for in a school. The receptionist provided materials clarifying the school's academic, character, and extracurricular programming. It was evident that this school had a clearly defined purpose and goals that were understood by staff. Shawn left the second school knowing that it was a perfect fit. She knew that her children's learning and growth would be valued, and if the receptionist could make her feel so welcome, she knew the teachers would do so as well. Shawn not only ended up purchasing a home so her children could attend school there, but started substitute teaching there and was hired as a teacher two months later.

This personal experience exemplifies how all practices in the district or school must align with the mission statement. Consider your own district or school. What would the staff say to the parents about the mission statement? What would they say about what the school values, and what systems and actions would parents see as a result of the mission of the school? Is what the school advertises in its mission statement a reality in the district or school? Now, consider a prospective family has been allowed to visit the classrooms, the playground, and the fine arts and physical education spaces. What would they say about their experiences in these areas? What would you hope to hear regarding what they observed? What were their observations of the learning taking place in the classrooms? What about the interactions among students and between staff and students? To the visitor, the mission should be a felt experience, but for the district and school leadership teams, it should be thoughtful, planned, and measurable. We must be intentional in examining our own evidence of a lived mission.

If the fundamental purpose of a school is to ensure learning, then our mission must call on our staff to act in a way to do so. Our mission statement is our truth—what we do every day for the students we serve. Let us be certain that our mission statement is just that, and we can demonstrate it in our daily actions.

We often assume the members of our district and our schools know what our mission is, whether that mission is written or not. We can easily think they know our collective why and will naturally behave in such a way that aligns with our mission. But that assumption creates an environment where individuals use their own why or reasons to drive their decision making and behaviors in their job. For example, a teacher might have had a poor educational experience as a child and felt not valued as a student. This teacher would then place a high priority on ensuring students in their class feel valued. This would be their overarching why for how they behave. Although making students feel valued is very important, we would also want the teacher to connect their why with the mission of the school. We must be intentional to ensure all staff have clarity on the why behind the mission.

Consider well-known companies like Apple, Amazon, and Disney. What do these companies have in common? They intentionally and tenaciously instill their mission within their organization. When employees not only understand the mission, but the why behind it and the actions and behaviors they are expected to demonstrate, they are then able to understand the fundamental purpose of the organization. The most successful companies connect people to their why. How can we apply this concept to our districts and schools, and why would it be important to do so? The same holds true for districts and schools. If the fundamental purpose is clear and well communicated, this assists employees in their decision making and actions to live out the mission.

In any organization, when employees feel a connection, they become passionate about the work. How effective is a mission statement if you aren't communicating it? Is it prominently displayed in places throughout the school where the staff can easily see it? And do you talk about how your behaviors and initiatives back up the mission? Do you celebrate when you see the mission in action? Great leaders in all industries and organizations communicate from the inside out, moving us from the why to the how and what.

It is important to connect to the district or school mission and have evidence to show we are living out the mission. In chapter 7 (page 241), we dive deeper into hiring practices and will share research surrounding why people choose to work where they do. Most importantly, connecting everyone with the why inspires each person to put the mission into action.

Taking a Deep Dive Into the Research for Developing a Mission

The importance of developing a mission has long been held as an undisputed fact in personal and business settings. Both business graduate programs and life coaches include setting a mission in their steps for success. The observational evidence on the impact of setting a mission is often held as so irrefutable that often the research is overlooked. However, noting the research findings on why having a mission is so effective in both personal and business settings and what conditions are required for a mission to produce the maximum benefits are both critical to achieving the desired positive results.

So, what does the research say about why having a mission makes such a difference? It turns out that it has a lot to do with how it makes us feel. In an organizational setting, when a shared mission clarifies a purpose that resonates with employees' own values, the resulting emotional connection positively affects autonomy in decision making, performance, and job satisfaction. A global research study conducted by Imperative (2015) and New York University in 2015 found that purpose-oriented employees are:

- 64 percent more likely to find fulfillment in their work
- 77 percent more likely to report that their work had a purposeful impact
- 30 percent more likely to be high performers
- 62 percent more likely to seek out opportunities for growth
- 54 percent more likely to remain at the same company for more than five years
- 47 percent more likely to positively promote their employers

In addition, a shared mission elicits passion for a shared purpose and inspires the commitment to perform, produce, and even change in order to achieve collective goals greater than those of the individual. An organizational culture is developed and sustained by a shared mission. According to researchers Inés Alegre, Jasmina Berbegal-Mirabent, Adrián Guerrero, and Marta Mas-Machuca (2018), the impact on employee motivation and behavior, as well as organizational performance, is clear and profoundly valuable.

Additional studies focused on the conditions that must be in place to maximize the value that a mission adds. In a meta-synthesis studying the impact of mission statements in schools, educator David Coker (2022) determined that while "a sentence by itself shows little promise of moving people and organizations," one that focuses on dimensions that produce value-added results does improve outcomes (p. 221). These findings are consistent with the explanation in *Learning by Doing* (DuFour et al., 2024) that the biggest mistake in creating a mission statement is "confusing *writing* a mission statement with *living* a mission" (p. 42). A mission statement should clarify priorities and sharpen the focus of the work of each individual in the organization. When each member of the group is clear on not only why they exist but also the areas affected by this why, they are better able to apply that why in their thoughts, discussions, and actions. This is reinforced in the study's further findings that "after developing visible, actionable, and usable mission statements, there exists a more important step: A development of an organization's commitment to the ideals of the organization, communication and knowledge sharing, culture building, and a focus on accomplishments" (Coker, 2022, p. 220).

Sailing Into Action for Each Stage of Developing a Shared Mission

The time frame for adopting or readopting your mission with the process we outline in the following pages will probably be the briefest of all the foundational pillars. If time is dedicated to this process weekly, it is reasonable to complete all the steps in as little as a month. One reason for this is that the basis for all school missions is rooted in the premise with which we opened the book: "The fundamental purpose of school is learning, not teaching" (DuFour et al., 2024, p. 153). Therefore, schools already have a jumping-off point for creating their own mission statements.

When preparing to create a shared mission, the first step is to determine your district's or school's current picture of reality using the "Mission Continuum (District)" (page 34) or "Mission Continuum (School)" (page 35). The Mission Continuum provides an overview of the indicators in each stage of the progress trajectory, from preinitiating to sustaining, that districts or schools typically follow when creating and establishing their mission. By studying the descriptors for each indicator across the continuum and noting which most closely do and do not describe your district or school, you are able to determine where in the process you are and what your next steps should be. After consulting the Mission Continuum and determining your reality, consult the applicable section that follows and follow the steps listed to create, refine, or sustain your district's or school's mission. We use the word "consult" because this isn't a lockstep process, nor are the tools provided under one indicator helpful only for schools that find themselves at that stage. We would caution you not to jump steps in the Mission Continuum (there are no shortcuts in this work) because there may be tools in sections at a previous or later stage that may be valuable to your school or district.

The Preinitiating Stage

A district or school in the preinitiating stage is one that has just opened, is brand new to the work of PLCs, or hasn't previously tackled the foundational pillars. These schools either don't have a mission statement at all or haven't previously engaged in a collaborative process to create one (that is, one was inherited or created in isolation by perhaps a superintendent or principal).

1. Begin with "What's My Why?" (page 37). This tool prompts staff to reflect on their personal why and educational beliefs. This is a critical step in connecting the why of individuals to the why of an organization to maximize both commitment and impact.

2. Engage staff in an analysis of the impact a school or district mission has on desired outcomes using either "The Power of a Mission Statement (District)" (page 38) or "The Power of a Mission Statement (School)" (page 41). This tool provides staff with a series of quotes to support the why of clarifying a mission. This time to read, reflect, and respond creates a collective understanding and desire to drive the work of creating or clarifying the shared mission.

3. To activate thinking and generate fruitful discussion surrounding a shared mission statement, lead staff in the "Mission Sort" (page 44) activity.

4. Guide staff in using the "Investigate and Create the Mission Statement" (page 45) activity. In this activity, staff will study examples of mission statements to analyze intended actions and outcomes through word choice and then create a potential mission statement for your district or school.

5. Have the guiding coalition synthesize potential mission statements generated by the staff to create a cohesive statement using the "Guiding Coalition Mission Formalization" (page 47) tool. This synthesis tool will aid the guiding coalition in creating a preliminary mission statement that represents the overarching ideas of what staff believe to be the district's or school's purpose.

6. Use the "Mission Proposal and Adoption (Step 1)" (page 48) and "Mission Proposal and Adoption (Step 2)" (page 49) tool to collect staff feedback for any possible revisions needed for them to commit to the proposed mission statement. The activity is the final step leading to the adoption and implementation of the new shared mission statement.

7. Systematically look for evidence of staff living out the mission and continue to celebrate the the ongoing work of the mission using the "Celebration Planning" (page 50) tool. This tool is designed to assist the guiding coalition in making celebration intentional for the staff by deliberately planning how and when to celebrate throughout the year. Another useful tool designed to assist with your your celebration is the "Mission in Action and Parent Celebration Certificates" (page 53), celebrating individuals who demonstrate living out the shared mission.

8. Monitor progress from the preinitiating stage to the initiating stage by collecting evidence corresponding with the indicators in the "Mission Continuum (District)" (page 34) and "Mission Continuum (School)" (page 35). The continuum serves as a road map indicating the major mile marker on your journey. The tool provides direction on the next steps needed to continue moving forward.

The Initiating Stage

A district or school in the initiating stage is one that has a mission statement, but that mission may not have been created collaboratively or with the current staff. This might also be a school that has a mission statement that was created collaboratively and with the current staff, but there is little impact on professional practice, possibly because of a lack of clarity.

1. Begin with "What's My Why?" (page 37). This tool prompts staff to reflect on their personal why and educational beliefs. This is a critical step in connecting the why of individuals to the why of an organization to maximize both commitment and impact.

2. Engage staff in an analysis of the impact a school mission has on desired outcomes using either "The Power of a Mission Statement (District)" (page 38) or "The Power of a Mission Statement (School)" (page 41). This tool provides staff with insight from thought leaders that is meant to promote collaborative learning and conversation to stimulate a common understanding of the impact of this foundational pillar. This time to read, reflect, and respond creates a collective understanding and desire to drive the work of creating or clarifying the shared mission.

3. Solicit staff feedback on the current mission statement using the "Mission Survey (District)" (page 54) or "Mission Survey (School)" (page 56) to determine whether the mission statement needs revision. The tool is designed

to gather insight and evidence of the current reality of school perceptions of the current mission statement.

4. The guiding coalition will use the "Mission Survey Analysis (District)" (page 58) or "Mission Survey Analysis (School)" (page 59) to analyze staff responses from the "Mission Survey (District)" (page 54) or "Mission Survey (School)" (page 56). The tool will guide the team in synthesizing feedback to prioritize the next steps in revising the shared mission to ensure it drives the decisions and actions of all staff. Note: If the survey shows that staff agree that the foundational aspects of the mission are in place, continue to step 5. If the survey shows that the foundational aspects of the mission are not agreed on, return to the preinitiating stage, beginning with step 3.

5. Use the "Mission Proposal and Adoption (Step 1)" (page 48) and "Mission Proposal and Adoption (Step 2)" (page 49) tool to collect staff feedback for any possible revisions needed for them to commit to the proposed mission statement. The activity is the final step leading to the adoption and implementation of the new shared mission statement.

6. Systematically look for evidence of staff living out the mission and continue to celebrate the ongoing work of the mission using the "Celebration Planning" (page 50) tool. This tool is designed to assist the guiding coalition in making celebration intentional for the staff by deliberately planning how and when to celebrate throughout the year. Another useful tool designed to assist with your celebration is the "Mission in Action and Parent Celebration Certificates" (page 51), celebrating individuals who demonstrate living out the shared mission.

7. Monitor progress from the initiating to the implementing stage by collecting evidence corresponding with the indicators in the "Mission Continuum (District)" (page 34) and "Mission Continuum (School)" (page 35). The continuum serves as a road map indicating the major mile marker on your journey. The tool provides direction on the next steps needed to continue moving forward.

The Implementing Stage

A district or school at the implementing stage is one that has a mission statement that was created collaboratively with the current staff. There is evidence that the mission statement provides greater clarity on what specifically students are to learn and how their learning will be monitored. However, full buy-in hasn't yet been achieved. This could look like teachers expressing concerns about how actions to support the mission affect their autonomy.

1. Engage staff in a review of the current mission statement and collect feedback by using the "Staff Reflections—Implementing Stage (District)" (page 60) or "Staff Reflections—Implementing Stage (School)" (page 61). This tool guides

staff through a reflective process of their current shared mission statement with guiding questions.

2. The guiding coalition conducts an analysis of staff reflections using the "Guiding Coalition Analysis—Implementing Stage" (page 62). This guide provides step-by-step procedures to analyze the feedback from the "Staff Reflections—Implementing Stage (District)" (page 60) or "Staff Reflections—Implementing Stage (School)" (page 61). Based on the reflections of the guiding coalition, prioritize the next steps to move from the implementing stage to the developing stage.

3. Consider the "School Action Plan—Implementing Stage" (page 64) resource designed to assist the guiding coalition in synthesizing the staff feedback and creating a clear, actionable path forward.

4. Systematically look for evidence of staff living out the mission and continue to celebrate the the ongoing work of the mission using the "Celebration Planning" (page 50) tool. This tool is designed to assist the guiding coalition in making celebration intentional for the staff by deliberately planning how and when to celebrate throughout the year. Another useful tool designed to assist with celebration is the "Mission in Action and Parent Celebration Certificates" (page 51) .

5. Monitor progress from the implementing stage to the developing stage by collecting evidence corresponding with the indicators in the "Mission Continuum (District)" (page 34) and "Mission Continuum (School)" (page 35). The continuum serves as a road map indicating the major mile marker on your journey. The tool helps clarify the next steps needed to continue moving forward.

The Developing Stage

A school or district at the developing stage is one that has a mission statement that was created collaboratively with the current staff or adopted by the staff. There is evidence that this mission statement clearly establishes the expectations for student learning and the monitoring of that learning in the actions of staff. Teachers are becoming more analytical in assessing evidence of student learning and then conducting inquiry into and adjusting instructional practices as needed to maximize student learning.

1. Engage staff in a review of the current mission statement and collect feedback by using the "Staff Reflections—Developing Stage (District)" (page 65) or "Staff Reflections—Developing Stage (School)" (page 66) tool. This tool guides staff through a reflective process of their current shared mission statement with guiding questions.

2. The guiding coalition conducts an analysis of staff reflections using the "Guiding Coalition Analysis—Developing Stage" (page 67) tool. This guide provides step-by-step procedures to analyze the feedback from the "Staff Reflections—Developing Stage (District)" (page 65) or "Staff

Reflections—Developing Stage (School)" (page 66) tool. Based on the reflections of the guiding coalition, prioritize the next steps to move from the developing to the sustaining stage.

3. Consider the "School Action Plan—Developing Stage" (page 69) resource designed to assist the guiding coalition in synthesizing the staff feedback and creating a clear, actionable path forward.

4. Systematically look for evidence of staff living out the mission and continue to celebrate the ongoing work of the mission using the "Celebration Planning" (page 50) tool. This tool is designed to assist the guiding coalition in making celebration intentional for the staff by deliberately planning how and when to celebrate throughout the year. Another useful tool designed to assist with your celebration is the "Mission in Action and Parent Celebration Certificates" (page 51).

5. Monitor progress from the developing to the sustaining stage by collecting evidence corresponding with the indicators in the "Mission Continuum (District)" (page 34) and "Mission Continuum (School)" (page 35). The continuum serves as a road map indicating the major mile marker on your journey. The tool helps clarify the next steps needed to continue moving forward.

The Sustaining Stage

A district or school at the sustaining stage is one that has a mission statement that was created collaboratively with the current staff. Staff demonstrate commitment to the mission by working collaboratively to clarify what students must learn, monitor learning in an intentional and ongoing way, and implement systematic intervention and extension. Teachers implement, examine, and adjust all practices and procedures for their impact on student learning.

1. Engage staff in a review of the current mission statement and collect feedback by using the "Staff Reflections—Sustaining Stage (District)" (page 70) or "Staff Reflections—Sustaining Stage (School)" (page 72). This tool guides staff through a reflective process of their current shared mission statement with guiding questions.

2. The guiding coalition conducts an analysis of staff reflections using the "Guiding Coalition Analysis—Sustaining Stage" (page 74) tool. This guide provides step-by-step procedures to analyze the feedback from the staff reflections tools to prioritize the next steps.

3. Consider the "School Action Plan—Sustaining Stage" (page 76) resource designed to assist the guiding coalition in synthesizing the staff feedback and creating a clear, actionable path forward.

4. Systematically look for evidence of staff living out the mission and continue to celebrate the ongoing work of the mission using the "Celebration Planning"

(page 50) tool. This tool is designed to assist the guiding coalition in making celebration intentional for the staff by deliberately planning how and when to celebrate throughout the year. Another useful tool designed to assist with your celebration is the "Mission in Action and Parent Celebration Certificates" (page 51), celebrating individuals who demonstrate living out the shared mission.

5. Monitor progress within the sustaining stage by collecting evidence and revisiting action steps. Remember, as new staff are hired, it's important to discuss the shared mission with them so they can have a sense of connectedness to it and understand how their role in the district or school supports the mission.

Staying Afloat Through Common Challenges to Developing a Mission

Creating your new mission is a process of collaboration to ensure all voices of the learning community are heard. We have designed the steps and tools to avoid some of the challenges we experienced; however, along the journey, you may find that some challenges may arise. The if-then chart shown in table 2.1 is intended to share some common challenges you might experience and potential steps to overcome those challenges successfully. For each statement on the left-hand side, the possible response listed on the right-hand side is intended as a jumping-off point for engaging in a conversation to develop a solution that best fits the specifics of your staff and their needs.

Table 2.1: If-Then Chart

If . . .	Then . . .
Some teachers or teams are aligning their practices to the mission while others are not.	Clarify with the latter teachers or teams the mission and expected evidence of alignment.
There is little to no evidence of student growth for *all* students.	Provide collaborative learning with all staff surrounding different student populations and their needs. Examine best practices utilized for students.
General education and special education teachers are not collaborating about students' needs.	Ensure time in the master schedule for staff to collaborate on a regular basis.
The mission statement is not student focused.	Revise to clearly prioritize student learning.
Staff are committed to the mission, but the statement is very lengthy.	Engage in revising the mission so that it is easy to understand, remember, and internalize.

Knowing the Ropes for Mission Development

As you and your colleagues work to establish your organization's mission, orient yourselves by keeping in mind the following.

- District and school mission statements must be student focused.
- The mission statement must ultimately align with the district or school vision.
- The mission statement should not be created by one person in isolation and should include other key members of the district or school.
- The mission statement should show that all students are valued.
- The mission statement should include the word "learning."
- Each word of the statement should be deliberate, illuminate the purpose and add value.

Celebrating the Mission

Once staff have created and adopted the mission statement, it is critical not to let the mission statement fall by the wayside. It will be important for the community of educators to keep it front and center. After all, the mission states why the school community exists. That is a pretty big deal! It will be important to acknowledge the efforts of individuals bringing the mission to life and also celebrate the impact the mission has made in guiding the work of the school community to the vision. The guiding coalition should brainstorm ideas of how the district or school will be intentional in noticing staff who are working to align instructional practices and decision making to the mission using the "Celebration Planning" (page 50) tool.

Ideas to start your brainstorming include the following.

- Add a five-minute agenda item to all meetings (guiding coalition, collaborative teams, administrative teams, and so forth) to celebrate actions and success stories aligned with the mission statement.
- Include shout-outs in the district or school newsletter highlighting examples of success aligned with the mission statement.
- Plan school or classroom visits that allow educators to visit colleagues' classrooms to celebrate actions and practices aligned with the mission statement (successful small-group intervention, extension activity, differentiated instructional practices, and so on).
- Create a celebration certificate that any educator can complete and give to the supervisor or principal to hand deliver with a treat to the faculty member who is living out the mission statement.
- In the faculty workroom or lounge, create a "Mission Possible" board to which any employee can add photo examples of living their collective mission in their classroom, work area, and so on.

- Have a notice posted in the front office or in school newsletters that displays the mission statement, along with a certificate for family or community members to complete when they see staff demonstrating the mission statement. They then turn the certificate in to the school office for the principal to acknowledge and celebrate recognized staff.

These are just a few ideas, and we know there are many more that your guiding coalition will brainstorm. There are several tools for celebration in our end-of-chapter reproducibles. The most important part of this process is to recognize and celebrate the work in your school or district that aligns with your mission statement. It keeps the mission front and center and clearly communicates the value of a community of educators working toward the same results. Be intentional and celebrate your faculty members as they live out the shared mission.

Stay the Course

Collecting evidence that a mission informs and guides daily decision making and aligns the efforts of staff is a good litmus test to gauge the strength of a mission. Monitoring the implementation and success of the mission statement will ensure that the district or school community continues to move toward success for the learning of all students. It will be critical for the guiding coalition to continue to utilize the tools and continue to measure the progress through the stages from preinitiating to sustaining. This not only sheds light on your current reality but also provides valuable insight into the next steps needed to continue your trajectory toward success in living out the mission.

Anchors Away!

The mission is the fundamental purpose of the district or school, so clarity is essential and the ability for employees to easily recall it is key. Far too often, districts and schools confuse mission and vision as being one and the same, so ensure all staff members are not only aware of each of these important foundational pillars but also know the difference. Everyone should feel the mission is calling them to their purpose; it's what they do each day in their positions, and hopefully, the word "learning" is part of that mission. After all, it's why we have schools. If your mission is not summoning you to greatness, it might be time for a change. If it is a call to action for your district or school, then we cannot wait to hear your success story!

Use the space provided to anchor your thoughts and chart your course for your next steps.

Mission Continuum (District)

Instructions: Individually, read the indicators that describe each stage from preinitiating through sustaining. Honestly assess the current reality of the establishment of your district mission. Consider what evidence or anecdotes support your assessment. Record your reflections in the space provided.

Shared mission: It is evident that learning for all is our core purpose.

Mission Continuum Stages

Preinitiating	Initiating	Implementing	Developing	Sustaining
☐ The purpose of the district has not been articulated with a mission statement. ☐ Most staff view the purpose of the district as to provide an education for students. ☐ The district operates from the assumption that although all students should have the opportunity to learn, responsibility for learning belongs to the individual student and will be determined by the student's ability and effort.	☐ An attempt has been made to clarify the purpose of the district through the development of a formal mission statement by a few staff. It does little to impact professional practices, decision making, or student learning. ☐ District-level leaders analyze state or summative assessment data.	☐ A process has been initiated to provide greater focus and clarity regarding the mission of learning for all. ☐ Decision making, policies, and practices occasionally align with the mission statement. ☐ District-level leaders analyze state or summative assessment data. ☐ Steps are being taken to clarify what, specifically, students are to learn in each grade, course, and content area. ☐ Leaders are looking for formal ways to monitor student learning.	☐ There is a clear shared mission statement with a focus on learning for all. ☐ Decision making, policies, and practices frequently align with the mission statement. ☐ District-level leaders routinely analyze the monitoring of student learning at each school and engage in discussions with school leaders for ongoing improvement. ☐ District and school leaders collaboratively commit to helping all students learn at high levels by establishing a guaranteed and viable curriculum. ☐ District and school leaders work together to become more analytical in assessing the evidence of student learning and to become more effective in assessing student learning and providing instructional practices and professional learning to teachers to enhance student learning.	☐ There is a clear shared mission statement with a focus on learning for all. ☐ Decision making, policies, and practices align with the mission statement. ☐ District-level leaders routinely analyze and monitor student learning and engage in discussions with school leaders for ongoing improvement. ☐ District and school leaders collaboratively commit to helping all students learn at high levels and establish a guaranteed and viable curriculum. ☐ Teachers are provided with ongoing professional learning related to district and school goals to ensure high levels of learning for all students. ☐ The district has created a process for implementing a systematic plan of intervention to students who need support. ☐ Educators in the district are willing to examine all practices and procedures in light of their impact on learning. ☐ Feedback is routinely collected from staff, families, and the community to determine the mission impact on student learning. ☐ The district routinely celebrates colleagues when they demonstrate behaviors and actions linked to the mission.

I believe our district is at the _____ stage based on the preceding indicators. The evidence to support my rationale includes:

Source: Adapted from DuFour, R., DuFour, R., Eaker, R., Many, T. W., Mattos, M., & Muhammad, A. (2024). Learning by doing: A handbook for Professional Learning Communities at Work (4th ed.). Bloomington, IN: Solution Tree Press.

Mission Continuum (School)

Instructions: Individually, read the indicators that describe each stage from preinitiating through sustaining. Honestly assess the current reality of the establishment of your school mission. Consider what evidence or anecdotes support your assessment. Record your reflections in the space provided.

Shared mission: It is evident that learning for all is our core purpose.

Mission Continuum Stages

Preinitiating	Initiating	Implementing	Developing	Sustaining
☐ The purpose of the school has not been articulated with a mission statement. ☐ Most staff view the mission of the school as teaching. They operate from the assumption that although all students should have the opportunity to learn, responsibility for learning belongs to the individual student and will be determined by the student's ability and effort. ☐ There is not enough time for teachers to collaborate during the school day.	☐ An attempt has been made to clarify the purpose of the school through the development of a formal mission statement by a few staff. It does little to impact professional practices, decision making, or student learning. ☐ Staff are committed to teaching all students who are assigned to them and offer support for students who need additional assistance to learn. ☐ There is time for teachers to collaborate during the school day if they desire to do so. ☐ Teachers are concerned that efforts to create a guaranteed and viable curriculum will deprive them of their academic freedom.	☐ A process involving several staff has been initiated to provide greater focus and clarity regarding the mission of learning for all. ☐ Staff are committed to helping all students in their class learn. ☐ Teachers view student learning as their primary responsibility. ☐ Teachers use the intended time in the school day to collaborate; however, they are unclear as to what to collaborate about during this time. ☐ Decision making, policies, and practices occasionally align with the mission statement. ☐ Steps are being taken to clarify what, specifically, students are to learn and to monitor their learning. ☐ Some teachers are concerned that these efforts will deprive them of academic freedom.	☐ There is a clear shared mission statement with a focus on learning for all. ☐ Staff are committed to helping all students learn. Teams view student learning as their collective responsibility. ☐ Teachers use the intended time in the school day to collaborate around the four critical questions of a professional learning community. ☐ Decision making, policies, and practices frequently align with the mission statement. ☐ School leaders and teachers work collaboratively to commit to helping all students learn at high levels by establishing a guaranteed and viable curriculum. ☐ Teachers are beginning to see evidence of the benefits of clearly established expectations for student learning and systematic processes to monitor student learning. ☐ Teachers are becoming more analytical in assessing the evidence of student learning and are looking for ways to become more effective in assessing student learning and providing instruction to enhance student learning.	☐ There is a clear shared mission statement with a focus on learning for all. ☐ Staff are committed to helping all students learn. Teams view student learning as their collective responsibility. ☐ Teachers use the intended time in the school day to collaborate around the four critical questions of a professional learning community. ☐ Decision making, policies, and practices align with the mission statement. ☐ School leaders and teachers work collaboratively to commit to helping all students learn at high levels by establishing a guaranteed and viable curriculum. ☐ Teachers routinely analyze and monitor student learning and engage in discussions for ongoing improvement. ☐ Staff are committed to working collaboratively to clarify what students are to learn in each unit, creating frequent common formative assessments to monitor each student's learning on an ongoing basis and implementing a systematic plan of intervention when students experience difficulty. ☐ Educators in the school are willing to examine all practices and procedures in light of their impact on learning. ☐ Educators are committed to ongoing professional learning related to school goals to ensure high levels of learning for all students. ☐ Feedback is routinely collected from staff, families, and the community to determine the mission impact on student learning. ☐ The school routinely celebrates colleagues when they demonstrate behaviors and actions linked to the mission.

I believe our school is at the _____ stage based on the preceding descriptors. The evidence to support my rationale includes:

Source: Adapted from DuFour, R., DuFour, R., Eaker, R., Many, T. W., Mattos, M., & Muhammad, A. (2024). Learning by doing: A handbook for Professional Learning Communities at Work (4th ed.). Bloomington, IN: Solution Tree Press.

REPRODUCIBLE

What's My Why?

> Insert Your District or School Logo Here

Why did you choose your profession?

_____

_____

_____

_____

Why did you choose to work at _____?

_____

_____

_____

_____

Why did you choose to work in your current position?

_____

_____

_____

_____

Name _____

Anchor Your Vision © 2025 Solution Tree Press • SolutionTree.com
Visit **go.SolutionTree.com/PLCbooks/AYV** and enter the unique access code
found on the book's inside front cover to access this reproducible.

The Power of a Mission Statement (District)

Instructions: The mission pillar focuses on our why, the reason our school district exists. The mission is set in the present tense and is typically short, clear, and powerful. The mission should energize people both in and out of the school district and explain why the staff in our organization do what they do. People need a purpose; they need to know that what they are doing is important and is making a difference to the overall success of their school district. Therefore, the mission must be an action-oriented statement that shares the primary purpose.

In relation to the school district, the mission statement asks, "What is the fundamental purpose of our district? If we believe the fundamental purpose in all our schools is student learning, not teaching, then how do we demonstrate that by the work we are doing at the district level? If new staff or educators from another district visited our schools, what would they see us doing? What evidence would we show them to support our mission?"

> What does our school district do well right now? What are we proud to share with our community?

Read the quotes that follow and highlight words and phrases that resonate with you and your educational philosophy of how a mission impacts a school district. Then, respond to the questions. These quotes are meant to stimulate thinking and understanding behind a district mission statement while also providing for meaningful collaboration among colleagues that is grounded in the ideas from experts to create a common understanding of the value of this foundational pillar.

"After developing visible, actionable, and usable mission statements, there exists a more important step: A development of an organization's commitment to the ideals of the organization, communication and knowledge sharing, culture building, and a focus on accomplishments" (Coker, 2022, p. 220).

"What matters is that you have a team with a vision that's on a mission. Make the time to create your mission and vision together and then make even more time to live it" (Gordon, 2018, p. 31).

In her article on the differences between traditional leaders, PLC lite leaders, and PLC leaders, Jasmine Kullar (2022) describes a PLC leader as someone who "collaboratively creates a mission statement and ensures everyone knows it—but also everyone believes in it and lives it. Behaviors are all aligned to the mission statement. It becomes the foundation of everything" (p. 18).

"When you promote your mission to your employees, it results in a higher level of employee engagement and positive work culture, keeping them invested in the good work your company does when they go about their day-to-day tasks" (Craig, 2018).

"Without consensus among staff regarding the school's mission, improvement efforts may drift around a few common assumptions rather than strong shared principles" (Gruenert & Whitaker, 2015, p. 92).

"The most deeply motivated people—not to mention those that are most productive and satisfied—hitch their desires to a cause larger than themselves. . . . Nothing bonds a team like a shared mission. The more people that share a common cause . . . the more your group will do deeply satisfying and outstanding work" (Pink, 2011, as cited in DuFour et al., 2016, p. 38).

"Leaders need the ability to develop a shared moral purpose and meaning as well as a pathway for attaining that purpose. . . . Great leaders connect others to the reasons they became educators—their moral purpose" (Fullan & Quinn, 2016, as cited in DuFour et al., 2016, p. 38).

"In White River School District, our mission is ensuring high levels of learning for each student and preparing them for success after high school. *Ensure* is a big verb—it requires alignment to the mission from every role. As we have said, hope is not a plan. We need to do more than just hope that each student achieves" (Keating & Rhoades, 2022, p. 11).

What research resonates with you, and why?

Do you believe all students should learn at high levels? If so, what does that look like?

How do educators in our school district work together to improve students' lives?

Does our district mission statement inspire our staff?

References

Coker, D. (2022). A mission statement does not a mission make: A mixed methods investigation in public education. *International Education Studies, 15*(1), 210–225. https://doi.org/10.5539/ies.v15n1p210

Craig, W. (2018, May 15). *The importance of having a mission-driven company.* Accessed at www.forbes.com/sites/williamcraig/2018/05/15/the-importance-of-having-a-mission-driven-company/?sh=2c3adf053a9c on October 31, 2023.

DuFour, R., DuFour, R., Eaker, R., Many, T. W., & Mattos, M. (2024). *Learning by doing: A handbook for Professional Learning Communities at Work* (4th ed.). Bloomington, IN: Solution Tree Press.

Fullan, M., & Quinn, J. (2016). *Coherence: The right drivers in action for schools, districts, and systems.* Thousand Oaks, CA: Corwin.

Gordon, J. (2018). *The power of a positive team: Proven principles and practices that make great teams great.* Hoboken, NJ: Wiley.

Gruenert, S., & Whitaker, T. (2015). *School culture rewired: How to define, assess, and transform it.* Alexandria, VA: ASCD.

Keating, J., & Rhoades, M. (2022). A new era in district and school improvement: The critical role of the superintendent and school board. *AllThingsPLC Magazine, 7*(2), 8–14.

Kullar, J. (2022). Are you a PLC leader, a PLC lite leader, or a traditional leader? *AllThingsPLC Magazine, 7*(2), 16–21.

Pink, D. H. (2011). *Drive: The surprising truth about what motivates us.* New York: Riverhead Books.

The Power of a Mission Statement (School)

Instructions: The mission pillar focuses on our why, the reason our school exists. The mission is set in the present tense and is typically short, clear, and powerful. The mission should energize people both in and out of the school and explain why the staff in our organization do what they do. People need a purpose; they need to know that what they are doing is important and is making a difference to the overall success of their school. Therefore, the mission statement must be an action-oriented statement and share the primary purpose.

In relation to schools, the mission statement asks, What is the fundamental purpose of our school? If we believe the fundamental purpose is learning, not teaching, then how do we demonstrate that by the work we are doing? If new staff or educators from another district or school visited, what would they see us doing? What evidence would we show them to support our mission?

What does our school do well right now?

Read the quotes and research that follow and highlight words and phrases that resonate with you and your educational philosophy of how a mission impacts a school community. Then, respond to the questions. These quotes are meant to stimulate thinking and understanding behind a school mission statement while also providing for meaningful collaboration among colleagues that is grounded in the ideas from experts to create a common understanding of the value of this foundational pillar.

"What matters is that you have a team with a vision that's on a mission. Make the time to create your mission and vision together and then make even more time to live it" (Gordon, 2018, p. 31).

In her article on the differences between traditional leaders, PLC lite leaders, and PLC leaders, Jasmine Kullar (2022) describes a PLC leader as someone who "collaboratively creates a mission statement and ensures everyone knows it—but also everyone believes in it and lives it. Behaviors are all aligned to the mission statement. It becomes the foundation of everything" (p. 18).

"The most deeply motivated people—not to mention those that are most productive and satisfied—hitch their desires to a cause larger than themselves. . . . Nothing bonds a team like a shared mission. The more people that share a common cause . . . the more your group will do deeply satisfying and outstanding work" (Pink, 2011, as cited in DuFour et al., 2016, p. 38).

"Leaders need the ability to develop a shared moral purpose and meaning as well as a pathway for attaining that purpose. . . . Great leaders connect others to the reasons they became educators—their moral purpose" (Fullan & Quinn, 2016, as cited in DuFour et al., 2016, p. 38).

"Without consensus among staff regarding the school's mission, improvement efforts may drift around a few common assumptions rather than strong shared principles" (Gruenert & Whitaker, 2015, p. 92).

What research resonates with you, and why?

Do you believe all students should learn at high levels? If so, what does that look like?

How does our school improve students' lives?

How will the mission be demonstrated and observable throughout the school?

Does our school mission statement inspire our staff?

References

DuFour, R., DuFour, R., Eaker, R., Many, T. W., & Mattos, M. (2024). *Learning by doing: A handbook for Professional Learning Communities at Work* (4th ed.). Bloomington, IN: Solution Tree Press.

Fullan, M., & Quinn, J. (2016). *Coherence: The right drivers in action for schools, districts, and systems.* Thousand Oaks, CA: Corwin.

Gordon, J. (2018). *The power of a positive team: Proven principles and practices that make great teams great.* Hoboken, NJ: Wiley.

Gruenert, S., & Whitaker, T. (2015). *School culture rewired: How to define, assess, and transform it.* Alexandria, VA: ASCD.

Kullar, J. (2022). Are you a PLC leader, a PLC lite leader, or a traditional leader? *AllThingsPLC Magazine, 7*(2), 16–21.

Pink, D. H. (2011). *Drive: The surprising truth about what motivates us.* New York: Riverhead Books.

Mission Sort

Instructions: Cut apart the company names and mission statements shown on the next page and place them in a bag for table teams. Give teams five minutes to match up the companies and mission statements based on what they know about each company, asking them to put their hands up as they complete this task. Keep track of the time the first team and last team finish sorting. After all teams have had the opportunity to complete sorting, provide teams with an uncut copy of the tool as an answer key. Celebrate the number of matches teams have correct and the time in which sorting was done. Connect for teams the speed and accuracy with which they were able to complete their sorting and the way that the companies make their mission visible in the way they do business. Then, discuss the reasons they paired the companies with the mission statements. What evidence have they seen or experienced when shopping or visiting these companies? Do they feel the companies are living out their missions? If so, how? If not, what could they be doing?

Tesla (2024)	To accelerate the world's transition to sustainable energy.
Ford (2024)	We are here for one purpose, to help build a better world, where every person is free to move and pursue their dreams.
Lamborghini (2024)	Turning our visionary ideas into stunning creations.
Dutch Bros Coffee (n.d.)	It's our mission to make a massive difference, one cup at a time.
Caribou Coffee (2024)	Together, we create day-making experiences that spark chain reactions of good.
Starbucks (2024)	To inspire and nurture the human spirit—one person, one cup and one neighborhood at a time.

References

Automobili Lamborghini S.p.A. (2024). *Lamborghini brand manifesto*. Accessed at https://www.lamborghini.com/en-en/beyond/brand-manifesto on April 19, 2024.

Caribou Coffee. (2024). About us. Caribou Coffee. Accessed at https://cariboucoffee.com on September 11, 2024.

Dutch Bros Coffee. (n.d.). *Our story*. Accessed at https://www.dutchbros.com/our-story on April 23, 2024.

Ford Motor Company. (2024). *About us*. Accessed at https://corporate.ford.com/about.html?gnav=footer-aboutford on April 19, 2024.

Starbucks Corporation. (2024). *Archive*. Accessed at https://archive.starbucks.com/record/our-mission on April 20, 2024.

Tesla. (2024). *About us*. Accessed at https://www.tesla.com on April 19, 2024.

Investigate and Create the Mission Statement

Instructions: As a group, analyze the example mission statements that follow, paying particular attention to how each statement is focused on taking action. Each word in a mission statement must be deliberately chosen for clarity.

Step 1: Discuss the example mission statements that have been completed for you in the first two rows.

Step 2: Work together as a team to analyze the example in the third row.

Step 3: Analyze your organization's existing mission statement and reflect and discuss using the questions that follow.

Mission Statement Examples	Actions	Desired Outcome(s)	For Whom?
To guarantee exceptional learning and growth for all students and staff.	Guarantee	Exceptional learning and growth	All students Staff
To engage each student and ensure a high-quality education that includes social, emotional, physical, and academic pursuits.	Ensure, engage	High-quality education Social, emotional, physical, and academic pursuits	Each student
Our school prepares every student for success in the 21st century by engaging them in rigorous and relevant learning that assures academic, physical, and emotional growth.			

Our mission statement	What is the action word?	What are we doing?	Who will this impact?

Is the action strong (guarantee, ensure, promise), or is it less definitive (provide, offer, help)?

Does our mission statement focus on the fundamental purpose of moving students to high levels of learning?

Are the right people listed in our mission statement? Whom do we want to impact?

Does the language of our mission statement allow for the opportunity to opt out? For example, are we providing opportunities or guaranteeing learning?

Does our mission statement explain why we exist?

How will our mission statement move our professional learning community toward our shared vision?

Guiding Coalition Mission Formalization

Instructions: The guiding coalition will collect and analyze the staff "Investigate and Create the Mission Statement" (page 45) activity to synthesize the ideas that staff brainstormed into one cohesive mission statement.

Mission Statement	Actions	Desired Outcomes	For Whom?

Is the action strong (guarantee, ensure, promise), or is it flimsy (provide, offer, help)?
Does our mission statement focus on the fundamental purpose of doing the work of moving students to high levels of learning?
Are the right people listed in our mission statement? Whom do we want to impact?
Does the language of our mission statement allow for the opportunity to opt out? For example, are we providing opportunities or guaranteeing learning?
How does our mission statement explain why we exist?
How will this mission statement move our professional learning community toward our shared vision?

Anchor Your Vision © 2025 Solution Tree Press • SolutionTree.com
Visit **go.SolutionTree.com/PLCbooks/AYV** and enter the unique access code found on the book's inside front cover to access this reproducible.

Mission Proposal and Adoption (Step 1)

Instructions: Add time to your guiding coalition meeting agenda to brainstorm and make plans to create a method to collect staff feedback for the mission statement. Use step 1 for brainstorming and planning. When creating a feedback form, consider how you will garner consensus, allowing all staff to indicate their commitment to the new or revised mission. This tool is based on the fist-to-five strategy with a 0–5 rating (DuFour et al., 2024).

> 0 = I cannot commit to this mission statement.
> 1 = I have strong reservations about the mission statement.
> 2 = I have some concerns about the mission statement.
> 3 = I feel the mission statement is good and I will support it.
> 4 = I feel the mission statement is strong and I will promote it.
> 5 = I believe in the mission statement and I will champion it.

Possible methods to share the new or revised mission and collect feedback to be reviewed by the guiding coalition are:

- Each team's guiding coalition representative presents the proposed mission at their next collaborative team meeting. Team members share their feedback on paper to be collected by the guiding coalition representative.
- The guiding coalition collaborates to create a digital survey (using Google Forms, Microsoft Forms, or another online platform) to share the proposed mission and solicit feedback.
- During a staff meeting, the proposed mission is presented to the whole staff by the guiding coalition. Feedback is collected during the staff meeting either on paper or digitally.
- Your idea:

_____

_____

_____

_____

_____

Reference

DuFour, R., DuFour, R., Eaker, R., Many, T. W., Mattos, M., & Muhammad, A. (2024). *Learning by doing: A handbook for Professional Learning Communities at Work* (4th ed.). Bloomington, IN: Solution Tree Press.

Mission Proposal and Adoption (Step 2)

Instructions: Once your guiding coalition has chosen a method to collect staff feedback, at the next guiding coalition meeting, the team will analyze the feedback. As you do so, note the degree of consensus. Use the table that follows to gather staff insight for possible revisions and determine next steps.

Proposed mission statement:

Average Score	Next Steps	Proposed Revisions
0–2	Gather feedback and revise the proposed mission statement.	
3	Gather feedback and clarify the proposed mission statement.	
4–5	Congratulations! It's time to adopt and celebrate your new shared mission statement.	

Total Score

0–2: Make revisions to the mission statement based on staff feedback and resubmit to the staff for another fist-to-five rating. Continue the cycle until the mission statement scores a 3, 4, or 5, paying attention to the proposed revisions. Once the score is a 4 or 5, you are ready to celebrate!

3: Analyze the feedback and decide as a guiding coalition if the suggestions add clarity to the mission statement. With your team's collective input, make changes or keep the existing proposed mission and move to the adoption stage.

4–5: Congratulations! Your school is ready to collectively adopt the new shared mission statement. Now it is time for your guiding coalition to create plans for a meaningful celebration of the mission statement for the staff.

Celebration Planning

Instructions: Dedicate fifteen minutes on a guiding coalition meeting agenda to plan how the mission statement can be celebrated. Think about celebrations throughout the year.

Mission statement:		
Celebration Strategy	**Time of Year (monthly, two times per year, ongoing)**	**Who is responsible for creating or follow-up?**

Anchor Your Vision © 2025 Solution Tree Press • SolutionTree.com
Visit **go.SolutionTree.com/PLCbooks/AYV** to download this free reproducible.

Mission in Action and Parent Celebration Certificates

Instructions: Any staff member can complete a celebration certificate for any other staff member or parent they want to celebrate for actively living the mission in their classroom and through their instructional practices or other forms of support of the mission. Once the certificate is complete, deliver it to the principal who will then determine a method of celebration (for example, reading the certificate on the announcements, posting certificates outside collaboration spaces, sharing certificates during staff meetings, presenting the certificate to the staff member or parent in front of their students, and so forth).

MISSION IN ACTION AWARD

GROWING OUR PROFESSIONAL LEARNING COMMUNITY

Mission statement: _____
_____

Our Mission in Action Award is presented to: _____

Thank you for bringing our mission into action by: _____
_____

Recognized by: _____

Principal signature: _____ Date: _____

PARENT CELEBRATION
GROWING OUR PROFESSIONAL LEARNING COMMUNITY

Mission statement: _____

Our Parent Celebration Certificate is presented to: _____

Thank you for living the mission and making an impact by: _____

Recognized by: _____ Date: _____

Principal signature: _____

Mission Survey (District)

Instructions: This survey is designed to collect information about our district's shared mission statement. For each of the statements that follow, please (1) indicate the extent to which you agree or disagree with the statement by circling one of the three letters provided and (2) provide evidence to support the leading indicator.

Our district's shared mission statement:				
Leading Indicators	**Disagree**	**Neutral**	**Agree**	**Evidence**
Foundation				
Our district has a clear and understandable mission statement.	D	N	A	
Our mission statement was developed or adopted collaboratively with current staff.	D	N	A	
Our mission statement is focused on our fundamental purpose: student learning.	D	N	A	
Our mission statement describes what our vision will look like in action.	D	N	A	
Refinement				
Our mission statement is measurable by our actions.	D	N	A	
Our mission statement is inspiring to the staff.	D	N	A	
Application				
Our mission statement is frequently referenced by faculty members in formal and informal meetings.	D	N	A	
Our policies and practices align with our district mission statement.	D	N	A	
Our decision making is aligned with our mission.	D	N	A	
Renewal				
We review our mission statement regularly and revise it when appropriate.	D	N	A	
Communication				
Our district families support our mission statement.	D	N	A	
Tally and Total				

Share your thoughts on our current mission statement and how it clarifies priorities and sharpens the focus of the work at our district.

What evidence does our district have that we are aligning our decisions with our mission?

How can we ensure that our mission is consistently and clearly communicated in our work daily with one another, students, and families?

Share additional feedback and ideas our guiding coalition should consider when reviewing the survey results.

Mission Survey (School)

Instructions: This survey is designed to collect information about our school's shared mission statement. For each of the statements that follow, please (1) indicate the extent to which you agree or disagree with each statement by circling one of the three letters provided and (2) provide evidence to support the leading indicator.

Our school's shared mission statement:				
Leading Indicators	**Disagree**	**Neutral**	**Agree**	**Evidence**
Foundation				
Our school has a clear and understandable mission statement.	D	N	A	
Our mission statement was developed or adopted collaboratively with current staff.	D	N	A	
Our mission statement is focused on our fundamental purpose: student learning.	D	N	A	
Our mission statement describes what our vision will look like in action.	D	N	A	
Our mission statement reflects the values of the school families and the community.	D	N	A	
Refinement				
Our mission statement is measurable by our actions.	D	N	A	
Our mission statement is inspiring to the staff.	D	N	A	
Application				
Our mission statement is frequently referenced by faculty members in formal and informal meetings.	D	N	A	
Our policies and practices align with our school mission statement.	D	N	A	
Our decision making is aligned with our mission.	D	N	A	
The school mission statement provides a clear sense of direction for staff.	D	N	A	
Renewal				
We review our mission statement regularly and revise it when appropriate.	D	N	A	

Communication				
Our school mission statement is regularly shared in a variety of ways.	D	N	A	
Our school families support our mission statement.	D	N	A	
Tally and Total				

Share your thoughts on our current mission statement and how it clarifies priorities and sharpens the focus of the work at our school.

What evidence does our school have that we are aligning our decisions with our mission?

How can we ensure that our mission is consistently and clearly communicated in our work daily with one another, students, and families?

Share additional feedback and ideas our guiding coalition should consider when reviewing the survey results.

Mission Survey Analysis (District)

Instructions: This analysis is intended to be conducted by the guiding coalition of the district in about one hour. Depending on the size of your guiding coalition, members will work in partnerships or small groups of up to four.

Step 1 (3–5 minutes)

Set the purpose of the collaborative time together as an inquiry into the effectiveness of the district's mission in each of the following in order to achieve the district's mission.

- Communicating the fundamental purpose
- Clarifying priorities
- Sharpening the shared focus

Step 2 (10–15 minutes)

Divide the completed district mission surveys among the partnerships or groups. Ask each partnership or group to review their set of surveys by section, summarize their findings for each section, and note any outliers.

Step 3 (10–15 minutes)

Share each partnership's or group's findings. Possible structures for sharing could include the following.

- Partnerships or groups verbally share their findings, section by section, with opportunity for clarifying discussion with the whole group after each section.
- Anchor charts titled with each section are displayed around the room. Partnerships or groups record their findings on sticky notes and post these on the corresponding anchor charts. Partnerships or teams then take a gallery walk of the anchor charts.

Step 4 (5 minutes)

Prioritize each section for next steps based on the shared findings of partnerships or groups.

Note: If surveys indicate a need for work in the Foundation section, this work will always be prioritized first and singularly. Work in other sections should be prioritized based on the level of need indicated by partnership or group findings and in consideration of the time of year. Work in other sections can occur in tandem.

Step 5 (10–15 minutes)

Create action steps, assignments, and timelines for the sections prioritized.

Step 6 (5 minutes)

Review the purpose and accomplishments of the collaborative time.

Mission Survey Analysis (School)

Instructions: With your guiding coalition, work in partnerships or small groups of up to four to follow these six steps. This process should take forty-five minutes to an hour and result in prioritized next steps for revising, refining, and implementing the shared mission as indicated by staff feedback.

Step 1 (3–5 minutes)

Set the purpose of the collaborative time together as an inquiry into the effectiveness of the school's mission in each of the following in order to achieve the school's mission.

- Communicating the fundamental purpose
- Clarifying priorities
- Sharpening the shared focus

Step 2 (10–15 minutes)

Divide the completed school mission surveys among the partnerships or groups. Ask each partnership or group to review their set of surveys by section, summarize their findings for each section, and note any outliers.

Step 3 (10–15 minutes)

Share each partnership's or group's findings. Possible structures for sharing could include the following.

- Partnerships or groups verbally share their findings, section by section, with opportunity for clarifying discussion with the whole group after each section.
- Anchor charts titled with each section are displayed around the room. Partnerships or groups record their findings on sticky notes and post these on the corresponding anchor charts. Partnerships or teams then take a gallery walk of the anchor charts.

Step 4 (5 minutes)

Prioritize each section for next steps based on the shared findings of partnerships or groups.

Note: If surveys indicate a need for work in the Foundation section, this work will always be prioritized first and singularly. Work in other sections should be prioritized based on the level of need indicated by partnership or group findings and in consideration of the time of year. Work in other sections can occur in tandem.

Step 5 (10–15 minutes)

Create action steps, assignments, and timelines for the sections prioritized.

Step 6 (5 minutes)

Review the purpose and accomplishments of the collaborative time.

Staff Reflections—Implementing Stage (District)

Instructions: Reflect and consider how our district is working toward fulfilling the district mission. Please provide evidence to support your thinking.

Our district mission:
Does our mission statement communicate why we exist? ☐ Yes ☐ No   Provide a rationale for your choice.
How do our instructional practices support the mission?
What evidence do we have of staff living out our mission in our district?
What success criteria could we use as evidence of attaining our district mission?
Do staff use our mission statement to guide day-to-day actions and decision making in our district? Provide specific evidence to explain your answer.
Will our mission enable us to achieve our vision? ☐ Yes ☐ No   If so, how? If not, why? Provide a rationale for your choice.
Does our district mission enhance or improve the lives of all students? Explain your answer.
Do we need to make any changes or updates to our district mission? If so, what are your suggestions?

Staff Reflections—Implementing Stage (School)

Instructions: Reflect and consider how our school is working toward fulfilling the school mission. Please provide evidence to support your thinking.

Our school mission:
Does our mission statement communicate why we exist? ☐ Yes ☐ No   Provide a rationale for your choice.
How do our instructional practices support the mission?
What evidence do we have of staff living out our mission in our school?
What success criteria could we use as evidence of attaining our school mission?
Do staff use our mission statement to guide day-to-day actions and decision making in our school? Provide specific evidence to explain your answer.
Will our mission enable us to achieve our vision? ☐ Yes ☐ No   If so, how? If not, why? Provide a rationale for your choice.
Does our school mission enhance or improve the lives of all students? Explain your answer.
Do we need to make any changes or updates to our school mission? If so, what are your suggestions?

Anchor Your Vision © 2025 Solution Tree Press • SolutionTree.com
Visit **go.SolutionTree.com/PLCbooks/AYV** and enter the unique access code found on the book's inside front cover to access this reproducible.

Guiding Coalition Analysis—Implementing Stage

Instructions: Break the guiding coalition into groups of two to three and divide the staff reflections among the groups. Groups will read through the responses, collecting thoughts across the reflections, and then discuss and jot essential observations and evidence on this worksheet.

Reflection Questions and Statements	Evidence	
Does the mission statement communicate why we exist?	Tally Marks for Yes	Tally Marks for No
Reasoning:		
Instructional practices that support the mission		
Evidence of staff living out our district or school mission in our district or school		
Future criteria for evidence of attaining our mission		

Evidence of day-to-day actions and decision making in our district or school		
Will our mission enable us to achieve our vision?	Tally Marks for Yes	Tally Marks for No
Reasoning:		
How our district or school mission enhances or improves the lives of all students		
Suggestions for changes or updates to our mission		

School Action Plan—Implementing Stage

Instructions: As a guiding coalition, discuss the common thoughts, insights, and evidence noticed across the guiding coalition analysis. Then, discuss the guiding questions that follow.

Our mission statement:

Discussion:

- What beliefs are needed to achieve our mission?
- What evidence demonstrates our school is committed to the mission of learning for all?
- Who is engaged in collaboration around the collective responsibility of what all students must learn?
- How do we currently clarify what students must learn in our grade or content area?
- What are the current practices we use to monitor student learning?

Action Plan:

Time Frame	Staff Responsible	Action

Staff Reflections—Developing Stage (District)

Instructions: Reflect and consider how our district is working toward fulfilling the district mission. Please provide evidence to support your thinking.

Our district mission:
What are the clear expectations for student learning in our district?
What processes does our district use to monitor student learning?
What evidence do we have to show high levels of learning for all students?
Who is involved in our data conversations and plans for intervention and extensions?
How does our district meet the needs of students when they do not show evidence of learning?
How does our district meet the needs of students when they already know essential knowledge and skills in the grade or content area?
What are ways our district can become more effective in ensuring learning for all students?
What evidence do we have of staff living out our mission in our district?
How do staff use our mission statement to guide day-to-day actions and decision making in our district?

Staff Reflections—Developing Stage (School)

Instructions: Reflect and consider how our school is working toward fulfilling the school mission. Please provide evidence to support your thinking.

Our school mission:
What are the clear expectations for student learning in our school?
What processes does our school use to monitor student learning?
What evidence do we have to show high levels of learning for all students?
Who is involved in our data conversations and plans for intervention and extensions?
How does our school meet the needs of students when they do not show evidence of learning?
How does our school meet the needs of students when they already know essential knowledge and skills in the grade or content area?
What are ways our school can become more effective in ensuring learning for all students?
What evidence do we have of staff members living out our mission in our school?
How do staff members use our mission statement to guide day-to-day actions and decision making in our school?

Guiding Coalition Analysis—Developing Stage

Instructions: Break the guiding coalition into groups of two to three and divide the staff reflections among the groups. Groups will read through the responses, collect thoughts across the reflections, and then discuss and jot essential observations and evidence on this worksheet.

Reflection Statements	Evidence
Expectations for student learning in our district or school	
Processes to monitor student learning	
Evidence of high levels of learning for all students	
Staff involved in our data conversations and plans for intervention and extensions	

The needs of students are met when mastery of skills is not met	
Enrichment for students who have achieved mastery of standards	
Ways our district or school can become more effective in ensuring learning for all students	
Staff living out our mission in our district or school	
Staff using our mission statement to guide day-to-day actions and decision making in our district or school	

School Action Plan—Developing Stage

Instructions: As a guiding coalition group, discuss the common thoughts, insights, and evidence noticed across the guiding coalition analysis. Then, discuss the guiding questions that follow.

Our mission statement:

Discussion:

- Do we need to make any changes to our current processes for monitoring student learning?
- Is there anything we need to address regarding all student groups demonstrating high levels of learning?
- How are we ensuring all learners show a year's worth or more of growth?
- How are we supporting students who require additional interventions or extensions?
- Who is engaged in collaboration around the collective responsibility of what all students must learn?
- Is there any professional learning we should consider to address current needs?

Action Plan:

Time Frame	Staff Responsible	Action

Staff Reflections—Sustaining Stage (District)

Instructions: Reflect and consider how our district is working toward fulfilling the district mission. Please provide evidence to support your thinking.

Our district mission:

What evidence demonstrates a collective responsibility in our district to ensure high levels of learning for all?

What evidence demonstrates a collaborative culture in our district surrounding learning for all?

How do we use common formative assessments throughout the district?

What processes does our district use to monitor student learning?

What evidence demonstrates teachers analyze, share, and adjust instructional practices in response to student learning data?

How does our district meet the needs of students when they do not show evidence of learning?

How does our district meet the needs of students when they already know essential knowledge and skills in the grade or content area?

What evidence do we have of staff members living out our district mission in our schools?

How do staff members use our mission statement to guide day-to-day actions and decision making in our district?

Staff Reflections—Sustaining Stage (School)

Instructions: Reflect and consider how our school is working toward fulfilling the school mission. Please provide evidence to support your thinking.

Our school mission:
What evidence demonstrates a collective responsibility in our school to ensure high levels of learning for all?
What evidence demonstrates a collaborative culture in our school surrounding learning for all?
How do we use common formative assessments throughout the school?
What processes does our school use to monitor student learning?

What evidence demonstrates teachers analyze, share, and adjust instructional practices in response to student learning data?

How does our school meet the needs of students when they do not show evidence of learning?

How does our school meet the needs of students when they already know essential knowledge and skills in the grade or content area?

What evidence do we have of staff members living out our school mission in our school?

How do staff members use our mission statement to guide day-to-day actions and decision making in our school?

Guiding Coalition Analysis—Sustaining Stage

Instructions: Break the guiding coalition into groups of two to three and divide the staff members' reflections among the groups. Groups will read through the responses, collecting thoughts across the reflections, and then discuss and jot essential observations and evidence on this worksheet.

Reflection Statements	Evidence
Demonstrating a collective responsibility in our district or school to ensure high levels of learning for all	
A collaborative culture in our district or school surrounding learning for all	
The use of common formative assessments throughout the district or school	
Processes used to monitor student learning	

Teachers analyzing, sharing, and adjusting instructional practices in response to student learning data	
The needs of students are met when mastery of skills is not met	
Enrichment for students who have achieved mastery of standards	
Staff members living out our mission in our district or school	
Staff members using our mission statement to guide day-to-day actions and decision making in our district or school	

School Action Plan—Sustaining Stage

Instructions: As a guiding coalition, discuss the common thoughts, insights, and evidence noticed across the Guiding Coalition Analysis Guide. Then, discuss the guiding questions that follow.

Our mission statement:

Discussion:

- Do we need to make any changes to our current processes for monitoring and responding to student learning?
- Is there anything we need to address regarding all student groups demonstrating high levels of learning? Consider both interventions and extensions.
- Are there any areas of concern surrounding a collective responsibility and collaborative culture for student learning?
- Is there anything we need to address ensuring assessments accurately reflect the rigor of the essential standards?
- How are we utilizing research-based best instructional practices in our school, and how are teachers learning from one another across the school?
- Is there any professional learning we should consider to address current needs?

Action Plan:

Time Frame	Staff Member Responsible	Action

CHAPTER 3
VISION

Vision is the art of seeing what is invisible to others.
—**JONATHAN SWIFT**

The year our school implemented our new school vision statement, we became much more intentional about its use for decision making. Katy Sue was a guiding coalition member on a grade-level team who encountered using the vision statement in their team's weekly collaborative team time to make an important decision. The science teacher had an agenda item about a national scientific contest designed for students to explore, research, and create scientific discoveries to impact our world. She shared her thoughts about this project as an opportunity to answer critical question 4, which focuses on extending learning. The team talked through the benefits of the program on student engagement and achievement and how it incorporated mathematics, social studies, and scientific reading and writing skills. They were excited about the project's potential to extend learning for the students.

However, when the science teacher shared the requirements for students and teachers in order to participate in the national project, such as due dates for activities, extended time needed to meet with students, lesson preparations, and activities to support the students' projects, the tone in the room shifted from excitement to hesitation.

When the science teacher came to the end of the proposal, she asked for feedback from the team before putting the new project to a fist-to-five vote. The room was silent for a bit. Then, one teacher spoke up, expressing concerns about the time requirements for teachers. Another teacher shared she was uncomfortable using any of her content time to allow students to work on the project. This could have been the end of this agenda item—and the end of a solid idea to meet students' needs for extension.

The concerns provided an opportunity for the team to first discuss the connection of the students' participation in the national science contest to the school vision—"We will be a globally recognized professional learning community that provides excellence in academic, cultural, and character education and prepares K–6 students to be positive leaders in a 21st century world." The team discussed how the science competition not only aligned with our school vision but provided an opportunity to fulfill it in a way not otherwise available to them. So they ultimately decided to collaborate on how topics in the science contest would align with cross-curricular essential standards, providing opportunities for creative ways to find the time and space needed for implementing the competition to ensure the possibility of reaching their school vision while extending learning in a meaningful way for students. The entire school was so proud of our science teacher's idea and leadership in bringing this opportunity to the students, along with the entire team's support of the projects. Their decision not only provided students with meaningful extensions of their learning, but one of their student teams won the regional competition and participated and placed in the national competition in Washington, DC. Talk about bringing parts of a school vision to reality!

Perhaps this sounds familiar to you. Educators frequently wrestle with the decisions facing them daily, such as adopting a new curriculum, determining master schedules, sharing students among the team, using common assessments, and employing grading practices. It is through the lens of our purpose created by a shared vision that Katy Sue's team was able to stay focused on the thoughts and actions that would drive the team's work of ensuring learning and growth for all students.

In this chapter, we outline the what, why, and how of establishing a school vision. We aim to further clarify the what so that districts and schools have a common understanding of both what they are aiming for and what guidelines could be used in determining success in the implementation of their district or school vision. In doing so, we place an emphasis on differentiating vision from mission, as these are often confused or unintentionally combined, which can cause confusion and diminish the value of their impact. We make a case for why every district and school needs a vision statement that describes their compelling future. Evidence is included from districts and schools where we have worked as practitioners, as well as districts and schools we have worked with throughout the United States as educational consultants. In addition, we include research from varied fields, including business, medicine, and education, and how other industries connect in the educational world through the foundational pillars. This evidence and research are intended both to inspire you to begin creating a vision with eagerness and intensity and to highlight the attributes of an organization's vision that make it most effective.

The majority of this chapter details steps to create or refine, implement, monitor, and celebrate a district or school vision. When describing these steps, we were careful to begin with soliciting input from all stakeholders, both in assessing which stage of development the organization is in and in the creation or revision of the vision, as the eliciting and inclusion of all voices is a necessity in making the vision shared. To allow most of the cognitive load to be dedicated to the collaboration and articulation of the vision rather than the logistics, we have included tools to support the work of each step.

Navigating the Vision

The vision pillar focuses on our compelling future of what we want to become. Here, we are thinking of the future of our district or school that we wish to create. The vision should be aspirational and ignite excitement for everyone in the organization to come together to create it. The vision is different from the mission. The mission is what we are doing right now that helps lead us to our vision. If you visited a district or school, you could see the actions and behaviors lived out by the mission. For example, if our mission is to ensure learning for all students, then the practices of intervention during the school day will be an actionable behavior you can see in action. The vision of all students in the school learning the guaranteed and viable curriculum hasn't occurred yet, but is obtainable if the staff live out the mission.

Creating a shared vision assists both district and school leaders by providing a foundational framework for prioritizing resources and initiatives. The purpose of a vision is twofold: (1) to provide a long-term goal of what the district or school will look like in five to ten years and (2) to align the staff around the work to be accomplished together. Richard DuFour (2015) states, "A vision statement that emerges on a poster from a board retreat is unlikely to impact the daily practices of an educator's life. A shared vision, however, can serve as a powerful catalyst for change" (p. 109).

All of the organization's stakeholders must know where they are going and a reason to go there. When efforts from the entire district or school are aimed at the same vision, the vision can become a reality versus simply a lofty goal or website banner. Think of the vision as an organization's North Star, an object that provides the direction of where the organization needs to go. The vision creates deep meaning for the hard work of educators and, in turn, can make a positive impact on the staff and students in the educational setting.

A common question in the work of creating a school vision is, Should visions be written at the district *and* school levels? The short answer is, ideally, yes. And here's why: The district vision is crucial for providing schools with an overarching sense of the purpose, priorities, or guiding principles at the district level. This clarity of focus allows schools to align their own vision statements in a way that moves the whole district toward the same goals (DuFour et al., 2021). However, we have worked with schools that do not have a district vision or that have a district vision that is not inspiring, measurable, or attainable. When we say measurable, we mean there are actions and artifacts to show efforts toward attaining the vision. We believe schools should not wait to begin creating a shared vision for their school if this is the case.

A powerful and meaningful shared vision statement is what it takes to communicate to all stakeholders the school or district's destination in order to streamline their daily decision making.

Examining Evidence of a Successful Vision

Shawn was working with a guiding coalition team in Stockton, California, and one of the team members brought a bag of chocolate candy to share with the team. Shawn hadn't seen this variety of chocolates before, so naturally, she had to try one for herself. However, on picking up the colorful bag of Tony's Chocolonely, she discovered something unique. The back of the bag of chocolate reads, "Crazy about chocolate, serious about people." While that statement might grab your attention with the bold red writing, it goes on to say the following: "Hi there, we're Tony's Chocolonely. We exist to end modern slavery and illegal child labor in the chocolate industry. Not just our chocolate but all chocolate worldwide.

The more people join us and share our mission, the sooner 100% slave free chocolate becomes the norm. The choice is yours. Are you in?" Wow! A company sharing their vision and mission right there on their product for all to read. Shawn loves to support a meaningful cause, especially those that directly impact children, so she went on their website to learn more.

Tony's Chocolonely, a Dutch chocolate company founded in 2005, has a vision to make a direct impact on children worldwide, and they are using their mission and road map with three pillars to pave the way to 100 percent exploitation-free chocolate. Tony's Chocolonely (n.d.b) shares on their website, "Right now there is illegal child labor and forced labor on cocoa farms in West Africa. This is a result of the unequally divided cocoa chain. Tony's Chocolonely exists to change that. Illegal child labor and forced labor are against the law—it needs to stop." Their fundamental purpose, their reason to exist, is clear.

How are they going to reach their vision? They have created a road map, the actionable steps they are taking to reach their vision. They call these their pillars. Their first pillar is focused on raising awareness. In addition to the eye-catching wrappers, each chocolate bar has unequal segments. In the frequently asked questions section on their website (Tony's Chocolonely, n.d.a), they share their reasoning for this: "The unevenly sized chunks of our 6 oz bars are a palatable way of reminding our choco friends that the profits in the chocolate industry are unfairly divided." Their second pillar is leading by example. They are fulfilling this pillar by their commitment to only make chocolate by their Tony's 5 Sourcing Principles, putting human rights at the center of their business. Their third pillar is inspiring others to act. Tony's Chocolonely shares with other chocolate companies, retailers, cocoa farmers, politicians, and even chocolate consumers (many of us) what they can do to help make 100 percent exploitation-free chocolate.

Whether it is a company like Tony's Chocolonely, a district, or a school, when you create a vision and then follow up with actionable steps toward the goals, the vision can be attained, and what a better place our world can be!

Taking a Deep Dive Into the Research for Developing a Vision

The development of a shared vision has a long history in management and organizational practices. It is well known among practitioners that the creation of a vision at the individual, team, or organizational level kindles a forward momentum beyond the current reality and toward an ambitious plan for the future. In recent years, empirical data have been compiled on the role of a shared vision in organizations from the perspective of both leaders and employees. In a study on the factors related to organizational vision integration among hospital employees, a marked increase was observed in organizational attractiveness as well as employee service effort and creative performance when those employees used the organization's vision for their daily decision making in their roles (Slåtten, Lien, & Mutonyi, 2022). These results provide research-based evidence that an organization's vision matters because of the substantial power to guide the efforts of employees. This also impacted employee productivity because it provided a framework for employees to take initiative, improve, and have autonomy in making decisions that streamlined processes and improved staff culture. When their employees have a clear lens through which to align their decision making, organizations become more efficient, productive, and innovative.

However, it's important to note this power is contingent on two factors: (1) the employee's perception of whether they know and have been informed of the vision and (2) whether the employee embraces the use of that vision as a guiding framework in their particular job. This supports the critical intentionality of including all stakeholders in the creation of a shared vision. In the field of higher education, researchers Kerice Doten-Snitker, Cara Margherio, Elizabeth Litzler, Ella Ingram, and Julia Williams (2021) analyzed several of the most well-known practitioner-driven change models and determined that employing practices of "co-orientation, formational communication, and collaboration to empower stakeholders" (p. 224) is a requirement to build a wider and stronger base for change. Leaders who intend to follow the how-to steps of creating a vision but do so in isolation will find their efforts insufficient in ensuring that employees accept the vision—therefore negating the impact of having a vision statement at all. Those whose efforts are integral to the success of an organizational vision must play a role in the creation of that vision because they "ultimately determine whether the vision statements will be ignored or accepted" (Slåtten, Mutonyi, & Lien, 2021). In an article published in the *Harvard Business Review*, this claim was reiterated in the findings of a study including the responses of tens of thousands of working people and one million leaders stating:

> Yes, leaders must ask, "What's new? What's next? What's better?"—but they can't present answers that are only theirs. Constituents want visions of the future that reflect their own aspirations. They want to hear how their dreams will come true and their hopes will be fulfilled. (Kouzes & Posner, 2009, p. 20)

The only visions that take hold and positively impact the future of the people and the organizations they are in are those that are shared. These shared visions are created when we listen closely to and appreciate the hopes and needs of others in the organization. After all, "in order to turn the vision of a school into reality, all stakeholders must have a place in the work" (Creswell, 2021). These are the compelling reasons we must have a shared vision in every district and every school.

Research states educators make upwards of 1,500 decisions a day (0.7 decision per minute) (Shavelson & Borko, 1979). There is little to no doubt that at least some of these decisions are stressful or difficult. This onslaught of possibilities can create "decision fatigue," adding additional stress. Having a clear shared vision reduces this stress by providing educator autonomy to confidently make decisions aligned with the vision. This supports educators because they have both guidance and power in decision making. When all stakeholders make decisions based on alignment with the shared vision, the decentralization of decision making—the need to run every decision up the chain of command—is eliminated because every district stakeholder, not just the superintendent of the district or the school principal, has clear parameters and purpose for making those decisions. A shared vision replaces other forms of control as the driver of consistency with the clarification of collective purpose within the organization. Regardless of the decision being made—whether to recall a dangerous medication or to implement a new science project at a school—the most productive and impactful organizations make these decisions with intentionality by aligning all actions to their vision; therefore, the significance of an organization's vision is critical to its success. When there is an absence of a shared vision, staff are left to their experiences and personal goals on which to base their decisions. Therefore, the variety of experiences and perspectives among educators in the same organization must be aimed at the shared vision in order to attain maximum impact.

The investment of staff in the vision is critical after a shared vision has been created. This creates energy, motivation, and enthusiasm from everyone in the organization in order to foster change and reach goals. When staff feel ownership of the shared vision, they have a sense of belonging and tend to put their hearts and souls into the school to help make the vision a reality. As demonstrated in the data from the medical research, employees in any organization will work harder when they feel connected to a larger purpose, yet just about half (51 percent) of employed Americans say they get a sense of identity from their job while 47 percent say their job is simply what they do for a living, according to recent data from the Pew Research Center (2016). When a vision statement is present, employees can get an idea of where the company is going, further building a connection between the employee and the organization. A vision statement brings together all stakeholders—staff, students, parents, and the community—to work together toward a common focal point and to align everyone toward the same goal.

Sailing Into Action for Each Stage of Developing a Shared Vision

While we hope that we have thoroughly built a case that districts and schools must have a shared vision, we expect you may be wondering, "But how?" How does a school approach the task of creating a vision that is powerful enough to incite change or empower stakeholders to achieve greatness? And how does that vision have lasting power to carry an organization across years? The action steps laid out in the chapter are meant to guide you through the creation of your vision and how to move to the sustaining stage on the continuum. The action steps are followed by tools to do the work.

A school shared vision is still necessary because, while a vision crafted at the district level should be applicable to all schools in the district, it would likely lack the specificity to embody the aspirations of every school, especially in a way that would impact the day-to-day operations of the educators at each school. For example, think about the possible difference in the goals set by a high school in comparison with an elementary school even in the same school district. Also, in larger districts, there may be diverse schools. Some may be located in a more rural area versus others in a more suburban area. Their school visions may be different based on the population of the students they serve and the community's industry. If a vision statement is to incite change, unite staff, and drive decisions, then it needs to be created by the members of the organization so they see a reflection of their own hopes and dreams for the school they wish to create. When staff of a school are engaged in the process, they have a sense of ownership and will more likely commit to seeing the school attain the vision.

An example of schools creating their vision statements particular to their school yet in alignment with the district vision follows.

Example District Vision

Our district and schools function as a high-performing professional learning community that takes collective responsibility to ensure all students learn at high levels while providing a physically and emotionally safe learning environment. We continually strive to grow our instructional practices and collaborate across the district and schools to provide exceptional professional learning for our educators. Our students will graduate with the knowledge, dispositions, and skills necessary for their future success in college or their chosen career field.

Example School Vision 1 (Elementary School)

We create a safe learning environment that enables every child to grow academically, socially, and emotionally while learning to value themselves and each other. We develop character education with our community service projects and daily lessons. We guarantee our students will master the academic and social skills to be successful in intermediate school and beyond.

Example School Vision 2 (Intermediate School)

Our school is a physically and emotionally safe school that takes a collective responsibility to ensure all students learn the knowledge and skills needed for success in high school by implementing best practices for instruction, gathering evidence of learning, and responding to these data with urgency. Our STEAM focus provides multiple learning opportunities for students to excel in their area of interest while learning all core content.

Example School Vision 3 (High School)

All students will develop a high level of intellectual, social, and personal growth in our physically and emotionally safe school. We ensure our students will be college and career ready by guaranteeing their learning of the essential knowledge and skills while providing them with opportunities to lead and excel in a variety of activities to connect students together in our school community.

To create a shared vision, the first step is to consider your district or school's current picture of reality using the "Vision Continuum" (page 94). Note that unlike some of the other chapters in this book, the same continuum is used for both district and school. The continuum provides an overview of the indicators in each stage of the progress trajectory, from preinitiating to sustaining, that districts or schools typically follow when creating and establishing their vision. The most beneficial way to use this continuum is to engage all staff in completing it to first determine which column mostly describes where your organization is (a clear picture of reality), and then study the next column over and determine what actions are needed to meet that description. In this way, districts and schools get a clear sense of where they are, where they are going, and what evidence or indicators would signify progress. After determining the district's or school's current reality, use the process and resources described in the next section to create, refine, or sustain your shared vision. For the initiating and implementing stages, the steps and tools are the same.

The Preinitiating Stage

A school or district in the preinitiating stage is a clean slate in regard to the work of creating a vision. This could look like a brand-new school open for its very first year or an existing district or school that does not have a vision statement. If this describes your district or school, the steps that follow can support your staff in creating your shared vision.

1. Begin with the "Vision Sort" (page 95) to set the focus and active thinking. This sorting activity is designed to engage the staff in a warm-up to activate their thinking about creating a shared vision. Through this activity, staff will make a connection between vision statements and how they communicate the organization's aspirations of what they wish to become.

2. Inspire staff to collaboratively create a shared vision using the tool "The Power of a Shared Vision (District)" (page 96) or "The Power of a Shared Vision (School)" (page 98). Utilizing this tool provides research on the rationale behind creating a shared vision. Staff will have the opportunity to reflect on key insight from thought leaders that is meant to promote collaborative learning and conversation to stimulate a common understanding of the impact of this foundational pillar.

3. Capture the hopes and dreams that staff have for their organization. This can be both exciting and inspirational. "Trending Stories (District)" (page 100) or "Trending Stories (School)" (page 102) guides participants to brainstorm what they value and dream the district or school will become in five to ten years. Once this activity is completed, the guiding coalition will collect and synthesize the information in the first steps of creating a shared vision.

4. Have the guiding coalition use the "Trending Stories Analysis" (page 104) to synthesize ideas and create a cohesive statement. The tool provides a lens through which the guiding coalition begins to craft the preliminary version of the shared vision statement.

5. Present the proposed shared vision statement to the staff using the "Proposal and Adoption (Step 1)" (page 107) and "Proposal and Adoption (Step 2)" (page 108) tool for feedback regarding the staff's willingness to commit to the proposed vision statement. Step 1 of the tool is designed to assist the guiding coalition in their planning of collecting input from the staff. Step 2 helps the guiding coalition determine if the vision statement is ready to adopt or needs further revision. The tool collects input and possible revisions and guides

staff through a cycle of creating clarity, with the goal of adopting a shared commitment to what the staff hope the school will become.

6. Use the "Plan to Celebrate!" (page 109) to plan the adoption and celebration of the shared vision. This tool is designed to help the guiding coalition plan a memorable celebration for the adoption of the shared vision. Planning with purpose is an important step in the process of bringing the vision to fruition.

7. Affirm staff and promote the continuation of positive practices and actions toward the shared vision through celebration. The "Advancing Our Vision" (page 110) is designed for staff to recognize one another's accomplishments as they take steps toward the shared vision throughout the year.

8. Monitor progress from the preinitiating stage to the initiating stage by collecting evidence corresponding with the indicators in the "Vision Continuum" (page 94).

The Initiating Stage

A district or school in the initiating stage is one that has a vision statement that staff may not know, understand, or support, perhaps because the vision is unclear, unattainable, or unmeasurable. This is often evidenced when the vision does not affect the day-to-day decisions or actions of the staff. If this describes your district or school, the same steps that guide the implementing stage can support your staff in refining or revising your school's vision—please see the next section.

The Implementing Stage

A district or school in the implementing stage is one that has a vision statement that staff may not know, understand, or support, perhaps because the vision is unclear, unattainable, or unmeasurable. This is often evidenced when the vision does not affect the day-to-day decisions or actions of the staff. If this describes your district or school, the steps that follow can support your staff in refining or revising your school's vision.

1. Review the current vision statement and provide staff an opportunity to share feedback by using the "Vision Survey (District)" (page 111) or "Vision Survey (School)" (page 113) tool. The survey is designed to collect feedback from the staff regarding progress toward attaining the district vision. The survey could be completed by staff either individually or with teams and offers the ability for anonymous feedback. We suggest using the survey on an annual or biannual basis to collect insights toward the attainment of the shared vision. The guiding coalition will use the survey results to make decisions for next steps.

2. Analyze staff reflections with the guiding coalition using the "Vision Survey Analysis (District)" (page 115) or "Vision Survey Analysis (School)" (page 116) tool to determine whether the vision is ready for readoption or to gather insight into areas for improvement. The guiding coalition uses this

analysis tool to provide insight into the progress of your school vision and guide the next steps to fulfill the vision.

3. If the vision statement is ready for readoption, present the shared vision statement to the staff using the "Proposal and Adoption (Step 1)" (page 107) and "Proposal and Adoption (Step 2)" (page 108) tool. This tool is designed to collect feedback regarding their willingness to commit to the proposed vision statement. Step 1 of the tool is designed to assist the guiding coalition in their planning of collecting staff input. Step 2 helps the guiding coalition determine if the vision statement is ready to adopt or needs further revision. The tool collects input and possible revisions and guides staff through a cycle of creating clarity with the goal of adopting a shared commitment to what the staff hope the school will become.

4. Celebrate the readoption of the shared vision using the "Plan to Celebrate!" (page 109) tool. Celebration is an extremely valuable way to affirm staff and promote the continuation of positive practices and actions toward the shared vision. This tool is designed to facilitate staff in recognizing one another as they see colleagues take steps toward the shared vision throughout the year.

5. Monitor progress from the implementing stage to the developing stage by collecting evidence corresponding with the indicators in the "Vision Continuum" (page 94).

The Developing Stage

A district or school that is working on developing their vision has a shared vision that staff collectively created or know well. They have endorsed the vision and use that description of the school they are trying to create to guide their improvement efforts and professional learning. However, the day-to-day efforts of the staff are impacted by the vision in a limited way or not at all. If this describes your district or school, the steps that follow can support your staff in creating your shared vision.

1. Review the current vision statement and provide staff an opportunity to share feedback by using the "Vision Survey (District)" (page 111) or "Vision Survey (School)" (page 113) tool. The survey is designed to collect feedback from the staff regarding progress toward attaining the district vision. The survey could be completed by staff either individually or with teams and offers the ability for anonymous feedback. We suggest using the survey on an annual or biannual basis to collect insights toward the attainment of the shared vision. The guiding coalition will use the survey results to make decisions for next steps.

2. Analyze staff reflections with the guiding coalition using the "Vision Survey Analysis (District)" (page 115) or "Vision Survey Analysis (School)" (page 116) tool to determine whether the vision is ready for readoption or to gather insight into areas for improvement. The guiding coalition uses this

analysis tool to provide insight into the progress of your school vision and guide the next steps to fulfill the vision.

3. Provide teams time to reflect on how the district's or school's shared vision guides their day-to-day efforts using the tool "Evidence of Impact (District)" (page 117) or "Evidence of Impact (School)" (page 118). With this tool, staff are prompted to consider how the district or school vision impacts day-to-day operations for everyone in the PLC. Through this process, staff will determine both the current reality of the district or school and the next steps. Responses collected could be used for further study by the guiding coalition or as part of celebrations.

4. Meet with the guiding coalition after they have reviewed teams' "Evidence of Impact (District)" (page 117) or "Evidence of Impact (School)" (page 118). Discuss celebrations and concerns and determine next steps. Consider the observations of the guiding coalition to identify opportunities to celebrate the efforts and progress toward making the school vision a reality.

5. Use the "Plan to Celebrate!" (page 109) tool to intentionally create, schedule, and assign celebrations of the evidence your district's or school's vision is being implemented and the efforts of staff. This tool is designed to help the guiding coalition plan a memorable celebration for the adoption of the shared vision. Planning with purpose is an important step in the process of bringing the vision to fruition. Celebration is an extremely valuable way to affirm staff and promote the continuation of positive practices and actions toward the shared vision. This tool is designed to facilitate staff in recognizing one another as they see colleagues take steps toward the shared vision throughout the year.

6. Monitor progress from the developing to the sustaining stage by collecting evidence corresponding with the indicators in the "Vision Continuum" (page 94).

The Sustaining Stage

A district or school at the sustaining stage has a shared vision that staff created or know well and demonstrate commitment to. Staff use the principles described in the vision statement to guide their day-to-day efforts, and they routinely assess the reality of the district or school against the aspirations of the vision. Staff seek out more effective strategies, practices, resources, and the like to become the district or school they are working to create.

1. Review the current vision statement and provide staff an opportunity to share feedback by using the "Vision Survey (District)" (page 111) or "Vision Survey (School)" (page 113) tool. The survey is designed to collect feedback from staff regarding progress toward attaining the district vision. The survey could be completed by staff either individually or with teams and offers the ability for anonymous feedback. We suggest using the survey on an annual or biannual

basis to collect insights toward the attainment of the shared vision. The guiding coalition will use the survey results to make decisions for next steps.

2. Analyze staff reflections with the guiding coalition using the "Vision Survey Analysis (District)" (page 115) or "Vision Survey Analysis (School)" (page 116) tool to determine whether the vision is ready for readoption or to gather insight into areas for improvement. The guiding coalition uses this analysis tool to provide insight into the progress of your school vision and guide the next steps to fulfill the vision.

3. Provide teams time to reflect on how the district's or school's shared vision guides their day-to-day efforts using the "Evidence of Impact (District)" (page 117) or "Evidence of Impact (School)" (page 118) tool. With this tool, staff are prompted to consider how the district or school vision impacts day-to-day operations for students, teachers, administrators, and support staff. Staff work in partnerships or teams to facilitate discussion as well as to collaborate and calibrate on what evidence to consider. Through this process, staff will determine both the current reality of the district or school and the next steps. Responses collected could be used for further study by the guiding coalition or as part of celebrations.

4. Meet with the guiding coalition after they have reviewed teams' "Evidence of Impact (District)" (page 117) or "Evidence of Impact (School)" (page 118). Set calendar dates for celebrations, discuss concerns, and determine next steps.

5. Continue to monitor the evidence in order for the district or school to maintain at the sustaining stage. Once the vision has become the reality of the district or school, celebrate! Then, follow the steps under the initiating descriptor to create your organization's next shared vision.

Staying Afloat Through Common Challenges to Developing a Shared Vision

When working to create your shared vision, expect that the process will not be completely linear. Districts and schools often find that, when this goal is best accomplished, the process is somewhat fluid in response to the varied backgrounds, knowledge, and values of their staff. The if-then chart shown in table 3.1 is a valuable troubleshooting resource addressing common challenges to be on the lookout for, as well as ideas to launch conversations among your leadership team regarding how you might best address these challenges to meet the needs of your staff.

Table 3.1: If-Then Chart

If . . .	Then . . .
The vision statement is more than three sentences.	Provide the guiding coalition members with a copy of the vision statement with each sentence on a separate piece of paper. Ask teams to consider each sentence individually, underlining the most important parts. Then, ask teams to consider the parts they underlined and compare each sentence to determine what could be combined, consolidated, or omitted.
The vision survey feedback shows many areas rated *neutral* or *disagree*.	Have the guiding coalition review the survey discrepancies and determine next steps.
The vision is unattainable or unmeasurable.	Gather teams to create examples of evidence to support the vision. Collectively adjust and refine the vision statement based on the ability or inability to create an example and the details of that example.
The vision statement restates what is already occurring at the school.	Have the guiding coalition collect evidence of the fulfillment of the shared vision and begin the process to create a new shared vision.
The district's or school's priorities and focus areas are overly abstract in the vision statement.	Create actionable steps to lead to attaining the vision.
The vision does not communicate the values of the district or school.	Incorporate what your district or school values into the vision statement by revisiting trending stories or host a meeting or survey with stakeholders to determine their hopes and dreams for the school.

Knowing the Ropes for Vision Development

As you and your colleagues work to establish your organization's vision, orient yourselves by keeping in mind the following.

- The vision statement should be inspiring and build hope for the future.
- Use concise statements that clearly communicate the direction and goals of the school.
- Keep it brief—between ten and twenty-five words—so everyone can easily recall it.
- The vision is the target for the future of the school.
- You can visit the All Things PLC website (www.allthingsPLC.info) to explore other schools' success stories.

Celebrating the Vision

A celebration of your collective effort in creating a meaningful shared vision to guide your daily work and efforts is important because the vision is the launch for attaining the district or school you wish to become. The recognition will provide momentum and ownership among all the stakeholders. By celebrating the work of a shared vision, you are communicating how valuable this work has been and how impactful a shared vision will be for your district or school moving forward with purpose and energy to ultimately ensure high levels of learning for all students.

Stay the Course

As with any work that is worthwhile to the growth of our organizations, you must take time to analyze progress and intentionally measure success. This evaluation provides opportunities to not only assess the impact of the work but also think about the small tweaks you may need to make, as well as next steps.

Monitoring the impact of your shared vision statement on the day-to-day actions and decisions of the school is essential. It is important to have a lens for what this evidence looks like. Consider using the "Vision Continuum" (page 94) as well as the "Evidence of Impact (District)" (page 117) or "Evidence of Impact (School)" (page 118) as monitoring tools across the year. Many districts and schools find that equipping a variety of stakeholders—administrators, guiding coalition members, teachers, even students—to periodically assess the reality of the organization toward their shared vision is an effective way to increase ownership and impact student learning and growth.

Anchors Away!

The vision statement is the North Star for where the district or school wants to go. The vision is rooted in the values of the district or school for what they wish to become in the future. It should be clearly written so everyone can connect with it while understanding what actionable steps they can take toward helping fulfill the vision. Remember the vision should be aspirational and ignite enthusiasm and determination for everyone to reach it. Remind the staff it will take the collective efforts of the entire organization, and each person can contribute to making it a reality.

Use the space provided to anchor your thoughts and chart your course for your next steps.

Vision Continuum

Instructions: Individually, read the indicators that describe each stage from preinitiating through sustaining. Honestly assess the current reality of the establishment of your vision. Consider what evidence or anecdotes support your assessment. Record your reflections in the space provided.

Shared vision: We have a shared understanding of and commitment to the district or school we are attempting to create.

Vision Continuum Stages				
Preinitiating	Initiating	Implementing	Developing	Sustaining
☐ No effort has been made to engage staff in describing the preferred conditions for the district or school.	☐ A formal vision statement has been created, but most staff are unaware of it.	☐ Staff have participated in a process to clarify the district or school they are trying to create, and leadership calls attention to the resulting vision statement on a regular basis. Many staff question the relevance of the vision statement, and their behavior is generally unaffected by it.	☐ Staff have worked together to describe the district or school they are trying to create. They have endorsed this general description and use it to guide their improvement efforts and their professional development.	☐ Staff can and do routinely articulate the major principles of the district's or school's shared vision and use those principles to guide their day-to-day efforts and decisions. They honestly assess the current reality and continually seek more effective strategies for reducing the discrepancy between that reality and the district or school they are working to create.

I believe our school or district is at the _____ stage based on the preceding indicators. The evidence to support my rationale includes:

Source: Adapted from DuFour, R., DuFour, R., Eaker, R., Many, T. W., Mattos, M., & Muhammad, A. (2024). Learning by doing: A handbook for Professional Learning Communities at Work (4th ed.). Bloomington, IN: Solution Tree Press.

Vision Sort

Instructions: Cut apart the company names and vision statements and place them in a bag for table teams. Give teams five minutes to match up the companies and vision statements based on what they know about each company. Then, discuss the reasons they paired the companies with the vision statements. What evidence have they seen or experienced when shopping or visiting these companies? Do they feel the companies are living out their visions? If so, how? If not, what could they be doing?

Tesla	To create the most compelling company of the 21st century by driving the world's transition to electric vehicles.
Ford	To become the world's most trusted company, designing smart vehicles for a smart world.
Uber	To ignite opportunity by setting the world in motion.
Amazon	To be the Earth's most customer-centric company, where customers can find and discover anything they might want to buy online.
Target	Guided commitments to great value, the community, diversity and the environment.
Walmart	To be the destination for customers to save money no matter how they want to shop.

Reference

Pereira, D. (2023, May 3). *Companies mission and vision statement.* The Business Model Analyst. Accessed at https://businessmodelanalyst.com/companies-mission-and-vision-statement/page/5/ on April 26, 2024.

The Power of a Shared Vision (District)

The vision pillar focuses on our compelling future of what we want to become. It embodies the hopes and dreams for the future of the district. What do we want our school district to look like in five to ten years? A vision statement provides a mental picture of the desired future.

Instructions: Read the quotes and research that follow and highlight words and phrases that resonate with you and your educational philosophy of how a vision impacts a school community. These quotes are meant to stimulate thinking and understanding behind a district vision statement while also providing for meaningful collaboration among colleagues that is grounded in the ideas from experts to create a common understanding of the value of this foundational pillar.

"You can have the greatest vision and purpose, but you must be connected and united in order to make it come to fruition" (Gordon, 2018, p. 80).

"A vision builds trust, collaboration, interdependence, motivation, and mutual responsibility for success. Vision helps people make smart choices, because their decisions are made with the end result in mind" (Blanchard, 2007, as cited in DuFour et al., 2016, p. 40).

"If the vision is truly shared, it will be evident in both the climate (how a school feels) and the culture (how business is done) of the school" (Robbins & Alvy, 2004, p. 9).

"If you're going to stir the souls of your constituents, if you are going to lift them to a higher level of performance, then this is what you need to know: It's not the leader's vision, it's the people's vision that matters most" (Kouzes & Posner, 2006, as cited in DuFour, 2015, p. 109).

"A vision statement that emerges on a poster from a board retreat is unlikely to impact the daily practices of an educator's life. A shared vision, however, can serve as a powerful catalyst for change" (DuFour, 2015, p. 109).

"A vision of the future is not simply a generic statement of positivity—it reflects a capacity to imagine a new reality and to understand all the components necessary to achieve and maintain it" (Gruenert & Whitaker, 2015, p. 49).

"Your school's vision can be specific, concise, and consistent, but if it fails to touch staff on an emotional level, it will fail and be doomed to a life of hanging on a wall or on your website banner. Your school's shared vision has to be large enough for every person to see his or her personal vision within it" (Williams & Hierck, 2015, p. 84).

What resonates with you about the purpose behind having a shared vision?

What values do you feel should be included in our district vision statement?

How do you see a shared vision benefiting all stakeholders?

How do you think a shared vision can impact the success of a school district community?

References

Blanchard, K. H. (2007). *Leading at a higher level: Blanchard on leadership and creating high performing organizations.* Upper Saddle River, NJ: Prentice Hall.

DuFour, R. (2015). *In praise of American educators: And how they can become even better.* Bloomington, IN: Solution Tree Press.

DuFour, R., DuFour, R., Eaker, R., Many, T. W., & Mattos, M. (2024). *Learning by doing: A handbook for Professional Learning Communities at Work* (4th ed.). Bloomington, IN: Solution Tree Press.

Gordon, J. (2018). *The power of a positive team: Proven principles and practices that make great teams great.* Hoboken, NJ: Wiley.

Gruenert, S., & Whitaker, T. (2015). *School culture rewired: How to define, assess, and transform it.* Alexandria, VA: ASCD.

Kouzes, J. M., & Posner, B. Z. (2006). *A leader's legacy.* San Francisco: Jossey-Bass.

Robbins, P., & Alvy, H. (2004). *The new principal's fieldbook: Strategies for success.* Alexandria, VA: ASCD.

Williams, K. C., & Hierck, T. (2015). *Starting a movement: Building culture from the inside out in professional learning communities.* Bloomington, IN: Solution Tree Press.

The Power of a Shared Vision (School)

The vision pillar focuses on our compelling future of what we want to become. It embodies the hopes and dreams for the future of the school. What do we want our school to look like in five to ten years? A vision statement provides a mental picture of the desired future.

Instructions: Read the quotes and research that follow and highlight words and phrases that resonate with you and your educational philosophy of how a vision impacts a school community. These quotes are meant to stimulate thinking and understanding behind a school vision statement while also providing for meaningful collaboration between colleagues that is grounded in the ideas from experts to create a common understanding of the value of this foundational pillar.

"You can have the greatest vision and purpose, but you must be connected and united in order to make it come to fruition" (Gordon, 2018, p. 80).

"A vision builds trust, collaboration, interdependence, motivation, and mutual responsibility for success. Vision helps people make smart choices, because their decisions are made with the end result in mind" (Blanchard, 2007, as cited in DuFour et al., 2016, p. 40).

"If the vision is truly shared, it will be evident in both the climate (how a school feels) and the culture (how business is done) of the school" (Robbins & Alvy, 2004, p. 9).

"If you're going to stir the souls of your constituents, if you are going to lift them to a higher level of performance, then this is what you need to know: It's not the leader's vision, it's the people's vision that matters most" (Kouzes & Posner, 2006, as cited in DuFour, 2015, p. 109).

"A vision statement that emerges on a poster from a board retreat is unlikely to impact the daily practices of an educator's life. A shared vision, however, can serve as a powerful catalyst for change" (DuFour, 2015, p. 109).

"A vision of the future is not simply a generic statement of positivity—it reflects a capacity to imagine a new reality and to understand all the components necessary to achieve and maintain it" (Gruenert & Whitaker, 2015, p. 49).

"Your school's vision can be specific, concise, and consistent, but if it fails to touch staff on an emotional level, it will fail and be doomed to a life of hanging on a wall or on your website banner. Your school's shared vision has to be large enough for every person to see his or her personal vision within it" (Williams & Hierck, 2015, p. 84).

What resonates with you about the purpose behind having a shared vision?

What values do you feel should be included in our school vision statement?

How do you see a shared vision benefiting all stakeholders?

How do you think a shared vision can impact the success of a school community?

References

Blanchard, K. H. (2007). *Leading at a higher level: Blanchard on leadership and creating high performing organizations.* Upper Saddle River, NJ: Prentice Hall.

DuFour, R. (2015). *In praise of American educators: And how they can become even better.* Bloomington, IN: Solution Tree Press.

DuFour, R., DuFour, R., Eaker, R., Many, T. W., & Mattos, M. (2024). *Learning by doing: A handbook for Professional Learning Communities at Work* (4th ed.). Bloomington, IN: Solution Tree Press.

Gordon, J. (2018). *The power of a positive team: Proven principles and practices that make great teams great.* Hoboken, NJ: Wiley.

Gruenert, S., & Whitaker, T. (2015). *School culture rewired: How to define, assess, and transform it.* Alexandria, VA: ASCD.

Kouzes, J. M., & Posner, B. Z. (2006). *A leader's legacy.* San Francisco: Jossey-Bass.

Robbins, P., & Alvy, H. (2004). *The new principal's fieldbook: Strategies for success.* Alexandria, VA: ASCD.

Williams, K. C., & Hierck, T. (2015). *Starting a movement: Building culture from the inside out in professional learning communities.* Bloomington, IN: Solution Tree Press.

Trending Stories (District)

Instructions: Imagine that five to ten years into the future your district has made the media's top posts, leading news, and trending stories of success. What would you like the media to report about your district?

Task 1: Independently reflect and respond to the following questions.

What would the articles highlight about student learning, growth, and achievement?	What would the articles highlight about the district culture?
What would the articles highlight about family and community involvement?	What would the articles highlight about awards, recognition, or special programs?

Task 2: Form groups as content or grade-band teams. Each group creates a trending-stories chart depicting headlines, illustrations, or captions that describe the hopes and dreams for your district from the perspective of students, staff, families, and the community. Be sure to include five to ten examples.

Here are some ideas to consider.

- Interviews of families or students
- Reviews from staff and community members
- Evidence of academic student achievement
- Advertisements for open positions or job fairs
- Notices of awards or recognition
- Invitations to special events

Task 3: Groups display their charts around the room and present their trending stories to the staff.

Task 4: After all groups have shared, review and reflect for possible revisions or additions.

Task 5: Consider what excites you most about the possible media trending stories, social media posts, and articles you've drafted for your district. Record which trending story resonates with you the most and why.

_____

_____

_____

_____

_____

_____

_____

Task 6: Take a moment to celebrate all the great news! Who wouldn't want to be a part of such a successful and impactful district? Congratulations!

Trending Stories (School)

Instructions: Imagine that five to ten years into the future your school has made the media's top posts, leading news, and trending stories of success. What would you like the media to report about your school?

Task 1: Independently reflect and respond to the following questions.

What would the articles highlight about student learning, growth, and achievement?	What would the articles highlight about the school culture?
What would the articles highlight about family and community involvement?	What would the articles highlight about awards, recognition, or special programs?

Task 2: Form groups as grade-level or content teams. Each group creates a trending-stories chart depicting the headlines, illustrations, or captions that describe the hopes and dreams for your school from the perspective of students, staff, families, and the community. Be sure to include five to ten examples.

Here are some ideas to consider.

- Interviews of families or students
- Reviews from staff and community members
- Evidence of student achievement
- Advertisements for open positions or job fairs
- Notices of awards or recognition
- Invitations to special events

Task 3: Groups display their charts around the room and present their trending stories to the staff.

Task 4: After all groups have shared, review and reflect for possible revisions or additions.

Task 5: Consider what excites you most about the possible media trending stories, social media posts, and articles you've drafted for your school. Record which trending story resonates with you the most and why.

_____

_____

_____

_____

_____

_____

Task 6: Take a moment to celebrate all the great news! Who wouldn't want to be a part of such a successful and impactful school? Congratulations!

Trending Stories Analysis

Your district or school has completed the trending-stories activity and dreamed of what your district or school can become. It will be important to synthesize this information to assist your guiding coalition in creating a vision that leads the district or school to the trending stories in five or ten years.

Instructions: Dedicate a guiding coalition meeting to collaborate on vision work. Display the trending-stories charts from the school or staff activity. Follow the task steps here to lead the work of the guiding coalition, gather staff input, and create the final vision statement.

Task 1: Individually, take a gallery walk to read the charts and observe any commonalities among them. Use this form to record common vocabulary, phrases, or concepts as they relate to the following ideas.

Student learning, growth, and achievement:	School culture:
Family and student involvement:	Awards, recognition, or special programs:

Task 2: Consider the preceding commonalities. Spend three to five minutes drafting a two- or three-sentence vision statement that encompasses the aspirations of the staff for your school.

Task 3: Reconvene partnerships to share their vision statements and spend three to five minutes combining their two statements into one.

Task 4: Combine partnerships to form groups. Each partnership shares their vision statements and then spends three to five minutes combining both vision statements into one statement.

Task 5: Continue combining groups until one vision statement has been drafted.

_____

_____

_____

_____

_____

Task 6: Guiding coalition members take this vision statement draft back to their collaborative teams using the fist-to-five rating scale and collect feedback.

Task 7: Bring the team's feedback to the guiding coalition. Collectively adjust the vision as needed based on team input. Publish the final vision statement.

_____

_____

_____

_____

_____

Task 8: Celebrate the adoption of the school vision in a way that builds excitement for the work ahead. Your district or school has just created a shared vision describing the district or school you aspire to become. Congratulations!

Proposal and Adoption (Step 1)

Instructions: Add time to your guiding coalition meeting agenda to develop a method to collect staff feedback for the vision statement. Use step 1 for brainstorming and planning. When creating a feedback form, consider how you will garner consensus, allowing all staff to indicate their commitment to the new or revised vision. This tool is based on the fist-to-five strategy with a 0–5 rating (DuFour et al., 2024).

> 0 = I cannot commit to this vision.
> 1 = I have strong reservations about the vision statement.
> 2 = I have some concerns about the vision statement.
> 3 = I feel the vision statement is good and I will support it.
> 4 = I feel this vision statement is strong and I will support it.
> 5 = I believe in the vision statement and I will champion it.

Possible methods to share the new or revised vision and collect feedback to be reviewed by the guiding coalition are as follows.

- Each team's guiding coalition representative presents the proposed vision at their next collaborative team meeting. Team members share their feedback on paper to be collected by the guiding coalition representative.
- The guiding coalition collaborates to create a digital survey (using Google Forms, Microsoft Forms, or another online platform) to share the proposed vision and solicit feedback.
- During a staff meeting, the proposed vision is presented to the whole staff by the guiding coalition. Feedback is collected during the staff meeting either on paper or digitally.
- Your idea:

_____

_____

_____

_____

_____

Reference

DuFour, R., DuFour, R., Eaker, R., Many, T. W., Mattos, M., & Muhammad, A. (2024). *Learning by doing: A handbook for Professional Learning Communities at Work* (4th ed.). Bloomington, IN: Solution Tree Press.

Proposal and Adoption (Step 2)

Instructions: Once your guiding coalition has chosen a method to collect staff feedback, at the next guiding coalition meeting, the team will analyze the feedback. As you do so, noting the degree of consensus, use the table that follows to gather staff insight for possible revisions and determine next steps.

Proposed vision statement:		
Average Score	**Next Steps**	**Proposed Revisions**
0–2	Gather feedback and revise the proposed vision statement.	
3	Gather feedback and clarify the proposed vision statement.	
4–5	Congratulations! It's time to adopt and celebrate your new shared vision statement.	

Total Score

0–2: Make revisions to the vision statement based on staff feedback and resubmit to the staff for another fist-to-five rating. Continue the cycle until the vision statement scores a 3, 4, or 5, paying attention to the proposed revisions. Once the score is a 4 or 5, you are ready to celebrate!

3: Analyze the feedback and decide as a guiding coalition whether the suggestions add clarity to the vision statement. With your team's collective input, make changes or keep the exhibiting proposed vision and move to the adoption stage.

4–5: Congratulations! Your school is ready to collectively adopt the new shared vision statement. Now it is time for your guiding coalition to create plans for a meaningful celebration of the vision statement for the staff.

Plan to Celebrate!

Use these questions to brainstorm with your guiding coalition leadership team to plan a moment of meaningful celebration for the organization when adopting the new vision. Remember—your vision is your school's or district's road map to success, so you want your celebration to highlight the importance and excitement of what staff have collectively envisioned for the organization's future. This is a pivotal moment for your school or district. Present the certificate, "Advancing Our Vision" (page 110) to those truly advancing the vision. Let's celebrate in a way that launches the entire team into the work ahead.

Who? • Who do we want to be included in this celebration? • How will we include *all* the stakeholders in the celebration?	
When? • When do we want to schedule this celebratory moment? 　◆ Before or after the workday for community participation? 　◆ Professional learning day? 　◆ Start of the school year? 　◆ Midyear launch? 　◆ Is this a daylong celebration?	
Where? • Where is the best location for the celebration? • Will the space accommodate all the stakeholders? • Where will we unveil or display the vision?	
How? • What ideas do we have to make this a celebration? • Do we want a theme? • Will there be refreshments?	
Launch • How will we brand the vision (posters to hang in classrooms or throughout the organization, notepads, website, social media, or newsletter)?	

Advancing Our Vision
GROWING OUR PROFESSIONAL LEARNING COMMUNITY

Vision statement: _____

Advancing Our Vision is presented to: _____

Thank you for advancing our shared vision by: _____

Recognized by: _____

Principal signature: _____

Date: _____

Vision Survey (District)

Instructions: This survey is designed to collect information about our district's shared vision statement. For each of the statements that follow, please (1) indicate the extent to which you agree or disagree with the statement by circling one of the three letters provided and (2) provide evidence to support the leading indicator.

Our district vision statement:				
Leading Indicators	**Disagree**	**Neutral**	**Agree**	**Evidence**
Foundation				
Our district has a clear and understandable vision statement.	D	N	A	
Our vision statement was developed or adopted collaboratively with current staff.	D	N	A	
The vision statement clearly describes what our district will look like in five to ten years.	D	N	A	
Refinement				
The vision statement is measurable.	D	N	A	
The vision statement is inspiring to staff, families, and the community.	D	N	A	
Application				
Our vision statement is frequently referenced by faculty members in formal and informal meetings.	D	N	A	
Our decision making is aligned with our vision.	D	N	A	
Resources—both financial and human—are allocated toward efforts that support our vision.	D	N	A	
District improvement efforts are aligned to the vision.	D	N	A	
Professional learning is aligned to the vision.	D	N	A	
Scheduling decisions support our vision.	D	N	A	
Hiring decisions are made with our vision in mind.	D	N	A	
Renewal				
We review our vision regularly and revise it when appropriate.	D	N	A	

	Communication			
Staff support our district vision.	D	N	A	
The families and community members support our district vision.	D	N	A	
Tally and Total				

Share your thoughts on our district vision statement and how it describes the type of school we are trying to create in five to ten years.

What success criteria should be used to evidence attainment of our district vision?

How do staff use the vision to guide day-to-day actions and decision making in our district? Provide specific evidence.

Does our vision inspire staff?

How will attaining our district vision enhance or improve the lives of students?

Vision Survey (School)

Instructions: This survey is designed to collect information about our school's shared vision statement. For each of the statements that follow, please (1) indicate the extent to which you agree or disagree with the statement by circling one of the three letters provided and (2) provide evidence to support the leading indicator.

Our school's vision statement:				
Leading Indicators	**Disagree**	**Neutral**	**Agree**	**Evidence**
Foundation				
Our school has a clear and understandable vision statement.	D	N	A	
Our vision statement was developed or adopted collaboratively with current staff.	D	N	A	
The vision statement clearly describes what our school will look like in five to ten years.	D	N	A	
Refinement				
The vision statement is measurable.	D	N	A	
The vision statement is inspiring to the staff.	D	N	A	
The vision is aligned to the district vision.	D	N	A	
Application				
Our vision statement is frequently referenced by faculty members in formal and informal meetings.	D	N	A	
Our decision making is aligned with our vision.	D	N	A	
Resources—both financial and human—are allocated toward efforts that support our vision.	D	N	A	
School improvement efforts are aligned to the vision.	D	N	A	
Professional learning is aligned to the vision.	D	N	A	
Scheduling decisions support our vision.	D	N	A	
Hiring decisions are made with our vision in mind.	D	N	A	

Renewal				
We review our vision regularly and revise it when appropriate.	D	N	A	
Communication				
School families support our school vision.	D	N	A	
The community supports our school vision.	D	N	A	
Tally and Total				

Share your thoughts on our school vision statement and how it describes the type of school we are trying to create in five to ten years.

What success criteria should be used to evidence attainment of our school vision?

How do staff use the vision to guide day-to-day actions and decision making in our school? Provide specific evidence.

Does our vision inspire staff?

How will attaining our school vision enhance or improve the lives of students?

Vision Survey Analysis (District)

Instructions: This analysis is intended to be conducted by the guiding coalition of the district in about one hour. Depending on the size of your guiding coalition, members will work in partnerships or small groups of up to four.

Step 1 (3–5 minutes)

Set the purpose of the collaborative time together as an inquiry into the effectiveness of the district's vision in each of the following in order to achieve the district's vision.

- Communicating a compelling future
- Describing what our district must become to accomplish our fundamental purpose
- Giving direction for what we should be doing and stop doing

---

Step 2 (10–15 minutes)

Divide the completed district surveys among the partnerships or groups. Ask each partnership or group to review their set of surveys by section, summarize their findings for each section, and note any outliers.

Step 3 (10–15 minutes)

Share each partnership's or group's findings. Possible structures for sharing could include the following.

- Partnerships or groups verbally share their findings, section by section, with an an opportunity for a clarifying discussion with the whole group after each section.
- Anchor charts titled with each section are displayed around the room. Partnerships or groups record their findings on sticky notes and post these on the corresponding anchor charts. Partnerships or teams then take a gallery walk of the anchor charts.

Step 4 (5 minutes)

Prioritize each section for next steps based on the shared findings of partnerships or groups.

Note: If surveys indicate a need for work in the Foundation section, this work will always be prioritized first and singularly. Work in other sections should be prioritized based on the level of need indicated by partnership or group findings and in consideration of the time of year. Work in other sections can occur in tandem.

Step 5 (10–15 minutes)

Create action steps, assignments, and timelines for the sections prioritized.

Step 6 (5 minutes)

Review the purpose and accomplishments of the collaborative time.

Vision Survey Analysis (School)

Instructions: This analysis is intended to be conducted by the guiding coalition of the school in about an hour. Depending on the size of your guiding coalition, members will work in partnerships or small groups of up to four.

Step 1 (3–5 minutes) Set the purpose of the collaborative time together as an inquiry into the effectiveness of the school's vision in each of the following in order to achieve the school's vision. • Communicating a compelling future • Describing what our school must become to accomplish our fundamental purpose • Giving direction for what we should be doing and stop doing
Step 2 (10–15 minutes) Divide the completed school surveys among the partnerships or groups. Ask each partnership or group to review their set of surveys by section, summarize their findings for each section, and note any outliers.
Step 3 (10–15 minutes) Share each partnership's or group's findings. Possible structures for sharing could include the following. • Partnerships or groups verbally share their findings, section by section, with an opportunity for a clarifying discussion with the whole group after each section. • Anchor charts titled with each section are displayed around the room. Partnerships or groups record their findings on sticky notes and post these on the corresponding anchor charts. Partnerships or teams then take a gallery walk of the anchor charts.
Step 4 (5 minutes) Prioritize each section for next steps based on the shared findings of partnerships or groups. *Note: If surveys indicate a need for work in the Foundation section, this work will always be prioritized first and singularly. Work in other sections should be prioritized based on the level of need indicated by partnership or group findings and in consideration of the time of year. Work in other sections can occur in tandem.
Step 5 (10–15 minutes) Create action steps, assignments, and timelines for the section(s) prioritized.
Step 6 (5 minutes) Review the purpose and accomplishments of the collaborative time.

Evidence of Impact (District)

Instructions: Work in partnerships or teams to reflect on the impact of your district's vision.

District vision statement:

Collaborate with your colleagues to discuss:

What evidence do we have that our vision impacts our day-to-day operations to achieve the district we are working to create?

Record evidence and next steps in the chart that follows.

Groups	Current Reality	Next Steps for Desired Future
Students		
Teachers		
Administrators		
Support Staff		
Resources		

Evidence of Impact (School)

Instructions: Work in partnerships or teams to reflect on the impact of your school's vision.

School vision statement:

Collaborate with your colleagues to discuss:

What evidence do we have that our vision impacts our day-to-day operations to achieve the school we are working to create?

Record evidence and next steps in the chart that follows.

Groups	Current Reality	Next Steps for Desired Future
Students		
Teachers		
Administrators		
Support Staff		
Resources		

CHAPTER 4
COLLECTIVE COMMITMENTS

Living into our values means that we do more than profess our values, we practice them. We walk our talk—we are clear about what we believe and hold important, and we take care that our intentions, words, thoughts, and behaviors align with those beliefs.

—BRENÉ BROWN

From our time coaching districts and schools across the country, the day that staff adopt their collaboratively created and agreed-on mission and vision always stands out in our memories as truly momentous. This accomplishment deserves a special kind of recognition—it's a red-letter kind of day that should be remembered in the history of the organization as the day educators set their collective purpose and the journey to attain it began. On this day in one particular school, staff were celebrating the creation of shared mission and vision statements—confetti poppers and Popsicles may have been involved—and as they closed their celebration, they paused the festivities and asked one simple question: "Now, how are we going to get there?" They knew that the work of setting the foundational pillars wasn't done just because they'd submitted the purchase order for the new vinyl cutout of their chosen phrases for their walls. They knew all the thought and effort they'd put into creating their shared mission and vision would be for naught if they simply stopped there. Their desire for lasting change demanded their next step must be the work of setting the third foundational pillar: collective commitments. To start this work, leaders asked staff to individually write out the attitudes, behaviors, and actions they thought they would need to commit to in order to fulfill their mission and vision. After giving staff time for reflection, discussion, and submission of ideas, the guiding coalition reviewed the responses, combining and synthesizing all ideas, to create the schoolwide collective commitments.

Once staff approved the commitments, they decided to make them just as public as their newly installed mission statement display. So a poster was created for all staff to sign. The poster was then hung in the entry of the school as a visual of the commitments they made. It not only was a constant reminder to the staff but also informed all family and community members what they could expect from the school, thereby serving as a method of both communication and accountability. This process created a shared knowledge of what the school staff valued, which, for both existing families and new families looking for a school home, made the values and actions clear and transparent.

And they didn't stop there. They discussed one more step to their process: addressing when collective commitments are not upheld. In their book *School Culture Rewired: How to Define, Assess, and Transform It*, a book focused on creating a positive school culture, Steve Gruenert and Todd Whitaker (2015) claim, "The culture of any organization is shaped by the worst behavior the leader is willing to tolerate" (p. 36). In addition, in *Revisiting Professional Learning Communities at Work: Proven Insights for Sustained, Substantive School Improvement*, Richard DuFour and colleagues (2021) write, "When individuals are allowed to consistently disregard and violate collective commitments, it creates a culture in which the school's mission, vision, values, and goals are merely a suggestion, and full participation is optional" (p. 113). With this knowledge in their tool belt, the school staff discussed how they wanted to address violations before they occurred, which created trust, honesty, clarity, and transparency throughout the school. With the third pillar firmly in place, they were equipped for success in living their mission and fulfilling their vision.

In this chapter, we define collective commitments and emphasize the need to create these collaboratively to bring the mission and vision to life. We use stories, experiences, and research from both businesses and schools to highlight the power of creating collective commitments on the success of an organization. To guide and support districts and schools in the creation of their collective commitments, we provide tools and procedures for drafting and implementing in ways that ensure the expectations for the attitudes, actions, and behaviors of the staff are clearly communicated, collectively embraced, consistently implemented, and celebrated.

Navigating the Collective Commitments

Collective commitments answer the question, How must we behave in order to live our mission and reach our shared vision? These are the promises group members make to one another for how they will behave and ensure the behaviors of each individual align and support the path toward the shared vision.

Collective commitments closely align with the values identified by the collective staff as they worked through the process of creating the shared vision and mission statements. However, it is crucial to move beyond simply discussing and naming these values or beliefs because, without action, naming alone will not sustain change in an organization. Through her work around values, Brené Brown found evidence supporting the importance of bringing beliefs into action. Brown (2018) says:

> If you're not going to take the time to translate values from ideals to behaviors—if you're not going to teach people the skills they need to show up in a way that's aligned with those values and then create a culture in which you hold one another accountable for staying aligned with the values—it's better not to profess any values at all. (p. 190)

Additionally, DuFour and colleagues (2021) state, "When educators clarify and commit to certain shared values, they are engaged in the essential ABCs of school improvement—identifying the actions, behaviors, and commitments necessary to bring mission and vision to life" (p. 106). They go on to clarify, "People make a conscious and deliberate effort to identify the specific ways they will act to improve their organizations, and then they commit to one another to act accordingly" (DuFour et al., 2021, p. 106). Clarifying how individuals must act in order to achieve meaningful work is a critical step that cannot be overlooked in the PLC. When created and implemented with thoughtful intention, collective commitments become the road map that details for educators what behaviors and actions are acceptable, expected, and celebrated.

Creating collective commitments begins with the leadership in the organization to lead the process. Marzano and colleagues (2018) explain that leaders play a crucial role in providing a clear understanding of the district or school values and collective commitments. Leaders of effective districts or schools realize the importance of clarity for all members in order to shift the narrative from "These are *my* students" to "These are *our* students," establishing that this is the work that *we* do. Clear communication, in both words and actions, of the organization's purpose, compelling future, and specific actions its members must commit to doing in order to achieve its goals is a requirement for turning the vision into reality.

Examining the Evidence of Successful Collective Commitments

Most schools and businesses don't advertise their collective commitments or make them public. However, shouldn't they? After all, when you are aware of the actions employees should demonstrate, you know when to bring compliments or concerns to the attention of the organization. Katy Sue visited a school, and as she walked in the front office area, she noticed the vision, mission, and values posted in the front foyer. She was excited to see the school valued respect, responsibility, and integrity. As she walked through the halls after morning arrival, she witnessed a teacher berating a student within view of classmates and other adults. The look on the student's face was one of embarrassment and devastation. At that very moment, Katy Sue knew that teacher did not value respect. This was a clear example of lack of articulation of the value. We can all say we have certain values; however, it is our behavior that truly provides evidence of what we value. The school had wonderful values in place, but they had not yet been articulated as behaviors or what we know as collective commitments. How must we behave to demonstrate that we value respect? If we value respect, then we must address students and adults with dignity and in an appropriate setting.

There are numerous businesses that list values on their company website. Let's use Starbucks as an example. Listed on their website, Starbucks shares that their values include:

> Creating a culture of warmth and belonging, where everyone is welcome. . . .
> Being present, connecting with transparency, dignity and respect.

Delivering our very best in all we do, holding ourselves accountable for results. We are performance driven, through the lens of humanity. (Peiper, 2023)

When Shawn's daughter, Grace, at the age of sixteen had finished her first day of work with Starbucks, she came home with enthusiasm not just about the fact that she'd landed her first job but also about the type of company for which she was working. She shared how the manager went over the mission, vision, and values of the company in detail, having an actual conversation about the why of the organization and how all the employees worked together to live out the mission and values. Grace felt like a true partner—which is exactly what Starbucks calls each of its employees—from day one, feeling like she was part of a team, part of something bigger than herself. She learned many things about making the perfect beverage and delicious food items, but what stuck with her most were the values of the organization she was joining and the actions expected of her in order to achieve them: asking customers for their names, learning frequent patrons' orders, and creating an inviting atmosphere for those who visited their stores.

Another example to consider is Mayo Clinic, which lists its core values on its website. The values that guide Mayo Clinic's (n.d.) mission are an expression of the vision and intent of the founders, the original Mayo physicians and the Sisters of Saint Francis:

Respect
Treat everyone in our diverse community, including patients, their families and colleagues, with dignity.

Integrity
Adhere to the highest standards of professionalism, ethics and personal responsibility, worthy of the trust our patients place in us.

Compassion
Provide the best care, treating patients and family members with sensitivity and empathy.

Healing
Inspire hope and nurture the well-being of the whole person, respecting physical, emotional and spiritual needs.

Teamwork
Value the contributions of all, blending the skills of individual staff members in unsurpassed collaboration.

Innovation
Infuse and energize the organization, enhancing the lives of those we serve, through the creative ideas and unique talents of each employee.

Excellence
Deliver the best outcomes and highest quality service through the dedicated effort of every team member.

Stewardship
Sustain and reinvest in our mission and extended communities by wisely managing our human, natural and material resources.

When Katy Sue's close relative became a patient of Mayo Clinic, she and her family knew they were at the right place for the treatment of their loved one. While they highly valued and respected the list of degrees and research expertise of each treating physician, it was the way they were made to feel while they were there that induced their complete trust in the organization. No matter the position within the company, through their everyday actions, staff adhered to the core values listed on the website—they were living their values. For a family facing a life crisis, these values made a difference not only to the patient but to the entire family.

In working with schools that aren't seeing the desired outcomes expected when operating as a PLC, we have often found that collective commitments aren't created collectively or explicitly stated, or there is a distinct inconsistency between the collective commitments and the actions of the staff. Through conversations with staff in these situations, we often discover that very few know the commitments. In cases where staff do know the collective commitments, we sometimes find an ambivalence or a belief that *they* aren't expected to utilize them in *their* positions. Much like a vision or mission statement that lives only on a website, collective commitments mean nothing without the knowledge, buy-in, and action orientation of staff. We asked ourselves, "What's the difference between these districts and schools and those that are high performing?" We discovered that although there isn't just one thing that makes a model school successful, having clear, transparent expectations for how to "do business" is critical. As we attend collaborative team meetings and watch informal and formal interactions among staff, families, and students, whether or not commitments are in place in a district or school setting is consistently an indicator of success.

Aisha Thomas, former principal of Zach Elementary School, worked to harness the power of collective commitments on the school's journey to become a National Blue Ribbon and Model PLC school. In speaking with us on the keys to her success, she explained how she and her colleagues read several articles written by Roland Barth from Harvard University. One key takeaway from their learning was discovering the number-one indicator for student success was the relationships among the adults in the school. Her school used this as a focal point to be clear on how they would and wouldn't treat one another. They discussed that in order to be a great school, adults needed to address concerns among themselves when appropriate, rather than relying on the principal to always step in. This work required the adults to learn how to have healthy dialogues. They focused on a book study to help them with the learning. They even created a video that was shared with the school families to aid in teacher and parent discussions. She explained that this was transformational in how adults in and out of the school building engaged in conversations with each other. In further discussions with Aisha, she detailed how the staff worked together to create shared collective commitments that aligned to their mission and vision.

The collective commitments:

- ***Healthy relationships:*** *We develop healthy relationships, based on trust, respect, and value.*
- ***Professional learning community:*** *We will, as collaborative teams, effectively use time and expertise to continuously improve.*
- ***Safe environment:*** *We are committed to sustaining a safe environment between staff, centered on trust and respect.*
- ***Shared leadership:*** *We arrive at consensus when all points of view have been heard and the "will of the group" is evident, even to those who are most opposed.*

Aisha also explained that staff agreed on a procedure of addressing instances in which educators weren't upholding those collective commitments, asking open-ended questions to seek understanding through healthy conversation. Over the course of six months, Aisha noticed major positive changes in their shift to a collaborative culture, and by the next year, the school culture became a "nirvana of highly effective educators who inspired each other and their students every day." Not only did Zach Elementary become a National Blue Ribbon School and a Model PLC school, but they moved in their state ranking from 89th to 13th and the school has continued to be one of the top-performing schools in Colorado (A. Thomas, personal communication, September 11, 2023).

The success story of Zach Elementary, just like those of Starbucks and Mayo Clinic, highlights how it is not simply the words we choose when developing our collective commitments but the attendant actions we take and observe that determine whether we achieve our vision.

Taking a Deep Dive Into the Research for Developing Collective Commitments

Much of the research supporting the need for collective commitments has already been stated in the mission (page 19) and vision (page 79) chapters of this book. When it comes to the establishment of a mission or vision, the point made over and over in the research is that these statements alone have little to no impact; instead, it is the alignment of the actions and behaviors of those within an organization to the mission and vision that provides measurable and meaningful benefits (Coker, 2022). The research of educators Valerij Dermol and Nada Trunk Širca (2018) also supports the concept that simply stating the mission and vision of a company does little to influence the performance of employees. Instead, employees must be connected to these aspects of the organization so that they "feel the meaning" of these statements and exercise them "passionately and positively" (Dermol & Širca, 2018, p. 542). So, how do we connect members of an organization to the collective commitments?

First, we must involve all staff to clarify, commit to, identify, and engage in the essential work of "identifying the actions, behaviors, and commitments necessary to bring mission and vision to life" (DuFour et al., 2021, p. 106). This highlights one way we can connect the members of an organization to its collective commitments: involvement. In their work

to study the impact of job involvement on performance, researchers Paul F. Rotenberry and Philip J. Moberg (2007) confirm that a high level of involvement leads to higher consistency of the efforts needed for the realization of organizational objectives. Additionally, motivation to implement the actions collective commitments describe becomes intrinsic versus extrinsic when staff are involved in the creation of these commitments. Studies also show that the internalization of the organization's purpose and teachers' intrinsic motivation to promote that purpose through their actions provides the maximum impact on organizational performance (Dermol & Širca, 2018). The level of involvement must be such that the aim is not merely for buy-in, or the willingness to support and participate in something, but for commitment: the dedication, devotion, or pledge to do something. When leadership meaningfully involves staff, soliciting and utilizing their voices to create or connect collective commitments, educators are better able to identify the effects of their individual actions on the success of the organization, and the more the employees perceive that their work contributes to the organization's achievements, the more they identify themselves with the organization's mission and values (Wright & Pandey, 2011). It is when the members of an organization come together to define the actions and behaviors that the mission and vision is brought to life.

Another way we can connect members of an organization to its collective commitments is through communication. Communication is essential for shaping and spreading organizational culture. Therefore, regarding collective commitments, it is vital not only for "companies to define such statements but [also to] spread such ideas among the employees" (Dermol & Širca, 2018, p. 542). Often, organizations focus on the external communication of their collective commitments—posting them on webpages and newsletters and referring to them when engaging with the surrounding community. However, a focus on clear and consistent internal communication of the collective commitments is also needed. Effective internal communication contributes to high performance through increased employee effectiveness, motivation, and creativity (Rogala, 2011). This could be attributed to the way effective internal communication builds loyalty and a sense of connectedness in the employee to the organization. It's important to note that "face-to-face conversation is the best and the most effective internal communication instrument" (Rogala, 2011, p. 4). This means that although we often have positive intentions such as expedience, efficiency, or respect for others' time when we choose to use digital communication—email, text, and so forth—when communicating the most important ideas in our organization, we need to devote the time and space for in-person conversations to connect all staff.

Sailing Into Action for Each Stage of Developing Collective Commitments

When deciding where to start with this work, use the "Collective Commitments Continuum" (page 137) to get a clear picture of your district's or school's current reality. Note that the same continuum is used for both district and school. First, identify the column that most describes the stage your school is in, and then, rather than looking to the next column to identify indicators for next steps, study the indicators at the developing and sustaining stages. That is, if you are at the initiating stage, the aim for the work to move your district or school forward will be to collaboratively articulate collective commitments endorsed by the staff from the very beginning as described in the developing and sustaining columns. This aim is supported in the steps we outline in the following pages.

When establishing collective commitments, the adage "Slower is better" may be valuable to follow. Taking the time to thoughtfully draft, apply, reflect on, and revise the commitments will make all the difference. We aren't saying it will take years to do this work; initial drafts through ratification should not take long. But when it comes to application, remember collective commitments are the promises we make for how we must *behave*, and behavior doesn't change overnight. This is how we would set about working with individual students on their behavior, keeping in mind the critical components of intentionality, consistency, and practice.

The Preinitiating Stage

A district or school in the preinitiating stage hasn't established its collective commitments, or it may have collective commitments that don't articulate the attitudes, behaviors, and actions necessary to forward the district's or school's mission and vision. The decisions, behaviors, and actions of the staff may be unaligned or based on assumptions communicated implicitly rather than explicitly.

1. Invite staff to consider and reflect on the impact collective commitments have on attaining desired outcomes using "The Power of Collective Commitments (District)" (page 138) or "The Power of Collective Commitments (School)" (page 140) tool.

2. Inspire staff to consider the impact of staff collective commitments on the educational experiences and successes of the students they serve using the tool "My Dreams for You" (page 142).

3. Provide staff the time and structure to brainstorm the ideal behaviors and actions needed in your district or school using the "Collective Commitments Wishlist (District)" (page 144) or "Collective Commitments Wishlist (School)" (page 145) tool.

4. Solidify the difference between beliefs and collective commitments using the "Beliefs and Collective Commitments Sort" (page 148).

5. Provide staff the time and structure to consider the actions needed in your district or school to achieve your mission and vision and then to draft commitment statements using the "Beliefs to Commitments (District)" (page 147) or "Beliefs to Commitments (School)" (page 148) tool. If desired, refer to "Example Beliefs to Commitments" (page 149).

6. Convene the guiding coalition to sort, combine, and synthesize the collective commitment statements submitted by the staff using the "Drafting Collective Commitments" (page 150) tool. The goal of this step is to generate a set of collective commitment statements that represent the voice and values of the organization as a whole.

7. After the guiding coalition has synthesized the collective commitments, submit them as a draft for staff feedback. This can be done using the "Ratification Survey" (page 153) or by creating a similar tool in a digital platform that allows for rating scales. All members of the organization will rate their commitment to the statement using the fist-to-five 0–5 scale, submitting specific feedback for a rating less than a 3.

8. Review the data collected from the "Ratification Survey" (page 153) with the guiding coalition. Discuss and adjust collective commitment statements if indicated and resubmit for ratification. Continue this process until all staff have indicated a 3 or higher for each commitment.

9. Once staff have ratified the collective commitments, use the "Collective Commitments Violations" (page 156) tool to brainstorm a list of ways staff may respond when a commitment is not upheld.

10. Intentionally celebrate evidence of the collective commitments being implemented throughout the district or school by using the tool "Celebration Planning" (page 157) to assist the guiding coalition in thoughtful planning of how and when these celebrations are scheduled throughout the year. Also plan for the use of the "Recognition Nomination" (page 158) form to celebrate individuals living the collective commitments.

11. Monitor progress from the preinitiating stage to the initiating stage by collecting evidence corresponding with the indicators in the "Collective Commitments Continuum" (page 137).

The Initiating Stage

A district or school in the initiating stage has collective commitments that a team of leaders (administrators or committee) have developed that communicate beliefs regarding the district's or school's purpose and direction. There has been an attempt to solicit feedback from staff as well as revisions made to the statements. However, these statements have little to no impact on the decisions, actions, and behaviors of the staff. In some ways, a district or school at this stage may feel that the commitment statements were created simply to check a box.

1. Invite staff to consider and reflect on the impact collective commitments have on attaining desired outcomes using "The Power of Collective Commitments (District)" (page 138) or "The Power of Collective Commitments (School)" (page 140) tool.

2. Inspire staff to consider the impact of staff collective commitments on the educational experiences and successes of the students they serve using the tool "My Dreams for You" (page 142).

3. Solidify the difference between beliefs and collective commitments using the "Beliefs and Collective Commitments Sort" (page 146).

4. Present the existing collective commitments to the staff and solicit input. Using the "Staff Feedback (District)" (page 159) or "Staff Feedback (School)" (page 160) tool, provide staff an opportunity to analyze and clarify their thoughts regarding the current commitments.

5. Provide staff the time and structure to consider the actions needed in your district or school to achieve your mission and vision and then to draft commitment statements using the "Beliefs to Commitments (District)" (page 147) or "Beliefs to Commitments (School)" (page 148) tool. If desired, refer to "Example Beliefs to Commitments" (page 149).

6. Convene the guiding coalition to sort, combine, and synthesize the collective commitment statements submitted by staff using the "Drafting Collective Commitments" (page 150) tool. The goal of this step is to generate a set of collective commitment statements that represent the voice and values of the organization.

7. After the guiding coalition has synthesized the collective commitments, submit them as a draft for staff feedback. This can be done using the "Ratification Survey" (page 153) or by creating a similar tool in a digital platform that allows for rating scales. All members of the organization will rate their commitment to the statement using a 0–5 scale, submitting specific feedback for a rating less than a 3.

8. Review the data collected from the "Ratification Survey" (page 153) with the guiding coalition. Discuss and adjust collective commitment statements if indicated and resubmit for ratification. Continue this process until all staff have indicated a 3 or higher for each commitment.

9. Once staff have ratified the collective commitments, use the "Collective Commitments Violations" (page 156) tool to brainstorm a list of ways staff may respond when a commitment is not upheld.

10. Take time to be intentional about celebrating evidence of the collective commitments being implemented throughout the district or school. Use the "Celebration Planning" (page 157) tool to assist the guiding coalition in thoughtful planning of how and when these celebrations are scheduled throughout the year. Plan to also use the "Recognition Nomination" (page 158) form to celebrate individuals living the collective commitments.

11. Monitor progress from the initiating to the implementing stage by collecting evidence corresponding with the indicators in the "Collective Commitments Continuum" (page 137).

The Implementing Stage

A district or school at the implementing stage has developed collective commitments collaboratively with the staff. These articulate more than beliefs and are stated as behaviors that forward the mission and vision of the district or school. However, there is evidence that not all staff have fully embraced these commitments or put them into action. There may be objections by some staff or a needed shift to personal ownership in the application of the collective commitments.

1. Provide teams and individuals an opportunity to consider the application of your district's or school's collective commitments in their attitudes, behaviors, and actions using the tool "Taking Ownership" (page 161). Teams and individuals will highlight the ways they already take ownership of the collective commitments and then create an action plan for deeper implementation.

2. Gather input from the staff for the existing collective commitments using the "Staff Feedback (District)" (page 159) or "Staff Feedback (School)" (page 160) tool. Provide your staff an opportunity to analyze and clarify their thoughts regarding the current commitments.

3. Use the "Collective Commitments Violations" (page 156) tool to brainstorm a list of ways staff can further align attitudes, behaviors, and actions of all staff by responding when a commitment is not upheld.

4. Monitor progress from the implementing stage to the developing stage by collecting evidence corresponding with the indicators in the "Collective Commitments Continuum" (page 137).

5. Take time to be intentional about celebrating evidence of the collective commitments being implemented throughout the district or school. Use the "Celebration Planning" (page 157) tool to assist the guiding coalition in thoughtful planning of how and when these celebrations are scheduled throughout the year. Plan to also use the "Recognition Nomination" (page 158) form to celebrate individuals living the collective commitments.

The Developing Stage

A school or district in the developing stage has collective commitments that staff created collaboratively and intentionally to advance the school vision. Staff continually endorse these commitments and put them into action.

1. Collect examples of evidence from staff actions that demonstrate the collective commitments and analyze how the collective commitments are impacting the goal of achieving the shared vision using the "Evidence of Action" (page 163) tool.

2. Use the "Collective Commitments Violations" (page 156) tool to brainstorm a list of ways staff can further align attitudes, behaviors, and actions of all staff by responding when a commitment is not upheld.

3. Twice a year, use the "Fulfilling Our Collective Commitments (District)" (page 164) or "Fulfilling Our Collective Commitments (School)" (page 165) tool to collect feedback on how well staff are living out the commitments.

4. Monitor progress from the developing to the sustaining stage by collecting evidence corresponding with the indicators in the "Collective Commitments Continuum" (page 137).

5. Take time to intentionally celebrate evidence of the collective commitments being implemented throughout the district or school. Use the "Celebration Planning" (page 157) tool to assist the guiding coalition in thoughtful planning of how and when these celebrations are scheduled throughout the year. Plan to also use the "Recognition Nomination" (page 158) form to celebrate individuals living the collective commitments.

The Sustaining Stage

A school or district at the sustaining stage has collective commitments that staff created and endorse. There is evidence that the decisions, behaviors, and actions of the staff align with these commitments to such an extent that the connection is observable even by those outside the school or district. Staff use the collective commitments as a definition of what the school or district stands for and actively challenge inconsistencies or misalignments in one another's decisions, behaviors, or actions.

1. At the beginning of and midway through the year, obtain feedback from the staff to ensure collective commitments remain at this stage using the "Status Survey (District)" (page 166) or "Status Survey (School)" (page 168).

2. Take time to intentionally celebrate evidence of the collective commitments being implemented throughout the district or school. Use the "Celebration Planning" (page 157) tool to assist the guiding coalition in thoughtful planning of how and when these celebrations are scheduled throughout the year. Plan to also use the "Recognition Nomination" (page 158) form to celebrate individuals living the collective commitments.

Staying Afloat Through Common Challenges to Developing Collective Commitments

Crafting collective commitments is often an unfamiliar process for districts and schools. This can often make it difficult to know what problems might arise through the process. The if-then chart shown in table 4.1 will help you navigate common challenges along the way. This is meant as a guide to support conversations with your leadership team to find the best solution for your district or staff needs.

Table 4.1: If-Then Chart

If . . .	Then . . .
The collective commitments are written as beliefs.	Work with staff to rewrite commitments as attitudes, behaviors, and actions.
There are too many commitments.	Work with the guiding coalition to determine which can be combined or synthesized to encompass several commitments as one statement.

If . . .	Then . . .
The commitments do not align to the mission or vision.	Revisit the mission and vision to determine whether any revisions might be needed.
The commitments are not used to guide day-to-day actions.	Revisit the tool designed to address collective commitments violations.
Staff are hesitant to address collective commitments violations.	Provide professional learning for staff around the work of crucial conversations to assist staff in having these important conversations.

Source: Adapted from DuFour et al., 2021.

Knowing the Ropes for Collective Commitments Development

As you and your colleagues work to establish your organization's collective commitments, keep in mind the following as your actions become your culture.

- Writing collective commitments provides clear expectations for adult behavior and accountability to one another.
- The guiding coalition members should both model the commitments and assist in the celebration of others by recognizing staff.
- Collective commitments should clearly articulate the actionable behaviors of the district or school.
- Collaborative teams are often familiar with norms, which are the commitments that articulate how members will behave to ensure a safe and productive collaborative team meeting. Collective commitments function similarly to the norms of a team at the district or school level.

Celebrating the Collective Commitments

Celebrating staff who are living the collective commitments highlights the behaviors you hope to see throughout your district or school. Acknowledging the actions that align with your values, purpose, and aspirations not only impacts student growth but also creates a culture of purposeful intention among the staff. The guiding coalition will want to add the planning of celebrations to meeting agendas to ensure the values and collective commitments are recognized and prioritized across the year. Ideas to consider for celebration planning can include the following.

- Gather insight from staff using the "Acknowledgment Survey" (page 170) for ideas of how they would like to be celebrated or to celebrate one another.
- Highlight a collective commitment each month on the announcements in the staff or school newsletter and include a variety of staff who exemplify the collective commitment.
- Encourage staff and parents to email the administrative team when a colleague has made an impact through their actions that live out the values of the school.

- At a monthly staff meeting, have staff jot down celebrations acknowledging colleagues who exemplify one of the collective commitments using the "Celebration Jot" (page 171) form and post these around the meeting room. Next, provide staff with stickers and colorful pens so that as everyone does a gallery walk to read the celebratory posts, they can add messages of congratulations, or note other examples of how the named members uphold the highlighted commitments. Disseminate the filled-out forms to the named staff after the meeting.

- Dedicate an area in or near the staff lounge as a graffiti wall of shout-out moments where collective commitments have made a difference in the school.

- Staff can nominate colleagues using the "Recognition Nomination" (page 158) form. This form can be completed and passed on to administrators to send notes home to the families of individual educators acknowledging the impact they're making at your district or school because of their dedication to the collective commitments.

Stay the Course

When visiting classrooms at the beginning of the school year, we often find teachers discussing classroom expectations with the students. Oftentimes, students are engaged in this work of determining the behaviors they would like to see from their classmates. Social contracts are commonplace, and collective accountability is the standard for the majority of classrooms. Just as teachers will find themselves struggling when infractions to classroom expectations are not addressed, so will educators in buildings when there are unaddressed violations of the commitments that have been made at the district or school level. In his book *In Praise of American Educators: And How They Can Become Even Better*, Richard DuFour (2015) confirms that "schools that do address the commitments pillar will not benefit from the process if staff members are unwilling to hold each other accountable when the commitments are violated" (p. 113). Since the commitments are the actionable ways we must behave to reach our vision, not only are the climate and culture of the school affected when violations are not addressed, but in turn, the vision will not become a reality for schools that elect not to adhere to the commitments. Protocols and consistency are essential for all educators, and accountability belongs to all, not just the district or school leaders, to follow through in both celebrating dedication to the commitments and addressing violations as they occur. We recommend using the "Fulfilling Our Collective Commitments (District)" (page 164) or "Fulfilling Our Collective Commitments (School)" (page 165) resource at least twice during the school year to monitor the effectiveness of the commitments.

Anchors Away!

Collective commitments are a critical pillar in the PLC foundation. These shared commitments bring the mission to life with behaviors and actions. Through the collective commitments, the mission becomes visible and impactful to the district or school. It shifts your professional learning community from buy-in to the PLC process to ownership. By committing to common beliefs that are now actionable through collective commitments, the district or school is set solidly on the path to reaching the shared vision. This is the work that will truly make the vision a reality.

Use the space provided to anchor your thoughts and chart your course for your next steps.

Collective Commitments Continuum

Instructions: Individually, read the indicators that describe each stage from preinitiating through sustaining. Honestly assess the current reality of the establishment of your collective commitments. Consider what evidence or anecdotes support your assessment. Record your reflections in the space provided.

Collective commitments (shared values): We have made commitments to one another regarding how we must behave in order to achieve our shared vision.

Collective Commitments Continuum Stages				
Preinitiating	Initiating	Implementing	Developing	Sustaining
☐ Staff have not yet articulated the attitudes, behaviors, or actions they are prepared to demonstrate in order to advance the mission of learning for all and the vision of what the district or school might become.	☐ Administrators or a committee of staff have created statements of beliefs regarding the district's or school's purpose and its direction. Staff have reviewed and reacted to those statements. Initial drafts have been amended based on staff feedback. There is no attempt to translate the beliefs into the specific commitments or behaviors that staff will model.	☐ A statement has been developed that articulates the specific commitments staff have been asked to embrace to help the school fulfill its purpose and move closer to its vision. The commitments are stated as behaviors rather than beliefs. Many staff object to specifying these commitments and prefer to focus on what other groups must do to improve the district or school.	☐ Staff have been engaged in the process to articulate the collective commitments that will advance the district or school toward its vision. They endorse the commitments and seek ways to bring them to life.	☐ The collective commitments are embraced by staff, embedded in the culture, and evident to observers of the district or school. They help define what it stands for. Examples of the commitments are shared in stories and celebrations, and people are challenged when they behave in ways that are inconsistent with the collective commitments.

I believe our school or district is at the _____ stage based on the preceding indicators. The evidence to support my rationale includes:

Source: Adapted from DuFour, R., DuFour, R., Eaker, R., Many, T. W., Mattos, M., & Muhammad, A. (2024). Learning by doing: A handbook for Professional Learning Communities at Work (4th ed.). Bloomington, IN: Solution Tree Press.

The Power of Collective Commitments (District)

Instructions: Read the research and quotes that follow and highlight words and phrases that resonate with you and your educational philosophy of how collective commitments impact a school community. Then, respond to the questions. These quotes are meant to stimulate thinking and understanding behind creating collective commitments at the district level while also providing for meaningful collaboration among colleagues that is grounded in the ideas from experts to create a common understanding of the value of this foundational pillar.

"Leaders of any effective organization must know the importance of clarity. Having clarity means communicating consistently in words and actions . . . the specific actions members can immediately take to achieve its goals" (Marzano et al., 2018, pp. 4–5).

"You must invest in the shared collective commitments you've identified as best practices to help your school live its mission and vision" (Williams & Hierck, 2015, p. 121).

"Research confirms that a collaborative school culture correlates positively with student achievement" (Gruenert, 2005 as cited in Gruenert & Whitaker, 2015, p. 51).

"A leader of the PLC process cannot verbally commit to a school mission of learning for all but then allow individuals within the organization to act in ways that are counterproductive to this commitment" (DuFour et al., 2016, p. 37).

"Develop commitment statements at each level within the district. The school board and superintendent team, district leadership team, building leadership team, and teacher collaborative teams should answer the question, What commitments do we need to make to improve student learning?" (Eaker, Hagadone, Keating, & Rhoades, 2021, p. 34).

"Your values are the soul of your leadership, and they drive your behavior" (Maxwell, 2011, p. 46).

"The values statement summarizes the core values of the company that act as cultural cornerstones for the entire corporation" (Shreim, 2020, p. 13).

What research or quote resonates with you, and why?

How could having collective commitments impact the culture in our district?

What collective commitments are needed to help us reach our district mission and vision?

References

DuFour, R., DuFour, R., Eaker, R., Many, T. W., & Mattos, M. (2024). *Learning by doing: A handbook for Professional Learning Communities at Work* (4th ed.). Bloomington, IN: Solution Tree Press.

Eaker, R., Hagadone, M., Keating, J., & Rhoades, M. (2021). *Leading PLCs at Work districtwide: From boardroom to classroom.* Bloomington, IN: Solution Tree Press.

Gruenert, S., & Whitaker, T. (2015). *School culture rewired: How to define, assess, and transform it.* Alexandria, VA: ASCD.

Marzano, R. J., Warrick, P. B., Rains, C. L., & DuFour, R. (2018). *Leading a High Reliability School.* Bloomington, IN: Solution Tree Press.

Maxwell, J. C. (2011). *The five levels of leadership.* New York: Hatchette Book Group.

Shreim, S. (2020). *Vision, mission, values, aspirations, do they matter?* Cambridge, MA: Business Model Hackers.

Williams, K. C., & Hierck, T. (2015). *Starting a movement: Building culture from the inside out in professional learning communities.* Bloomington, IN: Solution Tree Press.

The Power of Collective Commitments (School)

Instructions: Read the research and quotes that follow and highlight words and phrases that resonate with you and your educational philosophy of how collective commitments impact a school community. Then, respond to the questions. These quotes are meant to stimulate thinking and understanding behind creating collective commitments at the school level while also providing for meaningful collaboration among colleagues that is grounded in the ideas from experts to create a common understanding of the value of this foundational pillar.

"Leaders of any effective organization must know the importance of clarity. Having clarity means communicating consistently in words and actions . . . the specific actions members can immediately take to achieve its goals" (Marzano et al., 2018, pp. 4–5).

"You must invest in the shared collective commitments you've identified as best practices to help your school live its mission and vision" (Williams & Hierck, 2015, p. 121).

"Research confirms that a collaborative school culture correlates positively with student achievement" (Gruenert, 2005, as cited in Gruenert & Whitaker, 2015, p. 51).

"A leader of the PLC process cannot verbally commit to a school mission of learning for all but then allow individuals within the organization to act in ways that are counterproductive to this commitment" (DuFour et al., 2016, p. 37).

"Develop commitment statements at each level within the district. The school board and superintendent team, district leadership team, building leadership team, and teacher collaborative teams should answer the question, What commitments do we need to make to improve student learning?" (Eaker et al., 2021, p. 34).

"Your values are the soul of your leadership, and they drive your behavior" (Maxwell, 2011, p. 46).

"The values statement summarizes the core values of the company that act as cultural cornerstones for the entire corporation" (Shreim, 2020, p. 12).

What research or quote resonates with you, and why?

How could having collective commitments impact our school culture?

What collective commitments are needed to help us reach our school mission and vision?

References

DuFour, R., DuFour, R., Eaker, R., Many, T. W., & Mattos, M. (2024). *Learning by doing: A handbook for Professional Learning Communities at Work* (4th ed.). Bloomington, IN: Solution Tree Press.

Eaker, R., Hagadone, M., Keating, J., & Rhoades, M. (2021). *Leading PLCs at Work districtwide: From boardroom to classroom.* Bloomington, IN: Solution Tree Press.

Gruenert, S., & Whitaker, T. (2015). *School culture rewired: How to define, assess, and transform it.* Alexandria, VA: ASCD.

Marzano, R. J., Warrick, P. B., Rains, C. L., & DuFour, R. (2018). *Leading a High Reliability School.* Bloomington, IN: Solution Tree Press.

Maxwell, J. C. (2011). *The five levels of leadership.* New York: Hatchette Book Group.

Shreim, S. (2020). *Vision, mission, values, aspirations, do they matter?* Cambridge, MA: Business Model Hackers.

Williams, K. C., & Hierck, T. (2015). *Starting a movement: Building culture from the inside out in professional learning communities.* Bloomington, IN: Solution Tree Press.

My Dreams for You

Instructions: Staff should each bring in a picture of a child who is meaningful in their lives—perhaps a son or daughter, grandchild, niece or nephew, student, or family friend. Staff will complete this handout individually while keeping this child in mind.

Place photo here

Child's name:

_____

Educator's name: _____

My hopes for this child's future:

_____

_____

_____

What would you want the school to ensure for this child?

_____

_____

Describe the classroom culture.

Describe the observable ideal interactions among students and between students and adults.

Collective Commitments Wishlist (District)

Instructions: Independently and honestly describe behaviors and actions you wish to see in your district environment.

1. Describe behaviors and actions you would like present between colleagues.

2. Describe behaviors and actions you would like present between the district leaders and staff within the district office.

3. Describe behaviors and actions that would create family and community engagement within our district.

4. Describe behaviors and actions you feel are needed in order for the district to be committed to learning for all.

Anchor Your Vision © 2025 Solution Tree Press • SolutionTree.com
Visit **go.SolutionTree.com/PLCbooks/AYV** and enter the unique access code found on the book's inside front cover to access this reproducible.

Collective Commitments Wishlist (School)

Instructions: Independently and honestly describe behaviors and actions you wish to see in your school environment.

1. Describe behaviors and actions you would like present on your team between colleagues.

2. Describe behaviors and actions you would like present between the administrators and staff within the school.

3. Describe behaviors and actions that would create family and community engagement within our school.

4. Describe behaviors and actions you feel are needed in order for the school to be committed to learning for all.

Beliefs and Collective Commitments Sort

Instructions: Cut the beliefs and collective commitments apart. Hand them out to the staff to work in partnerships or small groups to match the actions that would exemplify the corresponding value.

Beliefs	Collective Commitments
We believe in treating one another with respect.	We seek to understand one another and value others' thoughts and opinions.
We believe all students can learn at high levels.	We will ensure that instruction aligns with the rigor of the standards.
We value collaboration.	We will work in collaborative teams to analyze learning expectations and outcomes.
We believe all students learn at different levels.	We will respond to data with systematic and targeted intervention to fill gaps in learning.
We value integrity.	We will follow through with our responsibilities and expectations.
We value clear communication.	We will actively listen and have direct, honest conversations with one another.
We believe celebration creates a positive culture.	We will acknowledge accomplishments and milestones toward our vision and mission.
We believe in ongoing learning for all.	We will seek out opportunities to grow in our professional practices.

Beliefs to Commitments (District)

Instructions: First, record your district's mission and vision. Then, list the overarching ideas described or implied by your shared mission and vision. Finally, by writing the specific attitudes, actions, or behaviors needed using the if-then statement framework to answer the question, What must we commit to do to become the district that fulfills our mission and vision?

Our district's mission:

Our district's vision:

Overarching ideas:			

If-then statements:
Example: "If we are to be a district that/where [overarching idea], then we must [attitude, action, or behavior]."

Beliefs to Commitments (School)

Instructions: First, record your school's mission and vision. Then, list the overarching ideas described or implied by your mission and vision. Finally, by writing the specific attitudes, actions, or behaviors needed using the if-then statement framework to answer the question, What must we commit to do to become the school that fulfills our mission and vision?

Our school's mission:

Our school's vision:

Overarching ideas:

If-then statements:

Example: "If we are to be a school that/where [overarching idea], then we must [attitude, action, or behavior]."

Example Beliefs to Commitments

Our school's mission:
Our school guarantees exceptional learning and growth for all students and staff.

Our school's vision:
Our school will be globally recognized as a model professional learning community that provides excellence in both academic and character education and prepares students to be positive leaders in their community.

Overarching ideas:

Exceptional learning	Exceptional growth	All (students and staff)	Academics
Character	Leadership	Global recognition	Model professional learning community

If-then statements:

Example: "If we are to be a school that/where [overarching idea], then we must [attitude, action, or behavior]."

- If we are to be a school that ensures exceptional learning for students, then we must commit to developing a guaranteed and viable curriculum and implementing that curriculum in our classrooms.
- If we are to become a model professional learning community, then we must commit to taking a collective responsibility to ensure all students learn the essential standards.
- If we are to be a school that ensures exceptional growth for students, then we must commit to providing additional time and support for student learning during the school day.
- If we are to be a school where the staff continually grows in their professional learning, then we must commit to providing time and opportunity for job-embedded professional learning.
- If we are to be a school that provides excellence in academic education, then we must commit to value all core content areas, providing the time, support, and opportunities.
- If we are to be a school that provides excellence in character education, then we must commit to teaching and modeling our character curriculum and intentionally create opportunities to practice, reinforce, and celebrate.
- If we are to be a school that prepares students to become positive leaders in their community, then we must commit to creating a variety of opportunities to practice leadership skills.

Drafting Collective Commitments

Step 1 Instructions: Divide the members of the guiding coalition into pairs and distribute copies of the staff's responses to the "Beliefs to Commitments (District)" (page 147) or "Beliefs to Commitments (School)" (page 148) tool. Partners will label one column with each of the overarching ideas listed by staff, combining similar ideas and adding a tally mark when the same idea is repeated. Then, partners will sort commitment statements by overarching idea. After sorting, partners will reread the commitment statements, combining, revising, and synthesizing statements as needed to draft one to two statements per overarching idea.

Idea:	Idea:	Idea:	Idea:
Tally:	Tally:	Tally:	Tally:
Idea:	Idea:	Idea:	Idea:
Tally:	Tally:	Tally:	Tally:

Partner Draft Commitment Statements:

Partner Draft Commitment Statements:

Step 2 Instructions: As a group, guiding coalition members will read out each collective commitment statement drafted by partners, discussing and sorting commitment statements by similarity as they are read. Once sorting is complete, the guiding coalition as a whole will combine, revise, and synthesize similar statements to create a set of collective commitment statements to submit to the members of the organization for ratification.

Guiding Coalition Draft Commitment Statements:

Ratification Survey

Instructions: Record the proposed collective commitments drafted by the guiding coalition. Invite staff to indicate commitment to each statement using a 0–5 scale (0 being the lowest and 5 the highest), submitting specific feedback if a 3 or less is selected.

Draft commitment statement:

0   1   2   3   4   5

Feedback:

Draft commitment statement:

0   1   2   3   4   5

Feedback:

Draft commitment statement:

0   1   2   3   4   5

Feedback:

Draft commitment statement:

◯ 0   ◯ 1   ◯ 2   ◯ 3   ◯ 4   ◯ 5

Feedback:

Draft commitment statement:

◯ 0   ◯ 1   ◯ 2   ◯ 3   ◯ 4   ◯ 5

Feedback:

Draft commitment statement:

◯ 0   ◯ 1   ◯ 2   ◯ 3   ◯ 4   ◯ 5

Feedback:

Draft commitment statement:

◯ 0   ◯ 1   ◯ 2   ◯ 3   ◯ 4   ◯ 5

Feedback:

Draft commitment statement:

◯ 0   ◯ 1   ◯ 2   ◯ 3   ◯ 4   ◯ 5

Feedback:

Draft commitment statement:

◯ 0   ◯ 1   ◯ 2   ◯ 3   ◯ 4   ◯ 5

Feedback:

Draft commitment statement:

◯ 0   ◯ 1   ◯ 2   ◯ 3   ◯ 4   ◯ 5

Feedback:

Collective Commitments Violations

Instructions: Divide collective commitments recorded on the "Beliefs to Commitments (District)" (page 147) or "Beliefs to Commitments (School)" (page 148) tool between pairs or groups of staff. Each pair or group will consider the collective commitment, imagine possible situations that would violate that commitment, and then brainstorm potential responses to ensure the commitment is upheld. After brainstorming, pairs or groups will combine with another pair or group to share their thinking and synthesize or add to their list of possible responses. Pairs and groups will continue to combine, repeating the same process, until all members' responses have been synthesized to create a single list of possible responses to commitment violations.

Collective commitment:

Possible violations:

Our group's ideas for response:

Our combined ideas for response:

Celebration Planning

Instructions: Dedicate fifteen minutes on a guiding coalition meeting agenda to plan how you can celebrate collective commitments. Think about celebrations throughout the year.

Collective Commitments:

Celebration Strategy	Time of Year (monthly, two times per year, ongoing)	Who is responsible for creating or follow-up?

Anchor Your Vision © 2025 Solution Tree Press • SolutionTree.com
Visit **go.SolutionTree.com/PLCbooks/AYV** to download this free reproducible.

REPRODUCIBLE

Recognition Nomination

Instructions: Use the brainstorming questions that follow to explain the actions you would like acknowledged for a colleague who is bringing the collective commitments to fruition. This information will be used to recognize your colleague in a way aligned with their preferences based on their responses to the "Acknowledgment Survey" (page 170).

Which individual educator would you like to acknowledge?
What actions demonstrate this person's impact on student growth aligned with our collective commitments?
How did these actions help guide the district or school toward the shared vision?
Provide a statement of how this impacted you to see this individual's commitment to supporting your school.

Anchor Your Vision © 2025 Solution Tree Press • SolutionTree.com
Visit **go.SolutionTree.com/PLCbooks/AYV** and enter the unique access code
found on the book's inside front cover to access this reproducible.

Staff Feedback (District)

Instructions: List your district's collective commitments in the chart that follows. Provide your feedback for each commitment. Is this a commitment you agree with? Does it align with the shared vision and mission? Provide a rationale for why or why not.

Collective Commitments	Feedback

Anchor Your Vision © 2025 Solution Tree Press • SolutionTree.com
Visit **go.SolutionTree.com/PLCbooks/AYV** and enter the unique access code
found on the book's inside front cover to access this reproducible.

Staff Feedback (School)

Instructions: List your school's collective commitments in the chart that follows. Provide your feedback for each commitment. Is this a commitment you agree with? Does it align with the shared vision and mission? Provide a rationale for why or why not.

Collective Commitments	Feedback

Anchor Your Vision © 2025 Solution Tree Press • SolutionTree.com
Visit **go.SolutionTree.com/PLCbooks/AYV** and enter the unique access code found on the book's inside front cover to access this reproducible.

Taking Ownership

Instructions: As a team, brainstorm a list of ways each collective commitment should be applied in the work of the team and the work of everyone. Review the list created, highlighting the ways that the team and individuals are already applying the commitments. Consider the parts not highlighted to create a next-steps action plan collectively and then individually for taking ownership of applying the collective commitments. Record the plans and set a review date for accountability.

Commitment	Team Application	Individual Application

Team's next-steps action plan:

Review date:

Individual's next-steps action plan:

Instructions: Record each teacher's personal action plan, one in each box below. Cut or tear along the lines and distribute so that each teacher has a recording of their plan to keep as a reminder.

Teacher name:	Commitments:	Review date:	Teacher name:	Commitments:	Review date:	Teacher name:	Commitments:	Review date:	Teacher name:	Commitments:	Review date:

Evidence of Action

Instructions: Divide staff into small groups to complete this task. Re-create the graphic organizer that follows on a piece of chart paper for each group and supply with markers. Distribute one collective commitment to each group to adhere to the center of the chart. Task each team with recording evidence of their collective commitments in action from across the school year and how those actions are leading toward the fulfillment of the shared mission and vision. Set a timer for five minutes, and then have teams rotate clockwise to each poster, first reading the evidence already recorded and then adding new ideas. Continue until all groups have had the opportunity to add to each chart and are back at their original chart. Ask groups to read through all the evidence and then share with the whole group.

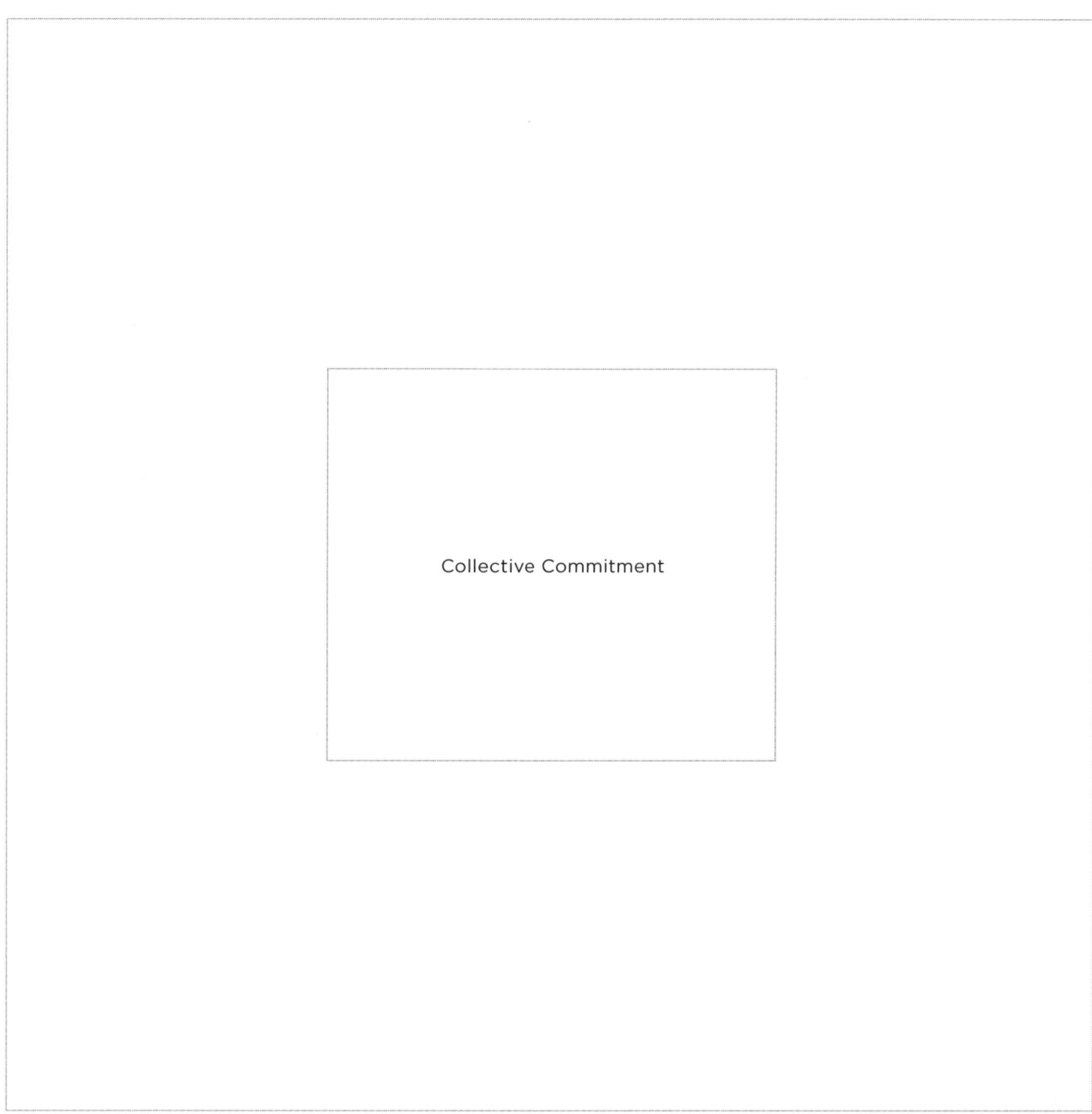

Fulfilling Our Collective Commitments (District)

Instructions: This survey is designed to collect information about how well our staff are adhering to our collective commitments. For each of the statements that follow, please (1) indicate the extent to which you agree or disagree with the statement by circling one of the three letters provided and (2) provide a rationale to support the leading indicator.

Our shared vision:

Our shared mission:

Leading Indicators	Disagree	Neutral	Agree	Rationale
Staff are fulfilling our collective commitments.	D	N	A	
Staff hold one another accountable for adhering to our collective commitments.	D	N	A	
Staff recognize and celebrate one another often for adhering to our commitments.	D	N	A	
Our collective commitments are frequently referenced by faculty members in formal and informal meetings.	D	N	A	
Decision making is aligned with our collective commitments.	D	N	A	
There is clear evidence of staff fulfilling the collective commitments.	D	N	A	
Our collective commitments are referenced frequently within our district.	D	N	A	
Collective commitments are in a location that can be viewed by visitors in our district office.	D	N	A	
Our leaders actively find ways to celebrate evidence of the collective commitments.	D	N	A	
Rituals, traditions, and stories reflect our collective commitments.	D	N	A	
Tally and Total				

Anchor Your Vision © 2025 Solution Tree Press • SolutionTree.com
Visit **go.SolutionTree.com/PLCbooks/AYV** and enter the unique access code found on the book's inside front cover to access this reproducible.

Fulfilling Our Collective Commitments (School)

Instructions: This survey is designed to collect information about how well our staff are adhering to our collective commitments. For each of the statements that follow, please (1) indicate the extent to which you agree or disagree with the statement by circling one of the three letters provided and (2) provide a rationale to support the leading indicator.

Our shared vision:

Our shared mission:

Leading Indicators	Disagree	Neutral	Agree	Rationale
Staff are fulfilling our collective commitments.	D	N	A	
Staff hold one another accountable for adhering to our collective commitments.	D	N	A	
Staff recognize and celebrate one another often for adhering to our commitments.	D	N	A	
Our collective commitments are frequently referenced by faculty members in formal and informal meetings.	D	N	A	
Decision making is aligned with our collective commitments.	D	N	A	
There is clear evidence of staff fulfilling the collective commitments.	D	N	A	
Our collective commitments are referenced frequently within our school.	D	N	A	
Collective commitments are in a location that can be viewed by staff, students, and families.	D	N	A	
Our administrators actively find ways to celebrate evidence of the collective commitments.	D	N	A	
Rituals, traditions, and stories reflect our collective commitments.	D	N	A	
Tally and Total				

Status Survey (District)

Instructions: This survey is designed to collect information about our district's collective commitments. For each of the statements that follow, please (1) indicate the extent to which you agree or disagree with each statement by circling one of the three letters provided and (2) provide a rationale to support the leading indicator.

Our shared vision:

Our shared mission:

Leading Indicators	Disagree	Neutral	Agree	Rationale
Foundation				
Our district has clear collective commitments.	D	N	A	
We have developed collective commitments that describe actions we will take to fulfill our vision.	D	N	A	
Our staff collaboratively developed our collective commitments.	D	N	A	
The collective commitments clearly describe behaviors we would see throughout the district departments.	D	N	A	
Refinement				
The collective commitments are supported by the staff.	D	N	A	
The commitments describe actions we should see in our district.	D	N	A	
Application				
The collective commitments are aligned to the vision and mission.	D	N	A	
The collective commitments clearly define how staff will work together to achieve the district's vision and carry out the mission.	D	N	A	
Staff hold one another accountable for adhering to our collective commitments.	D	N	A	

Leading Indicators	Disagree	Neutral	Agree	Rationale
Application				
Hiring decisions are made with our collective commitments in mind.	D	N	A	
Our collective commitments are frequently referenced by staff in formal and informal meetings.	D	N	A	
Renewal				
Decision making is aligned with our collective commitments.	D	N	A	
There is clear evidence of staff fulfilling the collective commitments.	D	N	A	
Collective commitments are revisited twice a year to assess staff alignment.	D	N	A	
Communication				
Collective commitments are in a location that can be viewed by staff and the community members.	D	N	A	
Our district actively finds ways to celebrate adherence to the collective commitments.	D	N	A	
Rituals, traditions, and stories reflect our collective commitments.	D	N	A	
Tally and Total				

Status Survey (School)

Instructions: This survey is designed to collect information about our school's collective commitments. For each of the statements, please (1) indicate the extent to which you agree or disagree with the statement by circling one of the three letters provided and (2) provide a rationale to support the leading indicator.

Our shared vision:

Our shared mission:

Leading Indicators	Disagree	Neutral	Agree	Rationale
Foundation				
Our school has clear collective commitments.	D	N	A	
We have developed collective commitments that describe actions we will take to fulfill our vision.	D	N	A	
Our staff collaboratively developed our collective commitments.	D	N	A	
The collective commitments clearly describe behaviors we would see in our school.	D	N	A	
Refinement				
The collective commitments are supported by the faculty.	D	N	A	
The commitments describe actions we should see in our school.	D	N	A	
Application				
The collective commitments are aligned to the vision and mission.	D	N	A	
Staff hold one another accountable for adhering to our collective commitments.	D	N	A	
The collective commitments clearly define how staff will work together to achieve the school's vision and carry out the mission.	D	N	A	

Leading Indicators	Disagree	Neutral	Agree	Rationale
Application				
Hiring decisions are made with our collective commitments in mind.	D	N	A	
Our collective commitments are frequently referenced by faculty members in formal and informal meetings.	D	N	A	
Renewal				
Decision making is aligned with our collective commitments.	D	N	A	
There is clear evidence of staff fulfilling the collective commitments.	D	N	A	
Collective commitments are revisited twice a year to assess staff alignment.	D	N	A	
Communication				
Collective commitments are in a location that can be viewed by staff, students, and families.	D	N	A	
Our school actively finds ways to celebrate evidence of the collective commitments.	D	N	A	
Rituals, traditions, and stories reflect our collective commitments.	D	N	A	
Tally and Total				

Acknowledgment Survey

Instructions: Individually complete the survey by placing a check in the box that best fits how you feel about the type of recognition.

Types of Acknowledgments	This would motivate me.	I am neutral.	This would not motivate me.
Recognition from your colleagues			
Recognition from your administrative team			
Your family receiving a note highlighting your accomplishments			
Receiving the gift of time			
Receiving a personal note of recognition			
A special delivery of your favorite treat to your classroom			
Receiving gifts to recognize accomplishments			
Celebrating accomplishments with others			
What are other ideas of ways you would like to be acknowledged for your success?			

Celebration Jot

Instructions: Complete the form about a colleague and return it to a school administrator. Include the educator's name, the collective commitment, and details about how this individual's actions, words, or behaviors exemplified the collective commitment to live the school mission while guiding the school toward the shared vision.

✂- -

Collective Commitment Celebration

Staff member:
Collective commitment:
Celebration:

✂- -

Collective Commitment Celebration

Staff member:
Collective commitment:
Celebration:

Anchor Your Vision © 2025 Solution Tree Press • SolutionTree.com
Visit **go.SolutionTree.com/PLCbooks/AYV** and enter the unique access code found on the book's inside front cover to access this reproducible.

CHAPTER 5
GOALS

Schools don't have goals; people do (or don't). If a faculty is unaware of the school's goals, there are no goals.

—RICHARD DuFOUR

For many educators, the start of the new school year can feel a lot like New Year's Day, when we feel the excitement of new beginnings and set goals to achieve our dreams for the year. Goals are a typical part of the beginning of the year for districts and schools, but creating an action plan to work toward and monitor those goals is unfortunately often left out—leading to unmet goals and a steep drop in the enthusiasm we feel toward those goals across the year.

When we first started this work, we began by creating schoolwide goals. The guiding coalition used the previous year's state assessment data to create the school goals for improvement on the number of students who met state standards. Teams created goals based on a variety of data sources such as state and district assessments, nationally normed assessments, and social behavior. Our school was frequently chosen by our district to pilot new curricular resources or instructional practices, so we set implementation goals. These types of goals were purposeful but we often lacked meaningful action steps and systems for monitoring progress along the way. For example, we might have had an end-of-year goal to increase the number of students mastering an essential standard, but did not create assessments to monitor, discuss, and reflect upon how students were progressing toward the end-of-year goal. Team goals were also not always connected to our school goal and therefore, we did not always accomplish our school goal due to the lack of alignment. We learned a valuable lesson on the impact of aligned goals through our mistakes along the way which helped us to improve in setting future goals with actionable steps, progress monitoring with meaningful feedback, and the significance of celebrating along the way.

After regrouping and reflecting, we adjusted our process. Our guiding coalition refined the school goals based on academic essential standards and skills and aligned them with the district goals. The school goals were then shared with teams and teams created goals that would directly impact the achievement of the school goal. Teachers also set individual student goals aligned to the team goal. This worked much better!

Once our goals were aligned, we worked on creating an action plan for achieving and monitoring those goals. In the grade levels with state assessments, data were used to pinpoint the essential standards on which students didn't score well. Next, teams focused on those standards by adjusting pacing calendars and instructional practices to plan for improvement. We conducted regular data discussions to analyze the results of high-stakes assessments that included these standards. However, the results didn't go quite as we expected. While we were able to excitedly celebrate the improvement of student performance on our lowest standards, we quickly realized we had accidentally excused ourselves from ensuring learning and growth on all essential standards by hyperfocusing only on the standards with the lowest scores. It was when we adjusted and aligned our goals to match our desired outcomes at every level—school, grade or content, teacher, and student—that we saw the success we were hoping to achieve. We believe Stephen R. Covey (2020) addresses this in writing about the importance of beginning with the end in mind: "It's incredibly easy to get caught up in an activity trap in the busyness of life, to work harder and harder at climbing the ladder of success only to discover it is leaning against the wrong wall" (p. 112). This quote hit home with us when we read it, and we find it to be a valuable reminder for the districts, schools, and teams we continue to work with. Fortunately, we can learn a process for creating powerful, meaningful goals at all levels that will lead to success for students.

This chapter explores an organization's goals and purpose while offering meaningful tools to assist you through the process of creating and aligning goals in order to attain academic success for all students. Since districts vary not only in size but also in the number of departments, we've included department-level tools to assist districts with multiple departments to implement aligned goals within the organization. As with the preceding chapters, in the following pages, we'll define goals, offer evidence and research for this pillar, include action steps and corresponding resources, and review common challenges, key points, celebrations, and notes on monitoring progress as you work toward establishing shared goals in your PLC.

Navigating the Goals

Goals compose the final foundational pillar of a PLC. This pillar is focused on answering the questions, How will we know if all of this is making a difference? and How will we monitor our progress? Goals are critical to support the work of the mission, vision, and collective commitments. They align the work with the organization's aspirations, purpose, and behaviors, which include both the visible and tangible targets.

Educators must consider a variety of goals throughout the organization when approaching this pillar. That is, goals at the district and school levels, within collaborative teams, among staff, and of individual students all play a part in propelling student learning. The pursuit and alignment of these goals is needed in order to maximize success.

According to Richard DuFour and Robert J. Marzano (2011), "The team goal should, however, contribute to and align with school and district goals. Every member should be clear on the goal, [and] how he or she can contribute to its achievement" (p. 78). When goals are aligned through all levels: district, school, teams, teachers and students, with actionable steps and progress monitoring, the end result will be higher levels of learning for all students.

Goals are most successful and effective when they have parameters to guide the process. The SMART acronym (Conzemius & O'Neill, 2014) is often used in both business and educational settings because it addresses key components that add clarity and purpose to a goal. Richard DuFour and colleagues (2021) describe SMART as a way for organizations to evaluate the progress and maintain focus on the important work of student growth. The SMART goal acronym isn't exclusive to the work of PLCs, but the definition of each of the letters varies slightly from other applications. In a PLC, the SMART acronym stands for:

- **S** refers to a goal being both strategic and specific—strategic in that it aligns with the organization's goals (district, school, team, teacher) and specific to avoid confusion or misinterpretation.
- **M** addresses the need for a goal to be measurable so there is an understanding of the baseline numbers by which comparisons can be made.
- **A** is the need for the goal to be attainable so the team can believe in the goal and the ability to collectively reach the goal.
- **R** is results oriented. This is a linchpin for goal setting. The members creating and striving for the goal must be hungry to find evidence that there is growth toward the goal. This is an essential piece on which important instructional decisions must be made.
- **T** is for time bound. This means the team must set expectations for instruction, monitoring, and achievement of the goal that have a clear time frame for doing so.

Team goals, whether districtwide, schoolwide, or at the department **(such as by content or population served, for example, special education)** or grade level, are created by the collaborative team. Teams must use data to drive goal setting with specific and focused intentions for high levels of student learning. It is important to have frequent progress checks toward goals. School teams may find a need to make instructional adjustments based on results, whereas district- or school-level teams may find a need to provide teachers with additional professional learning or coaching based on data points toward the goals. The SMART goal focuses the entire team by providing an action plan to reach the desired results.

When individual teachers create their professional goals that align with the team goals, these goals increase their own learning around concepts that impact student growth. For example, if a team is increasing the number of students reading on grade level or above, a teacher may set a professional goal to learn how to implement phonics instruction. When the teacher becomes more proficient in this skill of teaching phonics, it impacts the team goal of increasing the number of students reading at grade level. When school administrators support teachers in working toward professional goals and provide feedback through classroom observations, they help the teachers reach their individual professional goals. The key is meaningful feedback around the goal that helps the teacher learn and grow in a specific way that ultimately impacts student learning.

The goals pillar rounds out the work of the vision, mission, and collective commitments by adding intention and action to the foundation of the district's and school's purpose—learning and growth for all students.

Examining the Evidence of Successful Goals

The U.S. Department of Education awards the coveted distinction of National Blue Ribbon School to a small number of schools each year. The process is rigorous, and schools must show that they have "overall high academic achievement or success in closing the achievement gap among diverse groups of students" in order to even be considered (National Blue Ribbon Schools, n.d.). One such school is Tongue River Elementary School located in Ranchester, Wyoming, which received the National Blue Ribbon School award in 2021.

The school's principal, Annie Griffin, shared that her school was widely known as the school with the kindest kids. Being kind is definitely an important character trait and one that the school appreciated. However, leaders wanted to ensure the success of their students in both character skills and academics. They set to work getting a clear picture of their reality and then setting goals and creating their strategic plan for educating the whole student. Once they established their schoolwide goals in mathematics and reading, they guided teams to create SMART goals for every single essential standard. They collaborated across the building to ensure that team goals aligned with their school goals and all teams agreed that 100 percent of their students would meet those goals. Then, teachers worked with students to create individual student goals.

For example, the district wanted to increase state assessment scores in reading from 75 percent proficient and above to 80 percent proficient and above. At the school level, the school would consider their current reality and aim for an increase in their student performance level, using the SMART goal acronym to have actionable steps and monitor progress throughout the year. The school's increase in reading performance directly impacts the district-level goal. Grade-level teams or the reading department within the school would set SMART goals for reading as well, looking at their current and historical performance data. Then, teachers would set their goals, once again based on their previous data, and consider what instructional strategies or professional learning they would need to increase student performance. When the goals align, real growth can take place. Each SMART goal provides the structure to create meaningful and actionable change.

Across the year, goals were monitored and discussed in a timely way. These discussions allowed the teachers to deliberately make decisions based on data rather than opinions. With this careful and frequent progress monitoring, analyzing, and instructional adjustment, they continuously moved the needle toward their goals and attained them. By focusing on setting, monitoring, and adjusting to meet specific and meaningful goals, Tongue River is able to say that it is not just the school with the kindest kids but the school with the kindest academically successful students. Annie loves to share how proud staff and students were when they were recognized as a National Blue Ribbon School.

Taking a Deep Dive Into the Research for Developing Goals

A plethora of research on goals in the personal, business, and education fields has been conducted over the last fifty plus years. In the mid 20th century, Edwin Locke and Gary P.

Latham introduced goal-setting theory based on a substantial body of research. Their findings showed that clear goals with appropriate feedback increase motivation and productivity (Locke & Latham, 1990). In subsequent research, there has even been evidence to suggest that the extra clarity of creating written goals improves the likelihood of achieving them (Matthews, 2007). When the goals of an organization are clearly stated and staff understand the goal and their role in that goal's achievement, an action orientation is developed. When we create and follow an action plan and gather data-based feedback, even if only in the form of self-reflection shared with an accountability partner, we foster and sustain self-efficacy. In these ways, "results-oriented goals . . . foster interdependence and mutual accountability" (DuFour et al., 2021, p. 120).

The setting of goals as well as the monitoring of those goals increases the likelihood that the work of the members of an organization actually *will* make a difference. That is, goal setting is key to both change and improvement. Additional research emphasizes the importance of setting goals that are not just aligned with the desired outcomes but also challenging to achieve because the more challenging and valued a goal is, the greater the satisfaction and resulting motivation we experience following our success in attaining that goal (Locke & Latham, 2006). In fact, research shows a positive correlation between the difficulty of the goal and the effect size on performance (Kleingeld, van Mierlo, & Arends, 2011). To maximize the effect on continued motivation, self-efficacy, and achievement, goals must be attainable yet challenging.

We have worked with districts and schools that set goals but are frustrated when they do not attain them. A study by researchers Chris McChesney, Sean Covey, and Jim Huling (2012) indicated that for a goal to be met, there are five considerations for success.

- Clarity of the goal
- Commitment to obtaining the goal
- An action plan to achieve the goal
- Accountability for reaching the goal
- Prioritization to attain the goal

In the context of schools, this means we must set goals that ensure learning for all students at high levels and provide ongoing monitoring, support, and feedback to staff and students to attain these goals.

Sailing Into Action for Each Stage of Developing Goals

Once districts or schools have the first three foundational pillars in place, the work of goal setting should move quickly—both in setting the goals themselves and in moving through the stages of establishment. First, use the "Goals Continuum (District)" (page 186) or "Goals Continuum (School)" (page 187) to determine what stage your school or district is in. Then, similar to what you did for collective commitments, if you determine your current reality is at the preinitiating, initiating, or implementing stage, we suggest you look ahead across the continuum to the developing and sustaining stages. In this way, you aim to establish common goals that impact the organization at every level (district, school, team, teacher, and student) and have buy-in from all members right from the start. However, there is no need to jump from one stage to the next when utilizing the steps and tools created in this chapter, as we specifically designed the sequence and process for each stage to meet districts or schools where they are and move them to developing and sustaining. An important note for districts: The work of the developing stage hinges on individual teachers. At the district level, your work will progress from the implementing stage directly to the sustaining stage. Note that for the preinitiating and initiating stages, the steps and tools are the same.

Before starting your work on goals, assess the state of your guiding coalition—both the members and the time allotted for collaboration. It will be essential to have guiding coalition members who represent the teams in your district or on your school as well as routine meeting times set firmly in place to facilitate the creation of goals, the determination of the products for monitoring goals, the alignment of team goals to district and school goals, and the timely monitoring of data for achievement of goals across the year.

The Preinitiating Stage

A district or school in the preinitiating stage may or may not have goals explicitly stated, or the staff may not have engaged in the process of creating the goals that are in place. It's also possible that a school is at this stage if goals are explicitly stated and staff were engaged in creating them but those goals are not related to student learning. Schools and districts in this stage should follow the same steps as those listed for the initiating stage.

The Initiating Stage

A district or school in the initiating stage has established goals. However, these goals were established in isolation or were created by a team exclusively in connection with the formal school improvement process. Most staff would not be able to articulate these goals or explain how these goals are related to the work they do as teams.

1. Provide staff time to read, reflect on, and respond to quotes and research on the importance and impact of goals within an organization using the tool "Goals to Impact Student Learning (District)" (page 188) or "Goals to Impact Student Learning (School)" (page 190).

2. Collect and reflect on data with the guiding coalition using the tool "A Data Picture of Our District" (page 192) or "A Data Picture of Our School" (page 194) to get a clear picture of your current reality. If you do not yet have data for certain indicators that the team deems critical, consider ways to collect data for that indicator across the year.

3. Share the data collected in step 2 with the staff. Invite staff to study the data and identify high-need, high-leverage areas to monitor using the tool "Using Our Data Part 1: Studying Our Data (District)" (page 196) or "Using Our Data Part 1: Studying Our Data (School)" (page 197).

4. Once data have been analyzed for areas of celebration and concern, the next step is the creation of goals for these areas. Use the tool "Using Our Data Part 2: Setting Our Goals (District)" (page 198) or "Using Our Data Part 2: Setting Our Goals (School)" (page 199) to guide teams through creating goals.

5. To create a plan of actionable steps and progress monitoring that leads to growth, use the "Goals Action Plan (District)" (page 200) or "Goals Action Plan (School)" (page 201) to help create a road map for the year and put the plans into action.

6. Confirm alignment of district or school goals to the district or school mission and vision by soliciting feedback from staff using the "Goals Survey (District)" (page 202) or "Goals Survey (School)" (page 204).

7. Intentionally plan opportunities to celebrate progress. The "Creating Rituals and Celebrations" (page 206) form is designed to gather input from the staff on how best to create purposeful and meaningful celebrations. The "Plan to Celebrate!" (page 207) form helps the guiding coalition synthesize the staff input and create a plan for thoughtful celebrating of goals. Remember—your goals are impacting student growth in your school or district, so you want your celebration to highlight the importance and excitement of what the stakeholders are doing to reach those goals.

8. Move on to the implementing stage.

The Implementing Stage

A district or school at the implementing stage has staff who are aware of the long- and short-term goals, and tools and strategies for monitoring the progress of these goals have been implemented. However, the goals and the monitoring of goals are applied only at the global level. Goals have not been translated into meaningful targets at the team or individual teacher level.

1. Invite staff to reflect on the alignment of district or school goals to the district or school mission, vision, and goals by soliciting feedback from staff using the "Goals Survey (District)" (page 202) if you are part of a district department or "Goals Survey (School)" (page 204) if you are on a school-site team.

2. Provide teams time to consider their current reality and identify high-need, high-leverage areas to monitor using the tool "Data Analysis to Identify Department Goals" (page 208) or "Data Analysis to Identify Team Goals" (page 209). If you do not yet have data for certain indicators that the department or team deems critical, consider ways to collect data for that indicator across the year.

3. Once data have been analyzed for areas of celebration and concern, the next step is the creation of goals for these areas. Use the tool "Using Our Data Part 2: Setting Our Goals (District)" (page 198) or "Using Our Data Part 2: Setting Our Goals (School)" (page 199) to guide teams through creating goals.

4. Use the "Using Our Data Part 3: Goals Action Plan (District)" (page 200) or "Using Our Data Part 3: Goals Action Plan (School)" (page 201) to help create a clear plan for the year and put the plans into action.

5. Create a plan for monitoring the district, department, or school team progress toward achieving set goals, such as calendaring dates or creating meeting invites, and select a data protocol that explores different strategies for achieving goals to guide discussions.

6. Confirm alignment of district or school goals to the district or school mission and vision by soliciting feedback from staff using the "Goals Survey (District)" (page 202) or "Goals Survey (School)" (page 204).

7. Intentionally plan opportunities to celebrate progress. The "Creating Rituals and Celebrations" (page 206) form is designed to gather input from the staff on how best to create purposeful and meaningful celebrations. The "Plan to Celebrate!" (page 207) form helps the guiding coalition synthesize the staff input and create a plan for thoughtful celebrating of goals. Remember—your goals are impacting student growth in your school or district, so you want your celebration to highlight the importance and excitement of what the stakeholders are doing to reach those goals.

8. Move on to the developing stage.

The Developing Stage

A school or district at the developing stage has goals that staff know and embrace. These goals have been translated into specific targets for teams and teachers that directly impact student achievement. Teams and teachers monitor these goals and explore different strategies in order to achieve them.

1. Invite staff to reflect on the alignment of school team goals to the school mission, vision, and goals by soliciting feedback from staff using the "Goals Survey (School)" (page 204).

2. Provide teachers time to consider their individual current reality and identify high-need, high-leverage areas to monitor using the "Data Analysis to Identify Teacher Goals" (page 210). If teachers do not yet have data for certain indicators that they deem critical, consider ways to collect data for that indicator across the year.

3. Once data have been analyzed for areas of celebration and concern, the next step is the creation of goals for these areas. Use "Teacher SMART Goal" (page 211) as a guide to create these goals and create a plan of actionable steps and progress monitoring that leads to growth.

4. Invite teachers to share their individual goals with their team and discuss how they will support one another in the achievement of those goals. Teams will use

"Team Accountability Partners" (page 215) to commit to holding each other accountable.

5. Teachers work with students to set individual student goals which align to the team goals. Teachers will use "Student SMART Goal" (page 213) to create goals.

6. Intentionally plan opportunities to celebrate progress. The "Creating Rituals and Celebrations" (page 206) form is designed to gather input from the staff on how best to create purposeful and meaningful celebrations. The "Plan to Celebrate!" (page 207) form helps the guiding coalition synthesize the staff input and create a plan for thoughtful celebrating of goals. Remember—your goals are impacting student growth in your school or district, so you want your celebration to highlight the importance and excitement of what the stakeholders are doing to reach those goals.

7. Move on to the sustaining stage.

The Sustaining Stage

A school or district at the sustaining stage has goals that all staff embrace, support, and promote. Staff routinely pursue and monitor measurable goals within their classrooms and with their teams that directly link to the district or school goals. There is evidence that teams hold their members mutually accountable for the achievement of common goals. When goals are achieved, celebration has become part of the district or school culture.

1. Continually monitor the goals set from year to year and adjust as needed. Use "A Data Picture of Our District" (page 192) or "A Data Picture of Our School" (page 194) and "Studying Our Data (District)" (page 196) or "Studying Our Data (School)" (page 197) to refine current goals or identify new areas of need. If new goals are needed, use "Setting Our District Department or School Team Goals" (page 216) and the "Goals Action Plan (District)" (page 200) or "Goals Action Plan (School)" (page 201) to write the new goals and create a road map for implementation and monitoring.

2. Collect evidence in an ongoing way to ensure all staff are pursuing measurable goals directly linked to the district or school goals and that teams are holding each other mutually accountable to their team goals, that teachers are monitoring their goals, and that students are taking ownership of their SMART goals.

3. Continue to intentionally plan opportunities to celebrate progress. The "Creating Rituals and Celebrations" (page 206) form is designed to gather input from the staff on how best to create purposeful and meaningful celebrations. The "Plan to Celebrate!" (page 207) form helps the guiding coalition synthesize the staff input and create a plan for thoughtful celebrating of goals. Remember—your goals are impacting student growth in your school

or district, so you want your celebration to highlight the importance and excitement of what the stakeholders are doing to reach those goals.

Staying Afloat Through Common Challenges to Developing Goals

Creating and leveraging goals is a process that takes time, collaboration, and continual monitoring. This process can pose challenges along the way that should be addressed in a timely manner to ensure ongoing focus on achieving the goals. The if-then chart shown in table 5.1 reflects some common challenges you might experience and potential steps to overcome those challenges successfully.

Table 5.1: If-Then Chart

If . . .	Then . . .
Staff are unable to articulate district or school goals.	Revisit ways to improve communication of the goals with the guiding coalition.
There are no district- or school-level goals.	Have the district or school create goals that align with the district or school vision.
The district goals do not align with or support the school goals.	Consider the alignment of the school vision to the district vision. If these do not align, inevitably, the resulting goals will follow suit. This could signal a need for collaborative discussion to clarify the vision and goals across the district and school or a revision of one or the other—the district and school vision or the district and school goals. The school sets goals that align with the school's vision but considers district-level goals for alignment when possible.
The current goals are not clear on the actions needed to attain the goal.	Reassess the goals through the lens of the SMART acronym to add clarity.
There is no progress made toward the goal.	Have leaders take a deep dive into the data and engage in conversations to analyze both the curriculum and instructional practices.

Knowing the Ropes for Goal Development

As you and your colleagues work to establish your organization's goals, orient yourselves by keeping in mind the following.

- Begin the schoolwork on goals by looking at district goals, remembering that alignment and clarity are essential at all levels.

- Use a variety of methods to determine whether goals are communicated effectively, such as disseminating surveys, facilitating focus groups, listening to conversations in collaborative team meetings, and so forth.

- Set targets and dates to revisit the goals to celebrate work toward the goals.
- Students need goals too. Students can hit their learning targets more frequently when they are aware of those goals and are supported toward their progress.
- All employees should be able to articulate the goals of the district or school.

Celebrating the Goals

In the majority of classrooms, teachers frequently celebrate what they wish to see more of from their students. For example, a teacher may praise a student who shows academic growth from the beginning of a unit to the end of the unit. Some schools even have special ceremonies recognizing students weekly or monthly. Typically, the recognition feels wonderful, and the student is internally motivated to continue putting forth effort to learn and grow.

As adults, we, too, benefit and typically appreciate being recognized and celebrated for our work. When a goal involves the entire district or school to be on the same journey in order to achieve success, it's important to develop a culture that celebrates everyone's progress toward the shared goals and destination. Anthony Muhammad (2018) contends that by making rituals of celebration through intentional planning or impromptu events, we create a shift from staying mired in negativity to moving the culture toward one that seeks out positivity. It is through specific, monitored, and actionable shared goals that we can also create rituals to celebrate the success of our students, our personal pedagogical growth, and the success of our collective organization. Being intentional and taking time to celebrate impacts your school culture and helps all stakeholders stay focused on the shared vision and purpose of the organization.

Here are some suggestions as you determine which rituals for celebration will work best for your district or school.

- The guiding coalition can use the "Creating Rituals and Celebrations" (page 206) form to gather ideas from the staff to help plan rituals for celebrating throughout the year. Then, the guiding coalition will use the feedback to plan out the rituals across the year using the "Plan to Celebrate!" (page 207) form.
- Include goals and celebrations on meeting agendas to keep a focus on the goal but also provide opportunities to have frequent conversations of progress toward the goal along with celebrations of growth toward attaining the goal.
- Plan intentional rituals of celebrations at regular staff meetings. At a school we served, we had an award that was presented to a new team member or staff member each month. The "traveling award" was hung outside the team leader's room or outside the staff member's room for the month to acknowledge their effort to meet goals set by the team.
- Work together with your community leaders or parent-teacher organization to collect staff treats that can be used to reward teams that are making progress or achieving their goals.

- Acknowledge teachers who are reaching their personal and professional goals.
- Celebrate student growth on a regular basis in the classroom and at the district or school level.
- Use the staff newsletter as a means of highlighting progress toward a yearlong goal.
- Utilize social media to share the great news with families and the community.

Stay the Course

School leaders and teachers will be driven to maintain momentum if they feel others see and appreciate their efforts. Make an effort to acknowledge significant advancements in student achievement and attainment of team goals as progress is monitored. There may be times when goals need to be revised along the way. Be intentional about making decisions based on evidence rather than opinions. In order to accomplish this, set timely dates to review the predetermined data sources for evidence of progress toward achieving goals. Use data protocols to measure evidence of progress toward set goals. Identify the practices and processes that are impacting that data both positively and negatively. Finally, consider reflecting on all goals in alignment—from student to teacher to team to school to department to district—at each step. By closely aligning district and school goals and monitoring the progress, the unified result will be an amplified achievement for all students.

Anchors Away!

Shared goals focus the collective work of educators and make the intangible aspects of the foundational pillars tangible and measurable. As teams and teachers assess and analyze data on student progress toward goals, they identify both areas for growth and opportunities for celebration—both for students and for themselves. In this way, goals become guides for decision making about curricular resources, instructional strategies, and even professional development resulting in more effective teaching practices and better academic outcomes. Goals put the mission and vision of the district or school into action.

Use the space provided to anchor your thoughts and chart your course for your next steps.

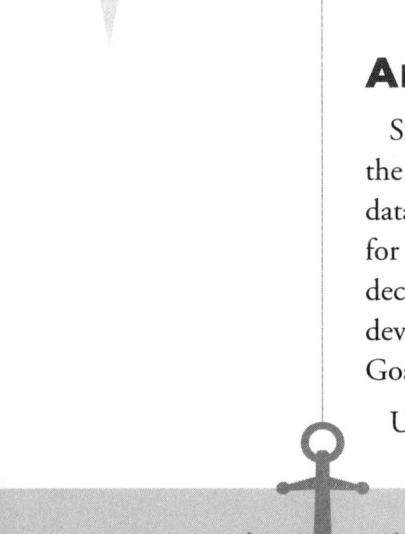

Goals Continuum (District)

Instructions: Individually, read the indicators that describe each stage from preinitiating through sustaining. Honestly assess the current reality of the establishment of your district goals. Consider what evidence or anecdotes support your assessment. Record your reflections in the space provided.

Common district goals: We have articulated our long-term priorities and short-term targets and timelines for achieving those targets.

Goals Continuum Stages

Preinitiating	Initiating	Implementing	Developing	Sustaining
☐ District leaders have established district goals as part of the formal district process for improvement.	☐ District leaders have established district goals as part of the formal district process for improvement.	☐ District leaders have established district goals as part of the formal district process for improvement. They have made school leaders aware of the long- and short-term goals for the district.	☐ District leaders have collaboratively established district goals as part of the formal district process for improvement. School leaders have an understanding of and commitment to the long- and short-term goals for the district.	☐ District leaders have collaboratively established district goals as part of the formal district process for improvement. School leaders have an understanding of and commitment to the long- and short-term goals for the district.
☐ Schools do not have goals, or they are not aligned to district goals.	☐ Schools have goals, but they are not all aligned with district goals.	☐ District departments have goals.	☐ District departments have goals loosely aligned to the district goals.	☐ All district departments strategically align goals to the district goals.
☐ Leaders have not made an effort to engage staff in establishing district improvement goals related to student learning.	☐ Most staff would be unable to articulate district goals or the why behind them.	☐ Schools have goals.	☐ Schools have created goals loosely aligned to district goals.	☐ All schools strategically align goals to the district goals.
		☐ Tools and strategies have been developed and implemented to monitor each school's progress toward the district goals.	☐ The district goals have been translated into specific goals that directly impact school and student achievement.	☐ Schools have created school and team goals that are strategically aligned to the district goals and directly impact student achievement.
		☐ Little has been done to translate the district goals into meaningful targets for schools and their teams.	☐ Teams in schools are exploring different strategies for achieving their goals that align with school and district goals.	☐ Teams work interdependently to achieve common goals for which members are mutually accountable.
				☐ Meaningful and timely celebration of the achievement of goals is part of the district culture.

I believe our district is at the _____ stage based on the preceding indicators. The evidence to support my rationale includes:

Source: Adapted from DuFour, R., DuFour, R., Eaker, R., Many, T. W., Mattos, M., & Muhammad, A. (2024). Learning by doing: A handbook for Professional Learning Communities at Work (4th ed.). Bloomington, IN: Solution Tree Press.

Goals Continuum (School)

Instructions: Individually, read the indicators that describe each stage from preinitiating through sustaining. Honestly assess the current reality of the establishment of your school goals. Consider what evidence or anecdotes support your assessment. Record your reflections in the space provided.

Common school goals: We have articulated our long-term priorities and short-term targets and timelines for achieving those targets.

Goals Continuum Stages

Preinitiating	Initiating	Implementing	Developing	Sustaining
☐ Leaders have not made an effort to create school goals or engage staff in establishing improvement goals related to student learning.	☐ The administration or school improvement team has established goals for the school as part of the formal district process for school improvement. ☐ Most staff would be unable to articulate a goal that has been established for their school.	☐ Leaders have made staff aware of the long- and short-term goals for the school; however, the goals are not aligned to district goals. ☐ Tools and strategies have been developed and implemented to monitor the school's progress toward its goals. ☐ Little has been done to translate the school goals into meaningful targets for either collaborative teams or individual teachers.	☐ The school goals are aligned with the district goals and have been translated into specific goals that directly impact student achievement for each collaborative team. ☐ If teams are successful in achieving their goals, the school will achieve its goals as well. ☐ Teams are exploring different strategies for achieving their goals. ☐ Teachers assist students with setting individual student SMART goals.	☐ The school goals are aligned with the district goals and have been translated into specific goals that directly impact student achievement for each collaborative team. ☐ All staff pursue measurable goals that are directly linked to the school's goals as part of their routine responsibilities. ☐ Teams work interdependently to achieve common goals for which members are mutually accountable. ☐ Students take ownership of their individual SMART goals. ☐ The celebration of the achievement of goals is part of the school culture and an important element in sustaining the PLC process.

I believe our school is at the _____ stage based on the preceding indicators. The evidence to support my rationale includes:

Source: Adapted from DuFour, R., DuFour, R., Eaker, R., Many, T. W., Mattos, M., & Muhammad, A. (2024). Learning by doing: A handbook for Professional Learning Communities at Work (4th ed.). Bloomington, IN: Solution Tree Press.

Goals to Impact Student Learning (District)

Instructions: Read the quotes that follow and highlight words and phrases that resonate with you and your educational philosophy of how goals impact a school or district. Then, respond to the questions. These quotes are meant to stimulate thinking and understanding behind creating district goals while also providing for meaningful collaboration among colleagues that is grounded in the ideas from experts to create a common understanding of the value of this foundational pillar.

The goals pillar focuses on answering the questions, How will we know if all of this is making a difference? and How will we monitor our progress? Goals are critical to support the work of the mission, vision, and collective commitments by aligning the work of the organization with the aspirations, purpose, and behaviors and making visible and tangible targets.

List a goal or goals our district is proud to celebrate.

"A meta-analysis of the research on the subject [goals] found that district leadership could have a significant impact on student achievement, but only if leaders at the district level are united in articulating and pursuing priorities (Marzano & Waters, 2009)" (DuFour & Fullan, 2013, p. 24).

"Successful systems develop shared coherence laterally as well as hierarchically. A shared mindset across peers is essential for systemwide success" (DuFour & Fullan, 2013, p. 24).

"Since the priority in schools should be higher levels of student learning, goals should have a direct and observable impact on student achievement" (DuFour et al., 2021, p. 114).

"When teachers feel they are making a professional contribution to their school, they enjoy their work more and accomplish far more than what any merit pay can yield" (Gruenert & Whitaker, 2015, p. 71).

"Goals play a key role in motivating people to honor their commitments so the school moves closer to fulfilling its fundamental purpose of learning for all students" (DuFour et al., 2016, p. 42).

"Even though setbacks and unanticipated challenges will undoubtedly occur, you need an overall sense of what you are working toward and what to expect. Having a clear goal makes it easier to navigate the unexpected" (Peek, 2023).

"Having a specific plan attached to your goals—knowing when and where you will do something—can more than double the likelihood of achieving a challenging goal. Having a clear plan is as important as motivation and willpower" (Burchard, 2017, p. 119).

"To achieve goals you've never achieved before, you need to start doing things you've never done before" (Covey, 2004, p. 286).

What research resonates with you, and why?

Do you think the district goals are clear and known throughout the organization?

Does your department have goals that align with the district goals?

Do our schools have goals that align to our district goals?

References

Burchard, B. (2017). *High performance habits: How extraordinary people become that way.* Carlsbad, CA: Hay House.

Covey, S. R. (2004). *The 8th habit: From effectiveness to greatness.* New York: Free Press.

DuFour, R., DuFour, R., Eaker, R., Many, T. W., & Mattos, M. (2024). *Learning by doing: A handbook for Professional Learning Communities at Work* (4th ed.). Bloomington, IN: Solution Tree Press.

DuFour, R., DuFour, R., Eaker, R., Mattos, M., & Muhammad, A. (2021). *Revisiting Professional Learning Communities at Work: Proven insights for sustained, substantive school improvement* (2nd ed.). Bloomington, IN: Solution Tree Press.

DuFour, R., & Fullan, M. (2013). *Cultures build to last: Systematic PLCs at Work.* Bloomington, IN: Solution Tree Press.

Gruenert, S., & Whitaker, T. (2015). *School culture rewired: How to define, assess, and transform it.* Alexandria, VA: ASCD.

Marzano, R. J., & Waters, T. (2009). *District leadership that works: Striking the right balance.* Bloomington, IN: Solution Tree Press.

Peek, S. (2023, June 22). *Management theory of Stephen Covey.* Accessed at www.business.com/articles/management-theory-of-stephen-covey/ on November 3, 2023.

Goals to Impact Student Learning (School)

Instructions: Read the quotes and research-based evidence that follow and highlight words and phrases that resonate with you and your educational philosophy of how goals impact a school. Then, respond to the questions. These quotes are meant to stimulate thinking and understanding behind creating school goals while also providing for meaningful collaboration among colleagues that is grounded in the ideas from experts to create a common understanding of the value of this foundational pillar.

The goals pillar focuses on answering the questions, How will we know if all of this is making a difference? and How will we monitor our progress? Goals are critical to support the work of the mission, vision, and collective commitments by aligning the work of the organization with the aspirations, purpose, and behaviors, and making visible and tangible targets.

> List a goal or goals our school is proud to celebrate.

"Much of what contributes to a strong learning climate is associated with the expectations and actions of teachers and other adults in the school building to work together around schoolwide goals. School staff support each other and hold each other accountable for the success of all students, not just those in their classroom" (Allensworth & Hart, 2018).

"Since the priority in schools should be higher levels of student learning, goals should have a direct and observable impact on student achievement" (DuFour et al., 2021, p. 114).

"When leaders monitor—pay attention to—the *quality of the products* teams produce and the results of each team's improvement efforts, the message is clear: this work is important" (Keating & Rhoades, 2022, p. 13).

"Goals play a key role in motivating people to honor their commitments so the school moves closer to fulfilling its fundamental purpose of learning for all students" (DuFour et al., 2016, p. 42).

"When teachers feel they are making a professional contribution to their school, they enjoy their work more and accomplish far more than what any merit pay can yield" (Gruenert & Whitaker, 2015, p. 71).

"Even though setbacks and unanticipated challenges will undoubtedly occur, you need an overall sense of what you are working toward and what to expect. Having a clear goal makes it easier to navigate the unexpected" (Peek, 2023).

"When the school is organized to focus on a small number of shared goals, and when professional learning is targeted to those goals and is a collective enterprise, the evidence is overwhelming that teachers can do dramatically better by way of student achievement" (Fullan, 2014, p. 83).

"Having a specific plan attached to your goals—knowing when and where you will do something—can more than double the likelihood of achieving a challenging goal. Having a clear plan is as important as motivation and willpower" (Burchard, 2017, p. 119).

"To achieve goals you've never achieved before, you need to start doing things you've never done before" (Covey, 2004, p. 286).

What research resonates with you, and why?

Please record your understanding of our schoolwide goals.

How do your team goals align with the schoolwide goals?

What professional goals do you have that align to team and school goals?

References

Allensworth, E., & Hart, H. (2018, March 12). *How do principals influence student achievement?* Accessed at www.edweek.org/leadership/opinion-how-do-principals-influence-student-achievement/2018/03 on November 3, 2023.

Burchard, B. (2017). *High performance habits: How extraordinary people become that way.* Carlsbad, CA: Hay House.

Covey, S. R. (2004). *The 8th habit: From effectiveness to greatness.* New York: Free Press.

DuFour, R., DuFour, R., Eaker, R., Many, T. W., & Mattos, M. (2024). *Learning by doing: A handbook for Professional Learning Communities at Work* (4th ed.). Bloomington, IN: Solution Tree Press.

DuFour, R., DuFour, R., Eaker, R., Mattos, M., & Muhammad, A. (2021). *Revisiting Professional Learning Communities at Work: Proven insights for sustained, substantive school improvement* (2nd ed.). Bloomington, IN: Solution Tree Press.

Fullan, M. (2014). *The principal: Three keys to maximizing impact.* San Francisco: Jossey-Bass.

Gruenert, S., & Whitaker, T. (2015). *School culture rewired: How to define, assess, and transform it.* Alexandria, VA: ASCD.

Keating, J., & Rhoades, M. (2022). A new era in district and school improvement: The critical role of the superintendent and school board. *AllThingsPLC Magazine, 7*(2), 8–14.

Peek, S. (2023, June 22). *Management theory of Stephen Covey.* Accessed at www.business.com/articles/management-theory-of-stephen-covey/ on November 3, 2023.

A Data Picture of Our District

Instructions: As a guiding coalition, collect, record, and reflect on the data pertaining to your district based on the indicators that follow.

Indicator	Three Years Ago	Two Years Ago	Last Year	Facts About Our Data
Student Achievement Results				
Based on Our School Assessment Data				
Based on Our District Assessment Data				
Based on Our State or Provincial Assessment Data				
Based on Our National Assessment Data				
Student Engagement Data				
Average Daily Attendance				
Percentage of Students in Extracurricular Activities				
Percentage of Students Enrolled in Most Rigorous Courses Offered				
Percentage of Students Graduating Without Retention				
Percentage of Students Who Drop Out of School				
Other Areas in Which We Hope to Engage Students, Such as Community Service				
Discipline				
Number of Referrals or Top Three Reasons for Referrals				
Number of Parent Conferences Regarding Discipline				
Number of In-School Suspensions				
Number of Detentions or Saturday School				
Number of Out-of-School Suspensions				
Number of Expulsions				
Other				
Survey Data				
Student Satisfaction or Perception Assessment				
Alumni Satisfaction or Perception Assessment				
Parent Satisfaction or Perception Assessment				

Indicator	Three Years Ago	Two Years Ago	Last Year	Facts About Our Data
Survey Data				
Teacher Satisfaction or Perception Assessment				
Administration Satisfaction or Perception Assessment				
Community Satisfaction or Perception Assessment				
Demographic Data				
Percent Free and Reduced Lunch				
Percent Mobility				
Percent Special Education				
Percent English as a Second Language				
Percent White (Not of Hispanic Origin)				
Percent Black				
Percent Asian				
Percent Native American / Indigenous				

Source: Adapted from DuFour, R., DuFour, R., Eaker, R., Many, T. W., Mattos, M., & Muhammad, A. (2024). Learning by doing: A handbook for Professional Learning Communities at Work (4th ed.). Bloomington, IN: Solution Tree Press.

A Data Picture of Our School

Instructions: As a guiding coalition, collect, record, and reflect on the data pertaining to your school based on the indicators that follow.

Indicator	Three Years Ago	Two Years Ago	Last Year	Facts About Our Data
Student Achievement Results				
Based on Our School Assessment Data				
Based on Our District Assessment Data				
Based on Our State or Provincial Assessment Data				
Based on Our National Assessment Data				
Student Engagement Data				
Average Daily Attendance				
Percentage of Students in Extracurricular Activities				
Percentage of Students Enrolled in Most Rigorous Courses Offered				
Percentage of Students Graduating Without Retention				
Percentage of Students Who Drop Out of School				
Other Areas in Which We Hope to Engage Students, Such as Community Service				
Discipline				
Number of Referrals or Top Three Reasons for Referrals				
Number of Parent Conferences Regarding Discipline				
Number of In-School Suspensions				
Number of Detentions or Saturday School				
Number of Out-of-School Suspensions				
Number of Expulsions				
Other				
Survey Data				
Student Satisfaction or Perception Assessment				
Alumni Satisfaction or Perception Assessment				
Parent Satisfaction or Perception Assessment				
Teacher Satisfaction or Perception Assessment				
Administration Satisfaction or Perception Assessment				
Community Satisfaction or Perception Assessment				

Indicator	Three Years Ago	Two Years Ago	Last Year	Facts About Our Data
Demographic Data				
Percent Free and Reduced Lunch				
Percent Mobility				
Percent Special Education				
Percent English as a Second Language				
Percent White (Not of Hispanic Origin)				
Percent Black				
Percent Asian				
Percent Native American / Indigenous				

Source: Adapted from DuFour, R., DuFour, R., Eaker, R., Many, T. W., Mattos, M., & Muhammad, A. (2024). Learning by doing: A handbook for Professional Learning Communities at Work (4th ed.). Bloomington, IN: Solution Tree Press.

Using Our Data Part 1: Studying Our Data (District)

Instructions: Study the data gathered using the tool "A Data Picture of Our District" (page 192). In teams, use the prompts that follow to determine high-need, high-leverage areas to monitor.

Data: List the indicator or indicators from each section that most closely align with your district mission and vision. Record the data you have for each indicator listed.

Section	Indicators	Data
Student Achievement Data		
Student Engagement Data		
Discipline		
Survey Data		
Demographic Data		

List any other indicators that need to be considered when developing district goals.

Section	Indicators	Data

Reflection:

Based on the preceding data, what are the biggest areas of celebration?

How can we continue or enhance these data trends?

Based on the preceding data, what are the biggest areas of concern?

How do we want to see these data trends improve?

Using Our Data Part 1: Studying Our Data (School)

Instructions: Study the data gathered using the tool "A Data Picture of Our School" (page 194). In teams, use the prompts that follow to determine high-need, high-leverage areas to monitor.

Data: List the indicator or indicators from each section that most closely align with your school mission and vision. Record the data you have for each indicator listed.

Section	Indicators	Data
Student Achievement Data		
Student Engagement Data		
Discipline		
Survey Data		
Demographic Data		

List any other indicators that need to be considered when developing school goals.

Section	Indicators	Data

Reflection:

Based on the preceding data, what are the biggest areas of celebration?

How can we continue or enhance these data trends?

Based on the preceding data, what are the biggest areas of concern?

How would we want to see these data trends improve?

Anchor Your Vision © 2025 Solution Tree Press • SolutionTree.com
Visit **go.SolutionTree.com/PLCbooks/AYV** and enter the unique access code found on the book's inside front cover to access this reproducible.

Using Our Data Part 2: Setting Our Goals (District)

Instructions: As a collaborative team, record the shared vision and mission statements. Review the tool "Using Our Data Part 1: Studying Our Data (District)" (page 196). Synthesize the collective data and information and collaboratively create district goals. Refer to the district mission and vision to ensure alignment.

District vision:
District mission:
What goals are needed to achieve our shared vision?
How will these goals directly impact student growth and achievement?

Using Our Data Part 2: Setting Our Goals (School)

Instructions: As a guiding coalition, record the shared vision and mission statements along with the district goals. Review the tool "Using Our Data Part 1: Studying Our Data (School)" (page 187). Synthesize the collective data and information and collaboratively create school goals. Refer to the school vision and mission and district goals to ensure alignment.

School vision:
School mission:
District goals:
What goals are needed to achieve our shared vision and mission and align with the district goals?
How will these goals directly improve student growth and achievement?

Using Our Data Part 3: Goals Action Plan (District)

Instructions: As a guiding coalition, create an action plan for each school goal identified in the "Using Our Data Part 2: Setting Our Goals (District)" (page 198). You will need to use a separate form for each goal.

District goal:
Short-term goal, targets, and timelines:
What assessment tools will be used to determine mastery toward the goal?
Are resources or professional learning needed in order to help us meet this goal?
How, when, and to whom will the goal be communicated?

Using Our Data Part 3: Goals Action Plan (School)

Instructions: As a guiding coalition, create an action plan for each school goal identified in the "Using Our Data Part 2: Setting Our Goals (School)" (page 199). You will need to use a separate form for each goal.

School goal:
Short-term goal, targets, and timelines:
What assessment tools will be used to determine mastery toward the goal?
Are resources or professional learning needed in order to help us meet this goal?
How, when, and to whom will the goal be communicated?

Goals Survey (District)

Instructions: This survey is designed to collect information about our district's goals. For each of the statements that follow, please (1) indicate the extent to which you agree or disagree with the statement by circling one of the three letters provided and (2) provide a rationale to support the leading indicator.

Our district's shared vision statement:

Our district's shared mission statement:

Leading Indicators	Disagree	Neutral	Agree	Rationale
Foundation				
Our district has specific goals.	D	N	A	
Our district goals are measurable.	D	N	A	
Our district goals are attainable.	D	N	A	
Our district goals are results oriented.	D	N	A	
Our district goals are time bound.	D	N	A	
Refinement				
Our goals are student focused.	D	N	A	
Our goals will ensure student learning.	D	N	A	
Application				
Our goals are frequently referenced by educators throughout the district in formal and informal meetings.	D	N	A	
School goals are aligned with the district goals.	D	N	A	
Our decision making is aligned with our goals.	D	N	A	

Renewal				
We review our goals regularly and revise them yearly.	D	N	A	
Communication				
Our goals are communicated to all stakeholders.	D	N	A	
The results of our efforts toward our goals are communicated to our educators and community members.	D	N	A	
Growth and attainment of district goals are celebrated.	D	N	A	
Tally and Total				

Share your thoughts on our district goals and how they will positively impact learning for our students.

What evidence does our district have that we are aligning our decision making with our goals?

How can we ensure that our district goals are clearly communicated to all stakeholders?

Share additional feedback and ideas regarding our district goals.

Goals Survey (School)

Instructions: This survey is designed to collect information about our school goals. For each of the statements that follow, please (1) indicate the extent to which you agree or disagree with the statement by circling one of the three letters provided and (2) provide a rationale to support the leading indicator.

Our school's shared vision statement:

Our school's shared mission statement:

Leading Indicators	Disagree	Neutral	Agree	Rationale
Foundation				
Our school has specific goals.	D	N	A	
Our school goals are measurable.	D	N	A	
Our school goals are attainable.	D	N	A	
Our school goals are results oriented.	D	N	A	
Our school goals are time bound.	D	N	A	
Refinement				
Our goals are student focused.	D	N	A	
Our goals will ensure student learning.	D	N	A	
Application				
Our goals are monitored throughout the school year.	D	N	A	
Our goals are frequently referenced by educators throughout the school in formal and informal meetings.	D	N	A	
Team goals are aligned to school goals.	D	N	A	

Leading Indicators	Disagree	Neutral	Agree	Rationale
Application				
Our decision making is aligned with our goals.	D	N	A	
Renewal				
We review our goals regularly and revise them yearly.	D	N	A	
Communication				
Our school goals are communicated to all stakeholders.	D	N	A	
The results of our efforts toward our goals are communicated to our staff and families.	D	N	A	
Growth and attainment of school goals are celebrated.	D	N	A	
Tally and Total				

Share your thoughts on our school goals and how they will positively impact learning for our students.

What evidence does our school have that we are aligning our decision making with our goals?

How can we ensure that our school goals are clearly communicated to all staff and our families?

Share additional feedback and ideas regarding our school goals.

Anchor Your Vision © 2025 Solution Tree Press • SolutionTree.com
Visit **go.SolutionTree.com/PLCbooks/AYV** and enter the unique access code found on the book's inside front cover to access this reproducible.

Creating Rituals and Celebrations

Instructions: Please share your ideas for ways we can celebrate each of the following items.

Growth toward schoolwide goals	
Achievement of the schoolwide goals	
Growth toward shared team goals	
Achievement of shared team goals	
Growth toward individual teacher-identified professional goals	
Achievement of individual teacher-identified professional goals	
Growth toward individual student-created goals	
Achievement of individual student-created goals	
Share additional feedback and ideas regarding a focus on celebrating our goals and creating rituals.	

Plan to Celebrate!

Instructions: With your guiding coalition, use the questions that follow along with the "Creating Rituals and Celebrations" (page 206) form to brainstorm ideas for and plan moments of meaningful celebration for the organization.

Who? • Who do we want to be included in this celebration? • How will we include *all* the stakeholders in the celebration?	

When?
• When do we want to schedule these celebratory moments?
  ◆ How frequently?
  ◆ Staff meetings?
  ◆ Professional learning day?
  ◆ Start of the school year?
  ◆ Midyear launch?
• Length of celebration?	

Where? • Where is the best location for the celebration? • Will the space accommodate all the stakeholders?	
How? • What ideas do we have to make this a celebration? • Are there a variety of ways we would like to celebrate?	
Launch • How will we celebrate the creation of our goals at the beginning of each year?	

Data Analysis to Identify Department Goals

Instructions: Determine data indicators that align with the attainment of the districtwide goals and record data (multiyear when available) associated with each of these indicators. Then, study the data gathered using the prompts that follow to determine high-need, high-leverage areas to monitor. Finally, use the reflection questions to collect your thoughts.

Data:

District Goal	Department Data Indicator	Department Data

List any other indicators that need to be considered when developing department goals.

Rationale	Indicator	Data

Reflection:

Based on the preceding data, what are our biggest areas of celebration?

How can you continue or enhance these data trends?

Based on the preceding data, what are the biggest areas of concern?

How do you want to see these data trends improve?

Data Analysis to Identify Team Goals

Instructions: Determine data indicators that align with the attainment of the schoolwide goals and record data (multiyear when available) associated with each of these indicators. Then, study the data gathered using the prompts that follow to determine high-need, high-leverage areas to monitor. Finally, use the reflection section to collect your thoughts.

Data:

School Goal	Team Data Indicator	Team Data

List any other indicators that need to be considered when developing team goals.

Rationale	Indicator	Data

Reflection:

Based on the preceding data, what are the biggest areas of celebration?

How can we continue or enhance these data trends?

Based on the preceding data, what are the biggest areas of concern?

How do we want to see these data trends improve?

Data Analysis to Identify Teacher Goals

Instructions: Determine data indicators that align with the attainment of the team goals and record data (multiyear when available) associated with each of these indicators. Then, study the data gathered using the prompts that follow to determine high-need, high-leverage areas to monitor. Finally, use the reflection section to collect your thoughts.

Data:

Team Goal	Teacher Data Indicator	Teacher Data

List any other indicators that need to be considered when developing teacher goals.

Rationale	Indicator	Data

Reflection:

Based on the preceding data, what are our biggest areas of celebration?

How can you continue or enhance these data trends?

Based on the preceding data, what are the biggest areas of concern?

How do you want to see these data trends improve?

Anchor Your Vision © 2025 Solution Tree Press • SolutionTree.com
Visit **go.SolutionTree.com/PLCbooks/AYV** and enter the unique access code found on the book's inside front cover to access this reproducible.

Teacher SMART Goal

Instructions: Create a professional goal for yourself that supports your school's mission, vision, and goals. You will need to use a separate form for each goal.

School goal:
My professional goal:

Is My Goal SMART?
Strategic and specific: Does my goal align with our team or school goal? Is it clear?
Measurable: How will I measure my goal?
Attainable: Is the goal a stretch goal? Make sure it is just right, not too easy or too challenging.
Results oriented: What evidence will I use to measure progress toward my goal?
Time bound: When will I meet this goal?

Reflection
How will this goal directly impact student growth and achievement?
How will this goal contribute to the attainment of our school goals?

Action Planning
Short-term goal, targets, and timelines:
How will I monitor this goal?
How will I support my learning to attain this goal?
How will I receive feedback to guide me toward this goal?
Who will be my accountability partner?

Student SMART Goal

Instructions: Students work with their teacher to create a SMART goal.

Name:

My personal learning goal:

Is My Goal SMART?

Strategic and specific:
What do I want to learn or know or be able to do?

Measurable:
How will I know I have learned?

Achievable:
Is the goal a stretch goal? Make sure it is just right, not too easy or too challenging.

Results oriented:
What will be the evidence to show I met my goal?

Time bound:
When will I meet this goal?

My Action Plan
How will this goal directly impact my future achievement?
How will I monitor my goal?
How will I get support if needed to attain this goal?
How will I receive feedback to guide me toward this goal?
Who will be my accountability partner?

Reflection
Did I meet my goal? Why or why not?
Teacher feedback:

Team Accountability Partners

Instructions: Record team goals, the related individual teacher professional goals, and the methods for monitoring those goals. Discuss and record the actions that you will commit to as a team for the purpose of holding each other mutually accountable for set goals.

Team Goal		
Related Teacher Goals	Methods for Monitoring	Actions for Accountability

Team Goal		
Related Teacher Goals	Methods for Monitoring	Actions for Accountability

Team Goal		
Related Teacher Goals	Methods for Monitoring	Actions for Accountability

Team Goal		
Related Teacher Goals	Methods for Monitoring	Actions for Accountability

Anchor Your Vision © 2025 Solution Tree Press • SolutionTree.com
Visit **go.SolutionTree.com/PLCbooks/AYV** and enter the unique access code found on the book's inside front cover to access this reproducible.

Setting Our District Department or School Team Goals

Instructions: As a collaborative team, review the data analysis to identify goals. Synthesize the collective information and collaboratively create SMART team goals that align with the schoolwide goals and support the school vision.

Are Our Goals SMART?
Strategic and specific:
Measurable:
Attainable:
Results oriented:
Time bound:
Reflection
How will these goals directly impact student growth and achievement?
How will these goals contribute to the attainment of our school goals?
How will these goals help us achieve our shared vision and mission?

Anchor Your Vision © 2025 Solution Tree Press • SolutionTree.com
Visit **go.SolutionTree.com/PLCbooks/AYV** and enter the unique access code found on the book's inside front cover to access this reproducible.

CHAPTER 6
MOTTO

A meaningful shared motto unites staff, students, families, and the community, creating a sense of belonging.
—SHAWN CRESWELL

When we first began implementing the PLC process, we started with creating a motto. In hindsight, it would have been best to do this work last in order to align our motto with our mission and vision. However, for us, the motto seemed like the best place to start at the beginning of the year because we felt unsure about exactly how to dive into creating the foundational pillars. We felt like we needed time not only to work with our guiding coalition but also to get feedback from staff and family members on our current vision and mission. We lacked the knowledge and tools to effectively do this work (which is one reason we created this book). In addition to our lack of direction to revisit and refine our vision and mission, our guiding coalition felt that we needed time to share the why behind potential changes in our vision and mission. For us, the motto revision ended up being a springboard for updating the mission and vision. The motto became a mini–mission statement by capturing in just a few words what our school valued. Although there is no right or wrong answer for when to create your motto, we do believe the alignment of a motto, mission, and vision really ties the work together. When the staff members understand the goal of connecting the work, it helps make the creation of a motto easier.

So, how did we do this work? When opening the new school, Shawn sent the staff a motto survey. The survey shared the why behind creating a motto and made clear we also wanted the motto to be an indicator of what we envisioned our school would be known for, and we wanted to make a connection to the students, staff, and families with the motto. We wanted it to inspire, share what we valued as educators, and be timeless so that we would not need to update it in years to come. The survey had a lengthy list of words for consideration to begin the brainstorming while leaving space for the staff to add words they thought would be important in the motto. The feedback from the survey had clear favorites, and the motto became *Believe. Grow. Achieve.* The staff felt that the chosen motto was important to teach students and remind staff that when we believe in ourselves, we can grow in any capacity of what we want to learn, and in turn, we can achieve our goals and aspirations. The motto was one that we believed our students would connect with, was easy for even our youngest learners to memorize, and was one we could teach in numerous ways.

Our motto became how we framed discussions with our students when goal setting. It was one way we motivated students and school staff with our motto chant and schoolwide attention signal. Through this process, we learned that a motto can be an impactful addition to our educational tool belt because our powerful motto kept staff, students, and families focused on what we believed.

In this chapter, we define the motto and communicate its value through one school's experience and examples of the way businesses utilize their mottoes. The "Motto Continuum" (page 228) guides leaders and staff through the process of identifying the current reality and the action steps to guide the work through the continuum to the sustaining level. We provide guidance through potential challenges and how to celebrate in a way that keeps the motto front and center. At the end of the chapter, we share insights on how to monitor the progress and impact of the motto.

Navigating the Motto

The motto is a unifying message used as a rallying call for all stakeholders. This three-to-five-word phrase is meant to express the common belief, purpose, and identity of the organization clearly and concisely while igniting a feeling of community. The motto often reflects the values, beliefs, or ideas that resonate across the shared vision and mission. The motto embodies what your organization promises and commits to the educational community. As Mike Mattos, Richard DuFour, Rebecca DuFour, Robert Eaker, and Thomas W. Many (2016) put it, "When a mission statement becomes too long for most people to commit to memory, the school community may embrace a motto that captures the essence of the mission statement. Examples of school mottoes include 'Learning for All,' 'Success for All,' and "Hand in Hand, We All Learn" (p. 13).

Examining the Evidence of a Successful Motto

If you ask people what company they think of when they hear the phrase "the happiest place on Earth," they will likely respond with "Disney." Walt Disney coined this phrase or motto when he opened Disneyland in 1955. Years before the opening of the park, Walt often spent Saturdays out with his daughters, taking them to zoos, carnivals, and parks, where they enjoyed riding the merry-go-round while Walt sat nearby enjoying the sight of his daughters filled with joy. But he wanted more than a few hours on a Saturday for his daughters and families. He envisioned a place where children and their families could enjoy fun together. This vision eventually became the first Disney theme park or, as many refer to it, "the happiest place on Earth." As a matter of fact, many refer to Disney theme parks by this simple phrase that embodies the intention for which Walt Disney created his world of wonder. We would agree from our experiences at the theme parks that the employees strive to create happy moments for their guests with the vision of making it the happiest place on Earth.

Can a district or school motto be created where students, families, and staff at all levels will be both connected and inspired by it? We believe the answer is an absolute yes!

At our first school, Coulson Tough Elementary, the motto we created with our staff—"Learn. Grow. Excel."—reminds both staff and students of the purpose of all we do at our school. It is about learning and growing to excel in all we do. The motto also lets our families and community know what we value in our school.

Taking a Deep Dive Into the Research for Developing a Motto

Research on mottoes in an organization largely focuses on company branding and market share as well as motto likability and memorability. But how does this apply to a district or school in its pursuit of becoming a high-functioning PLC? Well, in the same way that a company's motto can be an effective advertising tool for gaining consumer buy-in, a motto crafted to concisely convey the values of the district or school can promote buy-in of staff, students, and the community. To create an effective motto, research suggests aiming for short and clear. In the *Journal of Business Research*, educators Mayukh Dass, Chiranjeev Kohli, Piyush Kumar, and Sunil Thomas (2014) suggest mottoes that are most remembered are typically an average of three to five words long, decreasing cognitive overload and increasing the effectiveness and ability to remember the motto. To increase clarity, research suggests that a motto should articulate the objective and the benefits of the organization. With these parameters considered, a motto can become a powerful tool to continually communicate—and rally staff to—the values of the district or school.

Sailing Into Action for Each Stage of Developing a Motto

Use the "Motto Continuum" (page 228) to get started by getting a clear picture of your district's or school's current reality. Note that the same continuum is used for both district and school. Read the descriptors in each column and determine which best describes the stage of your district or school. Then, in the following pages, consult the steps listed in the respective stage to create an action plan. Note that for the preinitiating and initiating stages, the steps and tools are the same.

The time frame to create a motto is typically short, much like the motto itself. We suggest the prerequisite to this work is the establishment of a shared mission and vision. Teams will then be able to leverage this work in creating the district's or school's motto.

As you move through each stage, be sure to create a plan for engaging and inspiring new staff with the motto. Plans should include ways to share the meaning, purpose, and connection among the mission, vision, and motto.

The Preinitiating Stage

A district or school in the preinitiating stage does not yet have a motto. For such organizations, begin your work in the initiating stage at step 1, then skip to step 4.

The Initiating Stage

A district or school in the initiating stage has a motto either that is not connected to the mission or vision or whose creation did not reflect staff involvement, resulting in a phrase staff do not support or find valuable.

1. To activate thinking, engage staff in the activity outlined in the "Motto Sort" (page 229).

2. Provide staff time to share their thoughts on the current district or school motto by completing "The Power of a Motto (District)" (page 230) or "The Power of a Motto (School)" (page 231).

3. Facilitate the guiding coalition to synthesize the information and determine the the next steps using the "Analyze the Power of a Motto (District)" (page 232) or "Analyze the Power of a Motto (School)" (page 233) tool.

4. Begin the brainstorming process for creating a motto by engaging all staff in the "One Word" (page 234) activity.

5. Use the "Synthesizing the 'One Word'" (page 235) activity with the guiding coalition to create draft motto statements.

6. Submit draft motto statements to staff for feedback. Revise and resubmit the motto statement selected until consensus is reached, signaling the adoption of the motto statement.

7. Intentionally plan opportunities to celebrate progress. The "Celebrations Survey" (page 236) is designed to gather input from staff and stakeholders on how best to keep the motto front and center on a day-to-day basis. The "Celebration Planning" (page 237) form helps the guiding coalition synthesize the input and create a plan for how best to market and celebrate the shared motto. Remember—your motto is meant to unite your community of stakeholders, so it will be important to have fun with how to plan to inspire all stakeholders.

8. Monitor progress from the initiating to the implementing stage by collecting evidence corresponding with the indicators in the "Motto Continuum" (page 228). When ready, follow the steps outlined in the implementing stage to continue the momentum.

The Implementing Stage

A district or school in the implementing stage has a motto, and its alignment with the mission and vision is evident. Staff were involved in the creation of the motto and support it, but leaders don't utilize the motto for promoting and rallying staff, students, or the community to the values that the collective mission and vision capture.

1. Provide staff time to share their thoughts on the current district or school motto by completing "The Power of a Motto (District)" (page 230) or "The Power of a Motto (School)" (page 231).

2. Facilitate the guiding coalition to synthesize the information and determine the next steps using the "Analyze the Power of a Motto (District)" (page 232) or "Analyze the Power of a Motto (School)" (page 233) tool.

3. Based on the next steps outlined by the guiding coalition in the "Analyze the Power of a Motto (District)" (page 232) or "Analyze the Power of a Motto (School)" (page 233) tool, revise, update, or advance the implementation of the motto.

4. Intentionally plan opportunities to celebrate progress. The "Celebrations Survey" (page 236) is designed to gather input from staff and stakeholders on how best to keep the motto front and center on a day-to-day basis. The "Celebration Planning" (page 237) form helps the guiding coalition synthesize the input and create a plan for how best to market and celebrate the shared motto. Remember—your motto is meant to unite your community of stakeholders, so it will be important to have fun with how to plan to inspire all stakeholders.

5. Monitor progress from the implementing stage to the developing stage by collecting evidence corresponding with the indicators in the "Motto Continuum" (page 228). When ready, follow the steps outlined in the developing stage to continue the momentum.

The Developing Stage

A district or school in the developing stage has a motto, and its alignment with the mission and vision is evident. Staff were involved in the creation of the motto, support it, and use it to promote and rally others to the values that the mission and vision capture, but only within the district office or school building, among one another and with students.

1. Provide parents with "The Power of a Motto (Parent)" (page 238) survey to gather insight into the parent perspective of the school motto. When creating this tool to share with parents, be sure to include the school's vision, mission, and motto at the top of the form.

2. Work with staff to review and synthesize the results of "The Power of a Motto (Parent)" (page 238) survey using the "Analyze the Power of a Motto (Parent)" (page 239) tool.

3. Based on the next steps staff outline in the "Analyze the Power of a Motto (Parent)" (page 239) tool, revise, update, or advance the implementation of the motto.

4. Intentionally plan opportunities to celebrate progress. The "Celebrations Survey" (page 236) is designed to gather input from the staff and stakeholders on how best to keep the motto front and center on a day-to-day basis. The "Celebration Planning" (page 237) form helps the guiding coalition synthesize the input and create a plan for how best to market and celebrate the shared motto. Remember—your motto is meant to unite your community of

stakeholders, so it will be important to have fun with how to plan to inspire all stakeholders.

5. Monitor progress from the developing to the sustaining stage by collecting evidence corresponding with the indicators in the "Motto Continuum" (page 228). When ready, follow the steps outlined in the sustaining stage to continue momentum.

The Sustaining Stage

A district or school in the sustaining stage has a motto, and alignment to the mission and vision is evident. Staff were involved in the creation of the motto, support it, and use it to promote and rally others to the values that the mission and vision capture. The motto is known and used by staff, students, and the community to inspire and unite.

1. With the guiding coalition, set dates across the year to collect evidence corresponding to the indicators in the "Motto Continuum" (page 228).

2. Facilitate the guiding coalition in studying the evidence and engaging in the creation of action plans to continue implementation of the motto aligned with the sustaining stage.

3. Intentionally plan opportunities to celebrate progress. The "Celebrations Survey" (page 236) is designed to gather input from the staff and stakeholders on how best to keep the motto front and center on a day-to-day basis. The "Celebration Planning" (page 237) form helps the guiding coalition synthesize the input and create a plan for how best to market and celebrate the shared motto. Remember—your motto is meant to unite your community of stakeholders, so it will be important to have fun with how to plan to inspire all stakeholders.

Staying Afloat Through Common Challenges to Developing a Motto

When working to create a motto, challenges may arise for districts and schools in the process. The if-then chart in table 6.1 is a valuable troubleshooting resource identifying common challenges to look out for and ideas to address these challenges.

Table 6.1: If-Then Chart

If . . .	Then . . .
There is no motto in place.	Gather staff, families, and students together to discuss ways to create one. Remember—collaboration is always key, and creating a motto to inspire helps to unite the community.

The motto does not connect to the mission or vision.	Gather the guiding coalition together to discuss whether they feel a change is needed. If so, a survey of staff is the ideal place to begin the work.
The motto is written as a sentence and is too long to utilize.	Consider refining the slogan to a few of the key words for greater impact, keeping in mind that three to five words is ideal.

Knowing the Ropes for Motto Development

As you and your colleagues work to establish your organization's motto, orient yourselves by keeping in mind the following.

- Involve the stakeholders in district and school mottoes and elicit feedback or a vote on a final few. When people feel connected to the motto, they are more likely to use it and find it motivating.
- At the school level, consider students first. How might they connect to the motto and have feelings of excitement or school pride?
- Keep the motto short and simple so it's easy for students, families, and staff to remember and use.
- Consider meaningful words or attributes connected to the mission or vision.
- The more visible the motto is within the district or school, the more stakeholders throughout the organization will utilize it. The key is using it everywhere!

Celebrating the Motto

Celebrating the motto will be an ongoing process of ensuring that the motto is front and center in daily operations and communication. We suggest you market your message in places and ways that guarantee it impacts the way the organization operates. Because the motto is meant to motivate individuals, the intentional advertising of the motto will provide momentum for staff, students, and parents to aspire to the move toward a common belief.

- Put the motto on your website, on social media platforms, and in newsletters; say it during announcements; and so forth.
- Consider various items that might bear the motto—such as spirit wear, notepads, pens, cups, hats, posters, letterhead, and name badges.
- Determine how districts and schools can amplify the motto through chants, callbacks, and attention signals. For example, one way staff promoted our school motto in this manner was by saying to students, "Believe. Grow"—prompting them to reply, "Achieve!"
- Create recognition certificates for students, staff, and parents that are centered on exemplifying the message of the motto.

Stay the Course

Feedback is essential in any initiative, and the motto is no different. Perhaps there's already a district or school motto, and you're wondering whether it's one that might need to be replaced. Surveying is an easy way to obtain feedback from a variety of sources to give you feedback. Remember that, ultimately, the motto should create an emotional connection or positive feeling about the district or school.

Anchors Away!

A motto is not one of the foundational pillars of a PLC; however, it is an aspirational statement that many districts and schools use to unite the members of the organization around the foundational pillars. We believe a thoughtfully created motto aligned with the shared vision, mission, collective commitments, and goals connects the staff and students not only to the foundational pillars but also to each other. It can create an energy that relays the message of what is valued within the district or school. A well-crafted motto can be the battle cry for keeping the organization focused on the right work.

Use the space provided to anchor your thoughts and chart your course for your next steps.

Motto Continuum

Instructions: Individually, read the indicators that describe each stage from preinitiating through sustaining. Honestly assess the current reality of the establishment of your district or school mission. Consider what evidence or anecdotes support your assessment. Record your reflections in the space provided.

Shared motto: We have created a phrase that communicates, reminds, and motivates staff, students, and the community to achieve the shared beliefs outlined in our mission and vision.

Shared Motto Continuum Stages				
Preinitiating	Initiating	Implementing	Developing	Sustaining
☐ The district or school does not have a motto.	☐ The district or school has a motto; however, there is little to no alignment to the mission and vision. Staff were not involved in the creation, and many do not support or like the motto.	☐ The district or school has a motto that is aligned with the mission and vision. Staff were involved in the creation of the motto. Most staff support it or like it, but staff, students, families, and the community do not utilize it.	☐ The district or school has a known motto that is aligned to the mission and vision and that all staff created or support. Staff use the motto and refer to it with students, but families and the community are unaware of it and therefore do not have a connection to it.	☐ The district or school has a known motto that is aligned to the mission and vision and that all staff support. The motto is inspiring, creates a positive emotional response, or is a call to action. The majority of families and the community are aware of the motto and feel a connection to it. Students know the motto and are engaged with it. It is intentionally seen and used throughout the district or school and unites the district or school community.

I believe our school or district is at the _____ stage based on the preceding descriptors. The evidence to support my rationale includes:

Motto Sort

Instructions: Cut apart the company names and motto or slogan statements and place them in a bag for table teams. Give teams five minutes to match up the companies and motto or slogan statements based on what they know about each company. Then, have staff discuss their thoughts on why each business chose its motto or slogan and what the company is trying to communicate to consumers.

Nike	Just Do It
Apple	Think Different
McDonald's	I'm Lovin' It
Wheaties	Breakfast of Champions
Disneyland	Happiest Place on Earth
Ford	Built to Last
Burger King	Have It Your Way
Verizon	Can You Hear Me Now?
Sprite	Obey Your Thirst

Reference

Burns, R. (2024). *63 famous company slogans and taglines.* ActiveCampaign. Accessed at www.activecampaign.com/blog/company-slogans on April 25, 2024.

The Power of a Motto (District)

Instructions: After reading the paragraph that follows, respond to the motto prompts indicating your level of agreement and provide a rationale for your decision.

Motto (n.d.a, n.d.b) is defined by Cambridge Dictionary as "a short sentence or phrase that expresses a belief or purpose" and by the Merriam-Webster Dictionary as "a short expression of a guiding principle," Mottoes help communicate what is valued in an organization. When you think about company phrases that have stuck with you over the years, you'll notice how the most effective mottoes are short. This is because brief and concise statements are usually the most impactful.

Our shared vision:

Our shared mission:

District motto:

Leading Indicators	Disagree	Neutral	Agree	Rationale
Our district motto represents our purpose or what we value.	D	N	A	
Our district motto is connected to our vision and mission.	D	N	A	
Our staff are aware of the motto and connected to it.	D	N	A	
Our motto unites our community together.	D	N	A	
Our motto is inspiring, creates a positive emotional response, or is a call to action.	D	N	A	
Staff throughout our district use our motto in meaningful ways.	D	N	A	
Students throughout our district use the motto.	D	N	A	
Our district motto should not be revised.	D	N	A	
Our district motto should be revised.	D	N	A	
Tally and Total				
Share any additional thoughts regarding our district motto.				

References

Motto. (n.d.a). In *Cambridge dictionary*. Accessed at https://dictionary.cambridge.org/us/dictionary/english/motto on January 31, 2024.

Motto. (n.d.b). In *Merriam-Webster's online dictionary*. Accessed at www.merriam-webster.com/dictionary/motto on January 31, 2024.

The Power of a Motto (School)

Instructions: After reading the paragraph that follows, respond to the motto prompts indicating your level of agreement and provide a rationale for your decision.

Motto (n.d.a, n.d.b) is defined by Cambridge Dictionary as "a short sentence or phrase that expresses a belief or purpose" and by the Merriam Webster dictionary as "a short expression of a guiding principle." Mottoes help communicate what is valued in an organization. When you think about company phrases that have stuck with you over the years, you'll notice how the most effective mottoes are short. This is because brief and concise statements are usually the most impactful.

Our shared vision:

Our shared mission:

School motto:

Leading Indicators	Disagree	Neutral	Agree	Rationale
Our school motto represents our purpose or what we value.	D	N	A	
Our school motto is connected to our vision and mission.	D	N	A	
Our students are aware of our motto and connected to it.	D	N	A	
Our staff are aware of our motto and connected to it.	D	N	A	
Our motto unites our school community together.	D	N	A	
Our motto is inspiring, creates a positive emotional response, or is a call to action.	D	N	A	
Staff throughout our school use our motto in meaningful ways.	D	N	A	
Students throughout our school use our motto.	D	N	A	
Our school motto is ideal for our school.	D	N	A	
Our school motto should be revised.	D	N	A	
Tally and Total				
Share any additional thoughts regarding our school motto.				

References

Motto. (n.d.a). In *Cambridge dictionary*. Accessed at https://dictionary.cambridge.org/us/dictionary/english/motto on January 31, 2024.

Motto. (n.d.b). In *Merriam-Webster's online dictionary*. Accessed at www.merriam-webster.com/dictionary/motto on January 31, 2024.

Analyze the Power of a Motto (District)

Instructions: As a guiding coalition, use one copy of this tool to tally the responses from "The Power of a Motto (District)" (page 230). Use the data from tallies as well as the rationale to determine next steps. Possible next steps could include explicitly connecting the motto to an indicator, outlining opportunities for application and increasing consistency of use, or revising or updating the motto. Collaboratively discuss, decide, and implement next steps as a team.

Leading Indicators	Disagree	Neutral	Agree	Rationale
Our district motto represents our purpose or what we value.	D	N	A	
Our district motto is connected to our vision and mission.	D	N	A	
Our staff are aware of the motto and connected to it.	D	N	A	
Our motto unites our community together.	D	N	A	
Our motto is inspiring, creates a positive emotional response, or is a call to action.	D	N	A	
Staff throughout our district use our motto in meaningful ways.	D	N	A	
Students throughout our district use our motto.	D	N	A	
Our district motto should not be revised.	D	N	A	
Our district motto should be revised.	D	N	A	
Tally and Total				

Discuss comments left in this section. Share any additional thoughts regarding our district motto.

Collaborate and list possible action steps for what is next for the motto and plan the implementation of the next steps.

Analyze the Power of a Motto (School)

Instructions: As a guiding coalition, use one copy of this tool to tally the responses from "The Power of a Motto (School)" (page 231). Use the data from tallies as well as the rationale to determine next steps. Possible next steps could include explicitly connecting the motto to an indicator, outlining opportunities for application and increasing consistency of use, or revising or updating the motto. Collaboratively discuss, decide, and implement next steps as a team.

Leading Indicators	Disagree	Neutral	Agree	Rationale
Our school motto represents our purpose or what we value.	D	N	A	
Our school motto is connected to our vision and mission.	D	N	A	
Our staff are aware of the motto and connected to it.	D	N	A	
Our motto unites our community together.	D	N	A	
Our motto is inspiring, creates a positive emotional response, or is a call to action.	D	N	A	
Staff throughout our school use our motto in meaningful ways.	D	N	A	
Students throughout our school use our motto.	D	N	A	
Our school motto should not be revised.	D	N	A	
Our school motto should be revised.	D	N	A	
Tally and Total				

Discuss comments left in this section. Share any additional thoughts regarding our school motto.

Collaborate and list possible action steps for what is next for the motto and plan the implementation of the next steps.

One Word

Instructions: First, staff individually complete the first two prompts to generate and record a word that represents the organization's values and connects to the mission or vision, explaining why they chose it. After completing the first two prompts, staff form partnerships to share their responses and reflect, revise, or add to their thinking. Then, each partnership combines with another partnership to create a group of four and repeat the process. Groups of four join another group of four and repeat the process one more time. Staff then record ideas for potential mottoes.

One word that that connects to our mission and vision:

Why I chose this word:

After discussion in larger groups, share any ideas for a potential motto:

Anchor Your Vision © 2025 Solution Tree Press • SolutionTree.com
Visit **go.SolutionTree.com/PLCbooks/AYV** and enter the unique access code found on the book's inside front cover to access this reproducible.

Synthesizing the "One Word"

Instructions: Collect the "One Word" (page 234) from the staff and synthesize the information to create two to three drafts that can be shared with staff to vote on for the shared motto.

List all potential mottoes brainstormed by the staff:
List common words across the various potential mottoes:
After discussion in larger groups, share any ideas for two to three motto drafts:
Share the motto drafts with staff, students, and parents in a digital or analog format for a vote on stakeholder preference.

Anchor Your Vision © 2025 Solution Tree Press • SolutionTree.com
Visit **go.SolutionTree.com/PLCbooks/AYV** and enter the unique access code found on the book's inside front cover to access this reproducible.

Celebrations Survey

Instructions: Please complete the survey that follows, providing insight on how our district or school might promote and celebrate the shared motto in a way that creates a call to action and purpose for our motto.

Launch • How will we celebrate the creation of our motto?	
Who? • Who do we want to feel celebrated by living the motto? • How could we celebrate individuals, teams, students, parents, and staff who are purposeful in exemplifying the motto?	

When?
• When do we want to schedule these celebratory moments?
   ◆ How frequently?
   ◆ Staff meetings?
   ◆ Professional learning day?
   ◆ Start of the school year?
   ◆ Midyear launch?	

Where? • Where is the best location for celebrations? • Where could we market the motto?	
How? • What ideas do we have to make this a celebration? • Are there a variety of ways we would like to celebrate?	

Anchor Your Vision © 2025 Solution Tree Press • SolutionTree.com
Visit **go.SolutionTree.com/PLCbooks/AYV** to download this free reproducible.

Celebration Planning

Instructions: Dedicate fifteen minutes of a guiding coalition meeting agenda to plan how the motto can be celebrated and marketed. Think about celebrations throughout the year and creating marketing opportunities that inspire a call to action for stakeholders.

Motto:		
Celebration Strategy	Time of Year (monthly, two times per year, ongoing)	Who is responsible for creating or follow-up?
Marketing Ideas	Where, How, and When	Who is responsible for creating or follow-up?

The Power of a Motto (Parent)

Instructions: After reading the paragraph that follows, respond to the motto prompts indicating your level of agreement and provide a rationale for your decision.

Motto (n.d.a, n.d.b) is defined by Cambridge Dictionary as "a short sentence or phrase that expresses a belief or purpose" and by the Merriam-Webster Dictionary as "a short expression of a guiding principle." We want our school motto to communicate what we value.

Our shared vision:

Our shared mission:

School motto:

Leading Indicators	Disagree	Neutral	Agree	Rationale
I believe the school motto is connected to the school vision and mission.	D	N	A	
I am aware of the school motto and feel it represents our school.	D	N	A	
My child knows our school motto and likes it.	D	N	A	
I believe the motto unites our school community.	D	N	A	
I believe the school motto is inspiring.	D	N	A	
I notice that our motto is used throughout the school.	D	N	A	
I feel that the school motto is a great representation for our school.	D	N	A	
Tally and Total				

Share any additional thoughts regarding our school motto.

References

Motto. (n.d.a). In *Cambridge dictionary*. Accessed at https://dictionary.cambridge.org/us/dictionary/english/motto on January 31, 2024.

Motto. (n.d.b). In *Merriam-Webster's online dictionary*. Accessed at www.merriam-webster.com/dictionary/motto on January 31, 2024.

Analyze the Power of a Motto (Parent)

Instructions: As a staff, use one copy of this tool to tally the responses from "The Power of a Motto (Parent)" (page 238). Use the data from tallies as well as the rationale to determine next steps. Possible next steps could include to inform, connect, use, and advance the motto with parents. Collaboratively discuss, decide, and implement next steps as a team.

Leading Indicators	Disagree	Neutral	Agree	Rationale
I believe the school motto is connected to the school vision and mission.	D	N	A	
I am aware of the school motto and feel it represents our school.	D	N	A	
My child knows our school motto and likes it.	D	N	A	
I believe the motto unites our school community.	D	N	A	
I believe the school motto is inspiring.	D	N	A	
I notice that our motto is used throughout the school.	D	N	A	
I feel that the school motto is a great representation for our school.	D	N	A	
Tally and Total				

Discuss comments left in this section. Share any additional thoughts regarding our school motto.

Collaborate and list possible action steps for what is next for the motto and plan the implementation of the next steps.

CHAPTER 7
HIRING, CONNECTING, AND MAINTAINING

If you hire people just because they can do a job, they'll work for your money. But if you hire people who believe what you believe, they'll work for you with blood, sweat, and tears.

—SIMON SINEK

When the shared mission, vision, collective commitments, goals, and motto become the heart and soul of a district or school, the evidence of this work is the resulting high levels of learning for all students. In our experience, when staff are connected to their work, they are more motivated, and in return there is lower staff turnover with higher job satisfaction. Since the purpose of schools is learning, it makes sense to ensure not only that these foundational pillars are in place but also that they all work together and all staff embrace the learning culture.

When Shawn was a first-year principal, she had to hire for several positions before the start of the school year. She used a standard interview process and typical education-related questions for each interview and was able to hire applicants who were qualified and capable of doing the job. However, since she hadn't worked at the school previously and didn't know much about the school culture or the specific goals and needs for the coming year, once the school year began, she realized not all the hires were the best fit for the school culture. With a clearer picture of the culture and the direction the school needed to go, Shawn decided a new hiring process was needed for future positions. Rather than interviewing and hiring candidates on her own, or with just a few members of the staff, she wanted to involve several staff members from a variety of positions within the school to collaborate with her and determine how to best meet the needs of the educators and students in the building.

She started by surveying interested staff members to be part of a hiring committee and shared the goals of the committee, responsibilities, and the time commitment. When inviting members to join the committee, she was careful to set the expectation that it wouldn't matter which position the school had an opening for—this committee would hire for all positions. This was a shift from the way things had been done previously, where staff were hired to fill positions for which there was an opening either solely by the principal or by the principal and some members of the team, which often resulted in teams picking a candidate that they liked best based on their personalities and the status quo. However, the reality was that an applicant hired for one role might not stay in that role the following year—or, in some cases, even the same year—because of the fluctuating number of students per grade and resulting changes in allocations. When staff were required to change grade levels or roles, the existing hiring process that weighted the team's perspective so heavily was a detriment to the school and even the applicant. Once this committee was introduced, and their why for its work was explained, many staff eagerly embraced the premise, and the committee grew to include all those who were interested.

To get started, the committee conducted a book study on Patrick Lencioni's (2016) *The Ideal Team Player*. Based on their reading, team members discussed ideas presented in the book or ones the book inspired as well as highlights from their own interview experiences. From these discussions, they created a tiered interview process for each type of job opening they could have within the school. It didn't matter if the opening was for a teaching position, a support staff position, or even an administrative position—they decided the process would be the same and involve the entire committee. The committee created both verbal and written interview questions that aligned with the mission, vision, and goals of the school in order to home in on candidates who wanted to help attain the vision while committing to the work in the mission and goals. The committee understood that such candidates would be the ones that "will live the company's mission, vision, and values and those who will evangelize the brand internally and externally" (Cutting, 2022, p. vii). With this lens, the hiring process became more of a two-way conversation than a list of questions to which applicants would respond. The goal was to find individuals who really wanted to contribute to the learning-focused school culture that had been created and become part of the school family, adding value and contributing to reaching the vision.

Once new interview questions were established, the committee began working on rubrics to be used in the selection of applicants. These rubrics were created to be used after interviewing each applicant so that all committee members could share their reflections on the applicant and how they met the agreed-on criteria. Individually, each committee member completed a rubric for each applicant after conducting the interview but before any discussion occurred, which allowed for each person's thoughts to be their own and without the influence of other members of the committee. This process made clear which candidate the committee believed to be the best fit every single time. The result was a dramatic increase in successfully finding ideal staff members who, from the start, had a deep understanding of the school culture, the expectations, and the ways they would be able to contribute to achieving the school's goals.

After staff were hired, the new processes for ensuring staff were invested in the school's culture didn't end. The committee thoughtfully created and worked collaboratively to establish a meaningful onboarding process for each individual in addition to the human resources processes the district had in place. This process began with inviting new hires to breakfast at the school. During breakfast, new staff were connected to each other, assigned a mentor to support them their first year, and oriented to the culture of the school and the practices of a PLC. A focus on making new staff feel welcomed, connected, and supported was a high priority for the committee, in alignment with the school's culture and collective commitments. To accomplish this, the committee continued the onboarding process across the year, even taking turns each month to provide special treats with notes for the new staff and then delivering them during the day or placing them on their desk or work area as a special surprise to start the day. Intentional time was set aside throughout the school year to meet with new hires individually to check in; share additional details about the school, such as upcoming calendar items that would be new for them; and provide time to answer questions. These check-ins were also a great time to make plans for any additional support if it was determined to be wanted or needed.

This work was scaled to the district level of a large school district when Shawn moved into a district role and brought many of these practices and procedures to the district-level hiring process. After observing the success of this hiring committee process, many leaders from other departments began utilizing it as well. The impact on the hiring process was incredibly positive and increased the success rate on finding the best-fit candidate for the available positions. Leaders were also able to exhibit value for the insights and thoughts of their department members by including them in the process.

When creating collaborative hiring processes and onboarding procedures for the schools she led as a school principal, Shawn and the hiring committee were able to hire staff who wanted to be a part of creating a school that students wanted to attend each day, staff members were excited to be part of, families were thankful their children attended, and the community was proud to support. Creating a phenomenal school environment can be a reality for every school and district when intentional practices are put in place to align with the mission, vision, collective commitments, and goals. Of course, no school is perfect, but when all staff members unite around a vision to create this type of culture for a school and district, it can be attainable. All students, employees, families, and communities deserve it!

This chapter defines hiring, connecting, and maintaining the PLC foundational pillars and their purpose while offering meaningful tools to assist you through the process of aligning the pillars and motto in order to impact decision making. Since hiring, connecting, and maintaining the work entail different focuses and processes, we have created separate continuums to address each area. Hiring and connecting is one continuum, and maintaining is a separate continuum. There are also separate action-step sections to guide districts and schools through the stages of the continuums. Research-based evidence is included to enhance understanding of these steps in action and the importance of celebrating growth to create a shift to a high-functioning Model PLC.

Navigating Hiring, Connecting, and Maintaining the Work

The foundational pillars and motto guide the district or school toward a culture of collaboration focused on growth and learning for all students. This is impactful work, but it becomes much more powerful when the organization is intentional in using the foundational pillars to drive decision making.

We define *hiring* as the process through which an organization recruits, interviews, and employs individuals for roles in the district or school. When hiring, it is crucial to seek out individuals who understand and value the culture and expectations of the district or school, as they'll help to maintain the momentum that already exists. Once they're hired, ensuring those individuals understand and are excited to support and champion the vision, mission, collective commitments, and goals is the process we describe as *connecting*. Thoughtful onboarding of new staff with intentional mentorship that focuses on the expectations of behavior and actions aligned with the foundational pillars results in a smooth and successful transition into the culture of the organization. In his book *The Culture Playbook*, Daniel Coyle (2022) shares there are vast differences between weak and strong cultures that can be seen on a new employee's first day. He explains, "Weak cultures approach onboarding as a check-the-box routine" (p. 39). Examples of a weak culture might include a focus on completing forms or logistical checklists. In contrast, he notes that strong cultures "approach onboarding as an all-important opportunity to build safety and belonging" (p. 39). An employee's first day offers a fantastic opportunity to start creating a sense of being part of the team from the very beginning. A few ways to help the employee have a terrific first day could include a personalized welcome, a token of appreciation such as a thoughtful note from a leader, lunch with the team to get to know one another, or a solo meeting with a key leader (Coyle, 2022). We strived to make our new staff members' first days special by having breakfast or lunch with them and focusing on getting to know them personally. We always had a welcome note with school items such as branded notepads, pens, a cup, and a school shirt. We also made a point to check in with them at set meeting times throughout the year.

Maintaining the work is equally important to sustain the trajectory toward the shared vision. Again, this requires intentional actions to ensure the foundational pillars are consistently at the forefront of decision making. It is critical not to let your mission, vision, collective commitments, goals, and motto become a check mark of completion and simply posted on a wall or website. Continual action is required to make the maximum positive impact on culture and student growth. Embed intentional opportunities for the foundational pillars to drive conversations and question decisions, ensuring alignment of staff members' thoughts, actions, and behaviors to exemplify the shared commitments. The key words of this work are *intentionality* and *action*. Coyle (2018) professes that creating a strong culture requires that organizations create a place where individuals feel safe with a sense of belonging, have bonds of connection to share vulnerability, and feel a purpose. These three skills take intentional attention and planning. In other words, consistent action to the foundational pillars. Coyle (2018) states that "culture is a set of living relationships working toward a shared goal. It's not something you are. It's something you do" (p. xx).

Examining the Evidence of Successful Hiring, Connecting, and Maintaining the Work

As educators, we continually strive to find *the* thing that will result in the highest success for our students. As a profession, we purchase millions of dollars of resources year after year, yet we have not found one that ensures all students will be successful all the time. That's because it will never be about resources or something to purchase to attain this goal. It's about people. It's about having a united group of educators aiming at a shared vision to attain it. If you, like us when we started the work of being a PLC, want evidence, we have it. Every district and school that has become a Model PLC has a story, a vision, a mission, collective commitments, and goals. But beyond having those in place, they have more than that. They have continued yearly growth and success for students. Isn't that what we all want? Talking with and visiting districts and schools like yours can help you on your journey. We were honored when schools and districts came to visit our school and were always happy to share tools and resources we developed with others. We can all be part of an even larger PLC together, aiming for student success and learning from and growing with one another. Visit www.allthingsplc.info/evidence to learn from other districts and schools and see the evidence of success!

Taking a Deep Dive Into the Research for Hiring, Connecting, and Maintaining the Work

We feel it is important to point out the common thread across all chapters—being a PLC is an *ongoing, never-ending process*. As you look across the continuums for the foundational pillars, you'll notice that they begin with the preinitiating stage and seem to end with the sustaining stage. However, by definition, the word *sustaining* conveys that this work does not actually have an end. Improved outcomes and successes for staff and students year after year require "consistent, coherent effort over time" (Collins, 2001, p. 182). While at first the idea that this process is never ending may seem daunting, we encourage you to instead find it inspiring. There is not a finite end to this work in that at a certain date and time the seal is set on how things will be forevermore. Instead, there is the unlimited opportunity for improvement. We also hope you will find the never-ending aspect of this work less daunting by focusing on three areas we've found most valuable in achieving sustainability: leadership, launching, and celebration.

Depending on your experience with leadership, the word can have different connotations. Throughout this book and specifically in this chapter on sustainability, we intend for *leadership* to refer to all sorts of members of the organization, not just those with titles that convey a leadership position. For the work of a PLC to be sustained, administrators must provide clear direction and engage all members so that they are both inspired and empowered to act in alignment with the shared mission, vision, collective commitments, and goals of the organization. When looking at the work of Nitin Nohria and Michael Beer (2000) on process-driven versus people-driven change, the suggestion is that a mix of both is most effective. This means that there is a continued focus on not just structures and systems but also culture—and that although administrators set the direction, all members are intentionally engaged in an ongoing process of creating and carrying out action plans aligned with that direction. Soliciting the voices of and structuring staff to assess and reflect on progress toward the district's or school's shared mission, vision, and goals are two powerful ways to promote shared leadership.

Equally as important as supporting existing staff to take ownership and lead the work of maintaining the foundational pillars is the work of selecting and integrating new staff with the work already in place. There is a need for urgency to align new staff with our shared work. In a study surveying novice teachers published in 2021, it was found that teachers' perceptions of their person-organization fit were the strongest predictor of teacher retention (Miller & Youngs, 2021). These findings are reinforced as applicable to staff of all experience levels and across both educational and business settings by the *Harvard Business Review*'s reporting of a 2023 survey conducted by Paychex (Tsipursky, 2023). The report stated that 52 percent of new employees feel unprepared after onboarding, leading to a feeling of disengagement that could result in reduced productivity and retention (Tsipursky, 2023). The suggested fix for this was, in addition to the administrative tasks such as paperwork and orientation, that emphasis should be placed on providing new hires with a clear job description and performance expectations, helping them integrate with the team, and following up with them regularly. When considering how to support new staff in connecting with and taking up the existing shared mission, vision, collective commitments, and goals of the district or school, providing new hires with a clear description of the foundational pillars; the expectations of how those pillars affect the attitudes, behaviors, decisions, and actions of staff; time for discussion and support in integrating the pillars into their own practices; and routine and continued follow-up to clarify understanding and application is essential both for the improved job satisfaction of the individual and for the improvement of the organization.

In each chapter, we highlight opportunities to celebrate and want to continue that theme here. Celebration is crucial for existing employees and new hires alike. Because the work of maintaining the foundational pillars is both ongoing and—at times—hard, celebrating the efforts, progress, and achieved milestones along the way is essential. In *Learning by Doing* (DuFour et al., 2016), it is noted that "regular public recognition of specific collaborative efforts, accomplished tasks, achieved goals, team learning, continuous improvement, and support for student learning reminds staff of the collective commitment to create a PLC" (p. 221). In this way, celebration provides us the opportunity to affirm what we want to see more of, thereby clarifying the actions that align with our desired outcomes. Celebration also provides motivation. Psychologist B. J. Fogg (2019) suggests that celebration provides a shot of positive feeling and emotion that reinforces the small changes needed for big successes. Not only do we feel good when celebrated, but we feel seen, further connecting individuals to the shared purpose of the organization and fueling a desire to maintain the work.

Sailing Into Action for Each Stage of Hiring and Connecting the Work

Connecting the work of the foundational pillars and motto revolves around the recruiting, interviewing, hiring, and onboarding practices of your district or school. When referencing hiring practices in the steps that follow, we suggest the utilization of a hiring committee. In many districts and schools, the hiring personnel may be in the human resources department. What we are intending to convey is creating a committee whose members work to recruit, interview, recommend hiring, and support candidates for a position.

You will want to begin by evaluating your current reality using the "Hiring and Connecting New Staff Continuum (District)" (page 257) or "Hiring and Connecting New Staff Continuum (School)" (page 258). Once you have identified your current stage of establishment, use the action steps and tools provided that are associated with that stage in order to progress along the continuum toward the sustaining level. For the preinitiating through implementing stages, the steps and tools are the same. We have provided descriptors to clarify the indicators that would be present in each stage individually, followed by one list of the steps.

The Preinitiating Stage

In the preinitiating stage, the organization does not participate in the hiring process, and a generic set of questions is used during the interview process. There is not a connection between the candidate and the foundational pillars of the organization.

The Initiating Stage

In the initiating stage, a supervisor takes responsibility for the hiring process using an individually drafted set of interview questions to determine the best fit for the position. The candidate may be provided with a copy of the foundational pillars, but there is not a connection between their hiring and the organization's shared vision, mission, collective commitments, and goals.

The Implementing Stage

At the implementing stage, staff from a team or department now join the supervisor to sit in on the interview process using questions that reflect the department's or team's agreed-on criteria. A mentor is provided to support the new hire and reference the foundational pillars as part of the onboarding process.

1. The first step in thinking about hiring is to create a committee on hiring the ideal candidate. The "Hiring Committee Application" (page 259) tool explains the why behind creating a hiring committee along with an application that will guide the process of creating this valuable team.

2. Once the hiring committee has been established, review the professional commitments and create team norms using the "Hiring Committee Professional Commitments and Norms" (page 260) tool.

3. The hiring committee collaborates to create a "New Hire Onboarding" (page 261) tool to orient new hires with the district or school culture and expectations.

4. Convene the hiring committee to create the "Screening Criteria for a Vacancy" (page 263).

5. The hiring committee creates interview questions to match the criteria for the vacancy using the tool "Criteria-Based Interview Questions" (page 264).

6. After interviewing an applicant, each hiring committee member who is present in the interview completes the "Applicant Interview Rubric" (page 266). This

rubric will help the committee determine the most qualified candidate who matches the criteria.

7. Once the hiring committee has completed interviews of the selected applicants, the administrator uses the "Reference Question Examples (District)" (page 267) or "Reference Question Examples (School)" (page 268) to contact references for the two to three most qualified applicants based on the rubric.

8. When you are ready to offer a candidate the position, discuss with the candidate the document on the foundation of the district or school (see the section Sailing Into Action for Each Stage of Maintaining the Work, page 249) and ask the new hire to sign the collective commitments. Be sure they understand in advance of accepting the position that all staff are expected to adhere to the shared commitments and will be held accountable.

9. Celebrate new hires! Be sure to communicate who the new hires are and share a little about them. Current staff should intentionally seek out the new hires to make them feel welcome and part of the family.

10. The hiring committee uses the completed "New Hire Onboarding" (page 261) tool and refers to their created checklist, which includes thoughtfully assigning a mentor to support the newly hired colleague throughout the individual's first year, ensuring both parties understand their roles.

11. The hiring committee meets with new hires to welcome and orient them to the school. Ideally, mentors attend with their mentees. We suggest initiating a getting-to-know-you activity and having new hires complete "What's My Why?" (page 37 in chapter 2), which they share during the first meeting.

12. The hiring committee continually meets with the new hires the first year, typically on a quarterly basis. The committee creates agendas for each meeting, always building in a team-building activity and offering time for questions. Beginning work at a new district or school can be challenging for new hires with all there is to learn. Quarterly check-ins not only help them to acclimate more quickly but allow for intentional time to be set aside to value the new hires.

The Developing Stage

At the developing stage, a hiring committee and school hiring criteria have been established. Questions are created to reflect school criteria and gather insight on a candidate's connection to the foundational pillars. The department or grade-level team has processes in place to mentor the new hire and help support the individual in understanding the connection and alignment of the foundational pillars.

1. The staff complete the "Hiring and Connecting New Staff Continuum (District)" (page 257) or "Hiring and Connecting New Staff Continuum (School)" (page 258) on a yearly basis.

2. The guiding coalition members review the feedback and discuss what steps are needed in order to be at the sustaining stage.

The Sustaining Stage

At the sustaining stage, a hiring committee that has representation from different departments or teams is established. The committee collectively creates interview questions and a rubric aligned with the foundational pillars. The committee takes collective responsibility for onboarding the new hire into the culture of the school in a way that ensures as smooth a transition as possible for the individual.

1. Invite all staff to review the "Hiring and Connecting New Staff Continuum (District)" (page 257) or "Hiring and Connecting New Staff Continuum (School)" (page 258) and record their reflections on a yearly basis.

2. Convene the guiding coalition members to study the feedback given by staff on the "Hiring and Connecting New Staff Continuum (District)" (page 257) or "Hiring and Connecting New Staff Continuum (School)" (page 258), continually monitoring progress and creating action plans as needed to maintain alignment to the indicators in the sustaining stage.

Sailing Into Action for Each Stage of Maintaining the Work

The steps for this portion of the work look a little different from those of previous chapters. Maintaining the work of the foundational pillars and motto centers on the intentional and consistent use of the mission, vision, collective commitments, goals, and motto and is the driving force for decision making to ensure student learning. To begin, create a document that includes your vision, mission, collective commitments, goals, and motto. We created an example that can be found in the end-of-chapter reproducible "The Foundation of Our District or School—Example" (page 269). We also created a template for you to use called "The Foundation of _____ District" (page 270) or "The Foundation of _____ School" (page 271; fill in your district or school name) to create your district or school document. For the preinitiating through developing stages, the steps and tools are the same. We have provided descriptors to clarify the indicators that will be present in each stage individually, followed by one list of the steps.

The Preinitiating Stage

Districts and schools at the preinitiating stage may have some of the foundational pillars created but are not using them to make decisions to drive school operations and student learning. Staff are not connected to the foundational pillars.

The Initiating Stage

At the initiating stage, some of the foundational pillars are in place, but decision making is sporadically connected to the pillars to drive student learning. There is little evidence that staff feel connected to the foundational pillars in a way that impacts attitudes, behaviors, actions, or decisions.

The Implementing Stage

At the implementing stage, some of the foundational pillars are in place and focused on student learning and utilized in decision making focused on student learning. Staff feel connected to the foundational pillars and exhibit attitudes, behaviors, and actions that support them.

The Developing Stage

At the developing stage, the foundational pillars are created and consistently used in driving decision making, and evidence is collected to demonstrate student learning. Most staff are connected to and promote the foundational pillars. The school is intentional in celebrating evidence of connections to the foundational pillars.

1. Invite staff to complete the "Maintaining the Work Continuum (District)" (page 272) or "Maintaining the Work Continuum (School)" (page 273) to evaluate the current reality of implementation. Staff will provide support of their evaluation with reasons and evidence. Then, have them complete the "Maintaining the Work Planning Sheet (District)" (page 272) or "Maintaining the Work Planning Sheet (School)" (page 273).

2. Convene your guiding coalition to review staff feedback from the "Maintaining the Work Continuum (District)" (page 272) or "Maintaining the Work Continuum (School)" (page 273) and develop consensus on both the current stage and the reasons or evidence to support this stage using the "Guiding Coalition Synthesis" (page 276) tool.

3. Use the "Action Plan for Our Next Steps" (page 277) tool collaboratively with your guiding coalition. This plan should consider the indicators describing your current stage and the steps needed for attainment of the next stage.

4. Continue to take action and monitor progress from one stage to the next.

The Sustaining Stage

At the sustaining stage, all foundational pillars are created and drive the decision making of the organization. Staff are intentional in seeking evidence of student learning and are able to articulate the value of the foundational pillars. The foundational pillars are regularly celebrated with intention and in meaningful ways.

1. On an annual basis, invite staff to complete the "Maintaining the Work Continuum (District)" (page 272) or "Maintaining the Work Continuum (School)" (page 273) to evaluate the current reality of implementation. Staff will provide support of their evaluation with reasons and evidence.

2. Convene your guiding coalition to review staff feedback from the "Maintaining the Work Continuum (District)" (page 272) or "Maintaining

the Work Continuum (School)" (page 273) using the "Guiding Coalition Synthesis" (page 276) tool.

3. If the consensus continues to reflect that the current reality is the sustaining stage, use the "Action Plan for Our Next Steps" (page 277) tool collaboratively with your guiding coalition to intentionally maintain attainment of this stage. Otherwise, consider the indicators describing your current stage and the steps needed to move to the sustaining stage.

4. Continue to collect evidence and take action to maintain attainment of the sustaining stage.

Staying Afloat Through Common Challenges to Hiring, Connecting, and Maintaining the Work

Hiring, connecting, and maintaining the work is a process that must stay front and center in the planning of the PLC. Much like the foundation of a building that holds the structure firmly in place, it is the foundational pillars that hold the organizational structure and culture on a firm trajectory to achieving the shared vision. It takes time, attention, and intentional monitoring of the foundational pillars to maintain a strong foundation. This process can pose challenges along the way that should be addressed in a timely manner to ensure continued focus on maintaining the foundational pillars. The if-then chart shown in table 7.1 is intended to share some common challenges you might experience and potential steps to overcome those challenges successfully.

Table 7.1: If-Then

If . . .	Then . . .
You realize there are processes, practices, or resources that do not align with the foundational pillars.	Analyze all processes, practices, or resources using the lens of the foundational pillars in an effort to continue practices that fit and create a "stop doing" list for those that no longer align.
It is taking too long to create the foundational pillars.	Commit to making the foundational pillars a priority and understand that perfection is not the goal. There is always time to revise the foundational pillars along the way to make them better.
Staff do not have a clear understanding of the foundational pillars or cannot fully champion the work.	Find clear evidence from other districts or schools or within your own organization to demonstrate the positive impact of keeping the foundational pillars at the center of decision making.
Your pool of applicants is low, and you can't find a match for your criteria.	Consider if this is a position that must be filled versus a distribution of responsibilities within the school or district. If the position is needed, consider how the best candidate from the pool can be coached and supported.

Knowing the Ropes for Hiring, Connecting, and Maintaining the Work

As you and your colleagues engage in hiring, connecting, and maintaining the work surrounding the pillars and motto, orient yourselves by keeping in mind the following.

- Reviewing the strengths of departments and teams first when available positions occur guides setting criteria for the ideal candidate for the position. This is an ongoing process each time a position becomes available, as needs for the district and school will change and must reflect what is required to help reach the vision. If all team members have the same strengths, they don't grow as much from one another in their craft.

- Talking with a candidate's references is more important than most people tend to realize. On more than one occasion, our committee thought we found the ideal candidate, only to have references share another side of an applicant that we couldn't see from an interview. Asking the right questions and not making this process just a checkbox is important. After all, not only will new hires impact adults, but they'll impact students.

- Most people are prepared for the generic questions during interviewing and are ready with a response. Craft meaningful questions to best know applicants' skills and how they can contribute to the vision, mission, and goals of the organization.

- The most effective way to find ideal candidates is for them to spend time in the environment they would be in. Having a candidate teach a small-group lesson allows for the interview team to see how they interact with students in a real-life scenario. Oftentimes, applicants will shadow someone doing the job so that they, too, can see whether the position would be a good fit for them. Allowing applicants in the final round of the interview process to sit in on a collaborative team meeting is another suggestion. Again, the goal is an ideal fit for the organization and the new hire.

- Simply taking a tour of the workplace with one of the committee members allows for the candidate to ask questions and learn more about the place they would work.

- The more transparency you have with applicants about how the district or school works as a PLC and what that work entails prior to their accepting the position, the better fit it will be for both parties. Once the committee has narrowed down the applicants to a final few, share with the candidate the vision, mission, collective commitments, and goals.

- Keep in mind people typically stay with a district or school when they feel connected, valued, and appreciated. You can't wait to start this culture. As Cutting (2022) contends, "Right from the onboarding process, your employees need to feel like they matter, that what they're doing matters, and that they're helping move the needle forward" (p. vii). Be intentional and explicit in how your district or school communicates that every employee is needed and valued to be successful.

Celebrating Hiring, Connecting, and Maintaining the Work

Celebrations are one of the most powerful ways to nurture, encourage, sustain, and demonstrate what is valued. Recognizing individuals, teams, or departments promotes a culture of action toward the shared vision. When leaders acknowledge individual and team actions and contributions that align with the foundational pillars, they are reinforcing those actions both in the staff and within the district or school. Key ideas when considering celebrations include focusing on positive intentions; making celebrations a regular part of the district or school calendar; and creating meaningful rituals, traditions, and ceremonies. With these thoughts in mind, your intentional action toward celebration can help cement and sustain the work of a highly effective PLC. What follows are some ideas for how you might celebrate your foundational pillars.

- The foundational pillars and motto chapters ended with an adoption celebration for the specific area, but we must also remember to include ongoing smaller celebrations throughout the year for all aspects of our PLC. For example, we might celebrate when we notice a teacher or team doing something that aligns with the vision, mission, and collective commitments. This might be a shout-out in a newsletter, a social media post, or a unique staff award created at your district or school to honor teachers and teams that exemplify living out the school mission. At our first school, we had two spirit sticks that one of our teachers created. The spirit sticks were a traveling award presented to an individual teacher and to a team. The spirit stick hung outside the teacher's classroom or in the team hallway. Whoever received the spirit stick wrote their name on it and so as the spirit stick traveled around, all of the previous staff members' names remained on it. Staff members throughout the building would make a point of celebrating and acknowledging the teacher and team who were awarded the spirit sticks.

- Consider quarterly staff celebrations to publicly highlight what the leadership has seen in data conversations, classroom observations, and teacher growth that clearly supports the foundational pillars.

- Provide opportunities for staff to acknowledge and celebrate colleagues' efforts to operate in alignment to the foundational pillars and impact student learning.

- We believe that creating rituals infused with deep meaning is a meaningful way to celebrate what the district or school values. They help transform common experiences into uncommon events and continue to honor the culture of the PLC.

- Traditions are significant events that have a special history and meaning and occur year in and year out. Celebrating the foundational pillars through traditions underpins an intentional plan to continue valuing the work of the PLC. Traditions are part of the history of the district or school and tie people to its cultural roots. Thoughtful creation of traditions tied to the foundational pillars align efforts to collaborating around the right work.

- Ceremonies are one type of celebration that send a clear message of what your district or school values. They bind people together and shape unwritten cultural values. You may want to consider a monthly ceremony to recognize students achieving their growth goals, a regular ceremony celebrating staff who impact student achievement, or a ceremony inviting families and the community to the school to celebrate the collective effort to celebrate student achievement.

- Celebration comes in many forms. One way that organizations celebrate their culture and hard work is to hold tight to the stories that have created their current foundation and culture. We believe that honoring the work of the foundational pillars is to consider how you are going to maintain the history of your school and capture stories. Ideas include media recording stories; visual history with images; creating a platform for student, parent, and staff storytelling; and so on. Maintain a record of special events throughout your district or school's life and share this history with new staff and families. By holding tight to your history and revisiting these stories, it celebrates the work of creating the current culture while recommitting to the continued journey of a strong PLC.

- We believe it is imperative to be intentional in planning your celebrations. It can be as simple as dividing a piece of paper into the months of the year and mapping out the plan, using a more formal document, or digital format to share among your guiding coalition. Create a celebration action plan that works best for your district or school. The most important step is the journey to making celebrations intentional throughout the year and aligned to what you value and actions of which you hope to see more.

- A great way to celebrate your organization's commitment and dedication to functioning as a high-performing PLC is to apply to be a Model PLC district or school. The Model PLC flag is a symbol for your staff, students, parents, and community as a reminder of the important work and commitment to ensuring exceptional learning and growth in your organization. In addition, you will find applicants often seek to become staff of Model PLC districts and schools.

Stay the Course

We highly suggest monitoring the progress of the foundational pillars on an annual basis with the staff using the surveys and continuums, remembering that we monitor what we value. For us, no two years at the district or school level were alike—new staff were always joining our teams. Input from the whole staff on an ongoing basis is important to sustaining the work. Richard DuFour and Michael Fullan (2013) state, "A meta-analysis of the research on the subject [of coherent leadership] found that district leadership could have a significant impact on student achievement, but only if leaders at the district level are united in articulating and pursuing priorities" (p. 24). Not only do we need to articulate the priorities; we believe we must also monitor what we have created and value.

Anchors Away!

The most inspiring or wonderfully wordsmithed mission and vision still have little to no impact without the people who are inspired by that vision and live out that mission. This is why it is critical to get the people part right. By recruiting individuals who resonate with the district's or school's mission and vision, and then intentionally supporting them to connect their efforts with that mission and vision, a unified culture is created. When you make each hire with the mission and vision in mind, inevitably, you select individuals who are qualified for the job and, more importantly, passionate about contributing to the greater purpose.

Use the space provided to anchor your thoughts and chart your course for your next steps.

Hiring and Connecting New Staff Continuum (District)

Instructions: Individually, read the indicators that describe each stage from preinitiating through sustaining. Honestly assess the current reality of the establishment of your practices for hiring and connecting new staff. Consider what evidence or anecdotes support your assessment. Record your reflections in the space provided.

Hiring and connecting new staff: The district's shared mission, vision, collective commitments, goals, and motto are consistently used to drive hiring and onboarding processes in an effort to sustain the shared commitment to the foundational pillars.

Hiring and Connecting New Staff Continuum Stages				
Preinitiating	**Initiating**	**Implementing**	**Developing**	**Sustaining**
☐ An outside agency that is not employed in the district selects new staff. ☐ When hiring new staff, the agency selects candidates based on generic criteria. ☐ New staff do not receive a copy of the district's mission, vision, collective commitments, goals, and motto.	☐ Supervisors alone are responsible for selecting their direct reports. ☐ When hiring new staff, supervisors select candidates based solely on their own criteria. ☐ New staff receive a copy of the district's mission, vision, collective commitments, goals, and motto.	☐ Supervisors and members of the department for which there is an opening select new staff. ☐ When hiring new staff, supervisors and department members select candidates based on the department criteria. ☐ Procedures are in place for a mentor to support new staff and inform them of the district's mission, vision, collective commitments, goals, and motto.	☐ Supervisors and a committee select new staff. ☐ When hiring new staff, the hiring committee selects candidates based on the district criteria and considers how candidates will impact the district's collaborative culture. ☐ Procedures are in place for the team to support new staff in understanding and aligning to the district's mission, vision, collective commitments, goals, and motto.	☐ Supervisors and an established hiring committee whose members represent a variety of departments and positions across the district select new staff. ☐ When hiring new staff, the hiring committee selects candidates based on the district's set criteria and intentionally chooses candidates who will help the district reach its mission, vision, and school goals. ☐ Procedures are in place and all staff actively support new staff in understanding, aligning to, and championing the district's mission, vision, collective commitments, goals, and motto. ☐ There is evidence that new staff quickly adopt the district's foundational pillars and motto and align their attitudes, behaviors, actions, and decisions.

I believe our school or district is at the _____ stage based on the preceding indicators. The evidence to support my rationale includes:

Source: Adapted from DuFour, R., DuFour, R., Eaker, R., Many, T. W., Mattos, M., & Muhammad, A. (2024). Learning by doing: A handbook for Professional Learning Communities at Work (4th ed.). Bloomington, IN: Solution Tree Press.

Hiring and Connecting New Staff Continuum (School)

Instructions: Individually, read the indicators that describe each stage from preinitiating through sustaining. Honestly assess the current reality of the establishment of your practices for hiring and connecting new staff. Consider what evidence or anecdotes support your assessment. Record your reflections in the space provided.

Hiring and connecting new staff: The school's shared mission, vision, collective commitments, goals, and motto are consistently used to drive hiring and onboarding processes in an effort to sustain the shared commitment to the foundational pillars.

Hiring and Connecting New Staff Continuum Stages				
Preinitiating	Initiating	Implementing	Developing	Sustaining
☐ An administrator who does not work in the school selects new staff. ☐ When hiring new staff, the administrator selects candidates based on generic criteria. ☐ New staff are not oriented with the school's mission, vision, collective commitments, goals, and motto.	☐ Administrators alone are responsible for selecting new staff. ☐ When hiring new staff, administrators select candidates based on their own criteria. ☐ New staff receive a copy of the school's mission, vision, collective commitments, goals, and motto.	☐ Administrators and the grade-level or department team for which there is an opening select new staff. ☐ When hiring new staff, administrators and the grade-level or department team select candidates based on the grade-level or department team criteria.	☐ Administrators and a committee select new staff. ☐ When hiring new staff, the hiring committee selects candidates based on the school criteria and considers how candidates will impact the school's collaborative culture.	☐ Administrators and an established hiring committee whose members represent multiple grade levels or departments and positions across the building select new staff. ☐ When hiring new staff, the hiring committee selects candidates based on the school criteria and intentionally chooses candidates who will help the school reach its mission, vision, and school goals. ☐ Procedures are in place and all staff actively support new staff in understanding, aligning to, and championing the school's mission, vision, collective commitments, goals, and motto. ☐ There is evidence that new staff *quickly* adopt the foundational pillars and motto of the school and align their attitudes, behaviors, actions, and decisions.

I believe our school or district is at the _____ stage based on the preceding indicators. The evidence to support my rationale includes:

Source: Adapted from DuFour, R., DuFour, R., Eaker, R., Many, T. W., Mattos, M., & Muhammad, A. (2024). Learning by doing: A handbook for Professional Learning Communities at Work (4th ed.). Bloomington, IN: Solution Tree Press.

Hiring Committee Application

Our goal for our hiring committee is to have a representation of members from a variety of positions within the district or school. We value the insights of our staff and strive to hire candidates who will help us reach our shared vision and goals while honoring and adhering to our mission and collective commitments. According to Patrick Lencioni (2016):

> Many people will try to get a job even if they don't fit the company's stated values, but very few will do so if they know that they're going to be held accountable, day in and day out, for behavior that violates the values. (p. 180)

Through our process, we aim to select candidates who not only have needed skills for the position but who will match the vision and mission of our school or district. If you are interested in being part of this valuable committee, please complete the application that follows.

Instructions: Complete the application that follows to be considered for our hiring committee. Submit your completed application to _____ [name] by _____ [date].

First and last name:
Position:
Availability for hiring committee meetings and conducting interviews:
Why would you like to serve on the hiring committee?
Share your thoughts on processes or procedures you feel our hiring committee would possess.
Describe characteristics ideal candidates would possess for a position at our district or school.
Share your ideas for how our hiring committee should support new staff.

Reference

Lencioni, P. (2016). *The ideal team player: How to recognize and cultivate the three essential virtues.* Hoboken, NJ: Wiley.

Hiring Committee Professional Commitments and Norms

Instructions: Working together as a collaborative team, read through the professional commitments and add collective norms for the work you will be doing together.

Professional Commitments

As a member of the hiring committee:

- I am committed to ethical hiring practices and will adhere to state, provincial, or district guidelines and expectations.
- I will adhere to the processes and procedures of the hiring committee.
- I will maintain confidentiality within the hiring committee to include:
  - The list of applicants for screening
  - The list of candidates to interview
  - Résumés, interview questions, candidate responses, rubrics, hiring recommendations, and the like

Hiring Committee Norms

I commit to adhering to the professional commitments and team norms for the hiring committee.

Committee member: _____ School year: _____

New Hire Onboarding

Instructions: As a hiring committee, complete the following chart to include ideas to support new staff members in the onboarding process. Then, create an onboarding checklist for mentors or teams to use throughout the year as they support the new team members.

Topics	Ideas new staff need to know and how we might share those ideas to best support these individuals in our professional learning community
Vision	
Mission	
Collective commitments	
Goals	
Mentor and mentee roles and responsibilities	
Collaborative team expectations	
Building procedures	
Our shared rituals, traditions, and celebrations	
Ideas to make new staff members feel celebrated (snacks, treats, notes, and so forth)	

Onboarding Checklist:

Month	Actions	Staff Responsible
August		
September		
October		
November		
December		
January		
February		
March		
April		
May		

Screening Criteria for a Vacancy

Instructions: As a hiring committee, complete this form to create criteria for each vacancy and list applicants whose résumés meet the set criteria.

> **Criteria:** Consider criteria that would make the ideal candidate for your district or school.
>
> **Examples:** Certifications, experience, leadership skills, professional learning, knowledge, and experience with professional learning communities

List of Applicants Who Met Criteria	Date of Interview	Time of Interview

Anchor Your Vision © 2025 Solution Tree Press • SolutionTree.com
Visit **go.SolutionTree.com/PLCbooks/AYV** and enter the unique access code found on the book's inside front cover to access this reproducible.

Criteria-Based Interview Questions

Instructions: As a hiring committee, review the "Screening Criteria for a Vacancy" (page 263) tool and list the criteria in the space provided. Then, collaboratively create two to three criteria-based questions to pose to applicants for each of the indicated areas that follow. Consider which questions to communicate orally in the interview room and which to reserve for written responses.

Criteria from the "Screening Criteria for a Vacancy" (page 263) tool.

Interview Questions (indicate which will be asked orally and which will be written)

Topic: Focus on learning
Question bank:
Topic: Focus on collaboration and collective responsibility
Question bank:
Topic: Focus on results
Question bank:

Topic: Our mission
Question bank:

Topic: Our vision
Question bank:

Topic: Our collective commitments
Question bank:

Topic: Our goals
Question bank:

Applicant Interview Rubric

Instructions: After interviewing an applicant but before discussing as a committee, individually complete the rubric that follows based on interview questions and the applicant's responses. Individually and anonymously calculate scores and share before the committee's discussion of the applicant's qualifications. There are blank rows at the bottom of the rubric to incorporate additional criteria as needed.

Applicant Name: _____

Criteria	Score
Applicant's responses align with a focus on learning.	1 2 3 4 5
Applicant's responses align with a focus on collaborative culture and collective responsibility.	1 2 3 4 5
Applicant's responses align with a focus on results.	1 2 3 4 5
This applicant will contribute to the achievement of our:	
Mission	1 2 3 4 5
Vision	1 2 3 4 5
Goals	1 2 3 4 5
This applicant will complement the collaborative team.	1 2 3 4 5
This applicant will complement our professional learning community.	1 2 3 4 5
	1 2 3 4 5
	1 2 3 4 5
	1 2 3 4 5
	1 2 3 4 5
	1 2 3 4 5
Total Score	

Anchor Your Vision © 2025 Solution Tree Press • SolutionTree.com
Visit **go.SolutionTree.com/PLCbooks/AYV** and enter the unique access code found on the book's inside front cover to access this reproducible.

Reference Question Examples (District)

Instructions: When having a conversation with an applicant's professional reference, consider posing questions and prompts like the ones that follow in order to help identify the best-fit candidate for the available position. Provide an opportunity for the hiring committee to also assist in creating questions aligned to the position.

1. Our shared vision is _____
   _____ ,
   and we are looking for applicants who can help us achieve our vision. Please share how you think the applicant could contribute to fulfilling our vision.

2. Our shared mission is _____
   _____ .
   What experience do you have with the applicant to support how this individual could contribute to fulfilling our mission?

3. Our current goals are _____
   _____ .
   Please share what areas of expertise the applicant has that could assist us in achieving our goals.

4. We value working collaboratively and taking collective responsibility for ensuring learning for all students. Please share how the applicant's colleagues would describe what it is like to work with the applicant.

5. Please share the professional goals the applicant is working toward and the support needed to help this individual achieve those goals.

6. Please share how students would describe the applicant (if applicable to this person's current position).

7. Please share how school families would describe the applicant (if applicable to this person's current position).

Reference Question Examples (School)

Instructions: When having a conversation with an applicant's professional reference, consider posing questions and prompts like the ones that follow in order to help identify the best-fit candidate for the available position. Provide an opportunity for the hiring committee to also assist in creating questions aligned to the position.

1. Our shared vision is _____, and we are looking for applicants who can help us achieve our vision. Please share how you think the applicant could contribute to fulfilling our vision.

2. Our shared mission is _____. What experience do you have with the applicant to support how this individual could contribute to fulfilling our mission?

3. Our current goals are _____. Please share what areas of expertise the applicant has that could assist us in achieving our goals.

4. We value working collaboratively and taking collective responsibility for ensuring learning for all students. Please share how the applicant's colleagues would describe what it is like to work with the applicant.

5. Please share professional goals the applicant is working toward and the support needed to help this individual achieve those goals.

6. Please share how students would describe the applicant.

7. Please share how school families would describe the applicant.

8. Would you rehire the applicant for a position at your school?

Anchor Your Vision © 2025 Solution Tree Press • SolutionTree.com
Visit **go.SolutionTree.com/PLCbooks/AYV** and enter the unique access code found on the book's inside front cover to access this reproducible.

The Foundation of Our District or School—Example

Our shared mission: We ensure exceptional learning and growth for all students and staff.

Our shared vision: We will become nationally recognized as a professional learning community in which students thrive in a school setting where they are respected and valued. We focus on academic and social-emotional learning and growth so students become successful contributing members of their community.

Our collective commitments:
- We will identify our essential standards and commit to teaching our guaranteed and viable curriculum.
- We will communicate positively with our colleagues and students.
- We commit to collaborating with one another to ensure success for all our students.
- We take a collective responsibility for our students.
- We will set high behavior and academic expectations for ourselves and our students.
- We will analyze data to inform our instructional practices.
- We will commit to ongoing learning for ourselves in our profession.
- We will hold one another accountable for our commitments.

Our goals:
- All students will read on or above grade level.
- All students will demonstrate proficiency of the essential knowledge and skills for each grade, course, or content area.

Our motto: Learn. Grow. Excel.

The Foundation of _____ District

Our shared mission:

Our shared vision:

Our collective commitments:

Our district goals:

Our motto:

The Foundation of _____ School

Our shared mission:

Our shared vision:

Our collective commitments:

Our school goals:

Our motto:

Maintaining the Work Continuum (District)

Instructions: Individually, read the indicators that describe each stage from preinitiating through sustaining. Honestly assess the current reality of the establishment of your district practices in putting together and sustaining the collective foundational pillars. Consider what evidence or anecdotes support your assessment. Record your reflections in the space provided.

Maintaining the work: The district has an aligned shared **mission, vision, collective commitments, goals, and motto.** These are consistently used and celebrated throughout the district to drive decision making and create a culture of collaboration to ensure student learning.

	Maintaining the Work Continuum Stages			
Preinitiating	**Initiating**	**Implementing**	**Developing**	**Sustaining**
☐ Some of the foundational pillars and the motto are in place but are not aligned with a focus on student learning.	☐ Some of the foundational pillars and the motto are in place but are not aligned with a focus on student learning.	☐ Some of the foundational pillars and motto are in place and aligned with a focus on student learning.	☐ All the foundational pillars and motto are in place and aligned with a focus on student learning.	☐ All the foundational pillars and motto are in place and aligned with a focus on student learning.
☐ The mission, vision, collective commitments, goals, and motto are not utilized during decision making in the daily operations of the district.	☐ The mission, vision, collective commitments, goals, and motto are sporadically utilized during decision making in the daily operations of the district. There is little evidence that these decisions improve student growth and learning.	☐ The mission, vision, collective commitments, goals, and motto are often utilized during decision making in the daily operations of the district. There is some evidence that these decisions improve student growth and learning.	☐ The mission, vision, collective commitments, goals, and motto are consistently utilized during decision making in the daily operations of the district. There is clear evidence that these decisions improve student growth and learning.	☐ The mission, vision, collective commitments, goals, and motto are the driving force during decision making in the daily operations of the district. There is an abundance of evidence that these decisions improve student growth and learning.
☐ Most staff do not exhibit the foundational pillars in their attitudes, behaviors, actions, or decisions.	☐ Few staff exhibit the foundational pillars in their attitudes, behaviors, actions, or decisions.	☐ Some staff exhibit the foundational pillars in their attitudes, behaviors, actions, or decisions.	☐ Most staff consistently exhibit the foundational pillars in their attitudes, behaviors, actions, or decisions.	☐ Most staff champion and advocate for alignment of all attitudes, behaviors, and decisions to the foundational pillars and motto.
	☐ When staff speak about the foundational pillars that are in place, there are often inconsistencies or misunderstandings.	☐ When staff speak about the foundational pillars that are in place, there are sometimes inconsistencies or misunderstandings.	☐ Staff speak clearly and consistently about the foundational pillars and motto both within the district and in the community.	☐ Staff speak clearly, consistently, positively, and passionately about the foundational pillars and motto both within the district and in the community.
☐ The district does not celebrate the foundational pillars that are in place.	☐ The district celebrations are not routine or connected to the foundational pillars that are in place.	☐ The district routinely has celebrations connected to the foundational pillars that are in place.	☐ The district routinely has celebrations intentionally connected to the foundational pillars.	☐ The district routinely has celebrations intentionally connected to the foundational pillars. There is evidence that these celebrations affirm and motivate staff.
				☐ The district staff routinely celebrate their colleagues when they demonstrate behaviors and actions linked to the foundational pillars.

I believe our district is at the _____ stage based on the preceding indicators. The evidence to support my rationale includes:

Source: Adapted from DuFour, R., DuFour, R., Eaker, R., Many, T. W., Mattos, M., & Muhammad, A. (2024). Learning by doing: A handbook for Professional Learning Communities at Work (4th ed.). Bloomington, IN: Solution Tree Press.

Maintaining the Work Continuum (School)

Instructions: Individually, read the indicators that describe each stage from preinitiating through sustaining. Honestly assess the current reality of the establishment of your school practices in putting together and sustaining the collective foundational pillars. Consider what evidence or anecdotes support your assessment. Record your reflections in the space provided.

Maintaining the work: The school has an aligned shared mission, vision, collective commitments, goals, and motto. These are consistently used and celebrated throughout the school to drive decision making and create a culture of collaboration to ensure student learning.

Maintaining the Work Continuum Stages				
Preinitiating	Initiating	Implementing	Developing	Sustaining
☐ Some of the foundational pillars and the motto are in place but are not aligned with a focus on student learning.	☐ Some of the foundational pillars and the motto are in place but are not aligned with a focus on student learning.	☐ Some of the foundational pillars and motto are in place and aligned with a focus on student learning.	☐ All the foundational pillars and motto are in place and aligned with a focus on student learning.	☐ All the foundational pillars and motto are in place and aligned with a focus on student learning.
☐ The mission, vision, collective commitments, goals, and motto are not utilized during decision making in the daily operations of the school.	☐ The mission, vision, collective commitments, goals, and motto are sporadically utilized during decision making in the daily operations of the school. There is little evidence that these decisions improve student growth and learning.	☐ The mission, vision, collective commitments, goals, and motto are often utilized during decision making in the daily operations of the school. There is some evidence that these decisions improve student growth and learning.	☐ The mission, vision, collective commitments, goals, and motto are consistently utilized during decision making in the daily operations of the school. There is clear evidence that these decisions improve student growth and learning.	☐ The mission, vision, collective commitments, goals, and motto are the driving force during decision making in the daily operations of the school. There is an abundance of evidence that these decisions improve student growth and learning.
☐ Most staff do not exhibit the foundational pillars in their attitudes, behaviors, actions, or decisions.	☐ Few staff exhibit the foundational pillars in their attitudes, behaviors, actions, or decisions.	☐ Some staff exhibit the foundational pillars in their attitudes, behaviors, actions, or decisions.	☐ Most staff consistently exhibit the foundational pillars in their attitudes, behaviors, actions, or decisions.	☐ Most staff champion and advocate for alignment of all attitudes, behaviors, and decisions to the foundational pillars and motto. Staff are able to describe how their daily actions support the vision and mission.
	☐ When staff speak about the foundational pillars that are in place, there are often inconsistencies or misunderstandings.	☐ When staff speak about the foundational pillars that are in place, there are sometimes inconsistencies or misunderstandings.	☐ Staff speak clearly and consistently about the foundational pillars and motto both within the school and in the community.	☐ Staff speak clearly, consistently, positively, and passionately about the foundational pillars and motto both within the school and in the community.
☐ The school does not celebrate the foundational pillars that are in place.	☐ The school celebrations are not routine or connected to the foundational pillars that are in place.	☐ The school routinely has celebrations connected to the foundational pillars that are in place.	☐ The school routinely has celebrations intentionally connected to the foundational pillars.	☐ The school routinely has celebrations intentionally connected to the foundational pillars. There is evidence that these celebrations affirm and motivate staff.
				☐ The school staff routinely celebrate their colleagues when they demonstrate behaviors and actions linked to the foundational pillars.

I believe our district is at the _____ stage based on the preceding indicators. The evidence to support my rationale includes:

Source: Adapted from DuFour, R., DuFour, R., Eaker, R., Many, T. W., Mattos, M., & Muhammad, A. (2024). Learning by doing: A handbook for Professional Learning Communities at Work (4th ed.). Bloomington, IN: Solution Tree Press.

Maintaining the Work Planning Sheet (District)

Instructions: Individually determine the stage we are in based on the descriptors on the continuum and then provide rationale for each category. Then, read over the descriptors in the sustaining section of the continuum and share potential next steps that would help us move toward the sustaining stage.

Based on the "Maintaining the Work Continuum (District)" (page 272), I believe our district is at the _____ stage.

Category	Current Stage Rationale	Potential Next Steps
Alignment		
Decision making		
Connection		
Communication		
Celebrations		

Maintaining the Work Planning Sheet (School)

Instructions: Individually reflect on the stage you chose on the continuum and provide a rationale for selecting this stage of development. Then, read over the descriptors in the sustaining section of the continuum and share potential next steps that would help us move toward the sustaining stage.

Based on the "Maintaining the Work Continuum (School)" (page 273), I believe our school is at the _____ stage.		
Category	**Current Stage Rationale**	**Potential Next Steps**
Alignment		
Decision making		
Connection		
Communication		
Celebrations		

Guiding Coalition Synthesis

Instructions: After collecting the completed "Maintaining the Work Continuum (District)" (page 272) or "Maintaining the Work Continuum (School)" (page 273), tally the feedback provided by staff for each stage. Next, synthesize and record the rationale provided for current and potential next steps. Once this is completed, use the tool "Action Plan for Our Next Steps" (page 277).

Preinitiating	Initiating	Developing	Implementing	Sustaining

Based on the results, we are currently at the _____ stage.

Category	Current Stage Rationale	Potential Next Steps
Alignment		
Decision making		
Connection		
Communication		
Celebrations		

Anchor Your Vision © 2025 Solution Tree Press • SolutionTree.com
Visit **go.SolutionTree.com/PLCbooks/AYV** and enter the unique access code found on the book's inside front cover to access this reproducible.

Action Plan for Our Next Steps

Instructions: As a guiding coalition, discuss and plan the next steps based on the "Guiding Coalition Synthesis" (page 276) to move toward the sustaining stage. Then, discuss the questions that follow.

Discussion Questions:

- What are common ideas collected from the staff reflections?

- What is an appropriate timeline to consider for the actions?

- Who will lead the next steps?

- How will we communicate our action plan with the staff?

Action Plan		
Category	Next Steps	Timeline
Alignment		
Decision making		
Connection		
Communication		
Celebrations		

Anchor Your Vision © 2025 Solution Tree Press • SolutionTree.com
Visit **go.SolutionTree.com/PLCbooks/AYV** and enter the unique access code found on the book's inside front cover to access this reproducible.

EPILOGUE

Coming together is a beginning, staying together is progress, and working together is success.

—HENRY FORD

When we attended the PLC at Work institute, DuFour asked the question that stopped us in our tracks and started us on the journey to understanding, clarifying, creating, implementing, and living out the foundational pillars. Our journey included both high and low points that provided us invaluable insight into useful processes and tools to help ourselves and later guide others in more efficiently building the foundation for their own PLC.

Today we are blessed to work with educators across the United States. When we ask them to create their trending stories in an activity where they identify what they dream for their district or school to become, we hear headlines like the following.

- "Our school leads the nation for high academic success for all students."
- "Our district is a Model PLC."
- "Parents love how our school provides individualized learning for their children."
- "There is a long line at our district job fair every year because candidates want to join our staff."
- "Our graduates return year after year to express how prepared they are for their careers or continued education thanks to the dedication and commitment to learning our teachers provided."

It is exciting to hear the passion and enthusiasm of the educators dreaming big for their districts, schools, and students. What we've learned is that turning those visions into a reality takes intentional action and a laser focus on getting clear with the collective actions to reach those dreams. Our experience within our own schools and those we work with has proven that the foundational pillars are the way to make change and achieve those aspirations.

Before leaders of a district or school see a dramatic change, they must first clarify the change needed and connect everyone they lead to the why. Inspirational leaders are able to lead teams toward fulfilling the vision, ensuring staff are living out the mission daily, upholding collective commitments, and monitoring and achieving goals. Our objective in this book was to articulate both the why and the steps for doing this work in a way that guides you and your staff through the valuable process of creating your foundational pillars efficiently and collaboratively.

Each of us went into the field of education to make a difference in the lives of students, and we know working as a PLC built on a strong foundation of a shared vision, mission, collective commitments, and goals will make an impact for *all* students. We can transform our districts and schools worldwide through this process. We know this because we see evidence of tremendous success in student achievement and growth in districts and schools that have established strong foundational pillars. These districts and schools are leaps and bounds ahead of others who appear to be similar but lack the supportive foundation to focus the organization. Although the educational system has unique challenges, it is important to remember, "What lies behind us and what lies before us are tiny matters compared to what lies within us" (Oliver Wendell Holmes as cited in Covey, 2020, p. 110). We are thrilled when we get to play even a small part in helping districts and schools connect what is within them to their PLC journey. Thank you for reading our book and choosing the most noble profession that truly impacts students for life!

You must be the change you wish to see in the world.

—GANDHI

REFERENCES AND RESOURCES

Alegre, I., Berbegal-Mirabent, J., Guerrero, A., & Mas-Machuca, M. (2018). The real mission of the mission statement: A systematic review of the literature. *Journal of Management and Organization, 24*(4), 456–473.

Allensworth, E., & Hart, H. (2018, March 12). *How do principals influence student achievement?* Accessed at www.edweek.org/leadership/opinion-how-do-principals-influence-student-achievement/2018/03 on November 3, 2023.

Barnes, J. A. (2015). *The wisdom of Walt: Leadership lessons from the happiest place on Earth.* Lake Placid, NY: Aviva.

Bart, C. K., Bontis, N., & Taggar, S. (2001). A model of the impact of mission statements on firm performance. *Management Decision, 39*(1), 19–35.

Blanchard, K. H. (2007). *Leading at a higher level: Blanchard on leadership and creating high performing organizations.* Upper Saddle River, NJ: Prentice Hall.

Brown, B. (2018). *Dare to lead: Brave work, tough conversations, whole hearts.* New York: Random House.

Buffum, A., Mattos, M., & Malone, J. (2018). *Taking action.* Bloomington, IN: Solution Tree Press.

Burchard, B. (2017). *High performance habits: How extraordinary people become that way.* Carlsbad, CA: Hay House.

Burdon, P. C., Flowers, J. D., & Manchak, S. C. (2011). *Impact of students' self-assessment and creation of personal learning targets on reading comprehension and attitudes in elementary schools* [Online submission]. Accessed at https://files.eric.ed.gov/fulltext/ED529623.pdf on January 29, 2024.

Burns, R. (2024). *63 famous company slogans and taglines.* ActiveCampaign. Accessed at www.activecampaign.com/blog/company-slogans on September 22, 2024.

Chappuis, J., & Stiggins, R. (2016). *An introduction to student-involved assessment for learning.* Hoboken, NJ: Pearson.

Coker, D. (2022). A mission statement does not a mission make: A mixed methods investigation in public education. *International Education Studies, 15*(1), 210–225. Accessed at https://doi.org/10.5539/ies.v15n1p210 on May 25, 2024.

Collins, J. (2001). *Good to great: Why some companies make the leap—and others don't.* New York: HarperBusiness.

Covey, S. R. (2004). *The 8th habit: From effectiveness to greatness.* New York: Free Press.

Covey, S. R. (2020). *The 7 habits of highly effective people* (Rev. and updated ed.). New York: Simon & Schuster.

Coyle, D. (2018). *The culture code: The secrets of highly successful groups.* New York: Bantam Books.

Coyle, D. (2022). *The culture playbook.* New York: Bantam Books.

Craig, W. (2018, May 15). *The importance of having a mission-driven company.* Accessed at www.forbes.com/sites/williamcraig/2018/05/15/the-importance-of-having-a-mission-driven-company/?sh=2c3adf053a9c on October 31, 2023.

Creswell, S. (2021, August 10). *Turning a vision into a reality* [Blog post]. Accessed at www.allthingsplc.info/blog/view/459/turning-a-vision-into-a-reality on January 30, 2024.

Cutting, D. (2022). *Employees first!: Inspire, engage, and focus on the heart of your organization.* Newburyport, MA: Career Press.

D23. (n.d.). *Disney history.* Accessed at https://d23.com/disney-history/ on September 22, 2024.

Dass, M., Kohli, C., Kumar, P., & Thomas, S. (2014). A study of the antecedents of slogan liking. *Journal of Business Research, 67*(12), 2504–2511. Accessed at https://doi.org/10.1016/j.jbusres.2014.05.004 on May 28, 2024.

Dermol, V., & Širca, N. T. (2018). Communication, company mission, organizational values, and company performance. *Procedia, 238,* 542–551. Accessed at https://doi.org/10.1016/j.sbspro.2018.04.034 on May 26, 2024.

Doten-Snitker, K., Margherio, C., Litzler, E., Ingram, E., & Williams, J. (2021, March). Developing a shared vision for change: Moving toward inclusive empowerment. *Research in Higher Education, 62*(2), 206–229.

DuFour, R. (2015). *In praise of American educators: And how they can become even better.* Bloomington, IN: Solution Tree Press.

DuFour, R., DuFour, R., Eaker, R., Many, T. W., & Mattos, M. (2016). *Learning by doing: A handbook for Professional Learning Communities at Work* (3rd ed.). Bloomington, IN: Solution Tree Press.

DuFour, R., DuFour, R., Eaker, R., Many, T. W., Mattos, M., & Muhammad, A. (2024). *Learning by doing: A handbook for Professional Learning Communities at Work* (4th ed.). Bloomington, IN: Solution Tree Press.

DuFour, R., DuFour, R., Eaker, R., Mattos, M., & Muhammad, A. (2021). *Revisiting Professional Learning Communities at Work: Proven insights for sustained, substantive school improvement* (2nd ed.). Bloomington, IN: Solution Tree Press.

DuFour, R., & Fullan, M., (2013). *Cultures build to last: Systematic PLCs at Work.* Bloomington, IN: Solution Tree Press.

DuFour, R., & Marzano, R. J. (2011). *Leaders of learning: How district, school, and classroom leaders improve student achievement.* Bloomington, IN: Solution Tree Press.

DuFour, R., & Reeves, D. (2016, March 1). The futility of PLC lite. *Kappan.* Accessed at www.kappanonline.org/the-futility-of-plc-lite on April 20, 2024.

Eaker, R., Hagadone, M., Keating, J., & Rhoades, M. (2021). *Leading PLCs at Work districtwide: From boardroom to classroom.* Bloomington, IN: Solution Tree Press.

Fogg, B. J. (2019). *Tiny habits: The small changes that change everything.* Boston: Houghton Mifflin Harcourt.

Friziellie, H., Schmidt, J. A., & Spiller, J. (2016). *Yes we can!* Bloomington, IN: Solution Tree Press.

Fullan, M. (2014). *The principal: Three keys to maximizing impact.* San Francisco: Jossey-Bass.

Fullan, M., & Quinn, J. (2016). *Coherence: The right drivers in action for schools, districts, and systems.* Thousand Oaks, CA: Corwin.

Gabriel, J. G., & Farmer, P. C. (2009). *How to help your school thrive without breaking the bank.* Alexandria, VA: ASCD.

Gordon, J. (2018). *The power of a positive team: Proven principles and practices that make great teams great.* Hoboken, NJ: Wiley.

Gorenak, M., & Košir, S. (2012). *The importance of organizational values for organization.* Accessed at www.issbs.si/press/ISBN/978-961-6813-10-5/papers/ML12_117.pdf on January 30, 2024.

Gruenert, S., & Whitaker, T. (2015). *School culture rewired: How to define, assess, and transform it.* Alexandria, VA: ASCD.

Hall, B. (2022). *Powerful guiding coalitions: How to build and sustain the leadership team in your PLC at Work.* Bloomington, IN: Solution Tree Press.

Hamel, G., & Prahalad, C. K. (1993, March–April). Strategy as stretch and leverage. *Harvard Business Review, 71*(2), 75–84.

Hattie, J. (2012). *Visible learning for teachers: Maximizing impact on learning.* London: Routledge.

Johnson & Johnson. (n.d.). *Our credo.* Accessed at www.jnj.com/our-credo on January 31, 2024.

Jones, B. (2018, February 28). *3 principles Disney uses to enhance customer experience.* Accessed at https://hbr.org/sponsored/2018/02/3-principles-disney-uses-to-enhance-customer-experience on September 22, 2024.

Kanold, T. D. (2017). *Heart!* Bloomington, IN: Solution Tree Press.

Keating, J., & Rhoades, M. (2022). A new era in district and school improvement: The critical role of the superintendent and school board. *AllThingsPLC Magazine, 7*(2), 8–14.

Kenneth, C., & Baetz, M. C. B. (1998). The relationship between mission statements and firm performance: An exploratory study. *Journal of Management Studies, 35*(6), 823–853.

Kleingeld, A., van Mierlo, H., & Arends, L. (2011). The effect of goal setting on group performance: A meta-analysis. *Journal of Applied Psychology, 96*(6), 1289–1304.

Kotter International. (2018). *8 steps to accelerate change in your organization.* Accessed at www.kotterinc.com/wp-content/uploads/2019/04/8-Steps-eBook-Kotter-2018.pdf on January 30, 2024.

Kotter, J., & Whitehead, L. (2010). *Buy-in: Saving your good idea from getting shot down.* Boston: Harvard Business Review Press.

Kouzes, J. M., & Posner, B. Z. (2006). *A leader's legacy.* San Francisco: Jossey-Bass.

Kouzes, J. M., & Posner, B. (2009). To lead, create a shared vision. *Harvard Business Review, 87*(1), 20–21. Accessed at https://hbr.org/2009/01/to-lead-create-a-shared-vision on May 17, 2024.

Kullar, J. (2022). Are you a PLC leader, a PLC lite leader, or a traditional leader? *AllThingsPLC Magazine, 7*(2), 16–21.

Latson, J. (2014, September 29). How poisoned Tylenol became a crisis-management teaching model. *Time Magazine.* Accessed at https://time.com/3423136/ on March 1, 2024.

Lencioni, P. (2016). *The ideal team player: How to recognize and cultivate the three essential virtues.* Hoboken, NJ: Wiley.

Locke, E. A., & Latham, G. P. (1990). *A theory of goal setting and task performance.* Upper Saddle River, NJ: Prentice Hall.

Locke, E. A., & Latham, G. P. (2006). New directions in goal-setting theory. *Current Directions in Psychological Science, 15*(5), 265–268.

Loewus, L. (2021, May 4). *Why teachers leave—or don't: A look at the numbers.* Accessed at www.edweek.org/teaching-learning/why-teachers-leave-or-dont-a-look-at-the-numbers/2021/05 on April 4, 2023.

Marzano, R. J., Warrick, P. B., Rains, C. L., & DuFour, R. (2018). *Leading a High Reliability School.* Bloomington, IN: Solution Tree Press.

Marzano, R. J., & Waters, T. (2009). *District leadership that works: Striking the right balance.* Bloomington, IN: Solution Tree Press.

Matthews, G. (2007). The impact of commitment, accountability, and written goals on achievement. *Psychology/Faculty Presentations.* Accessed at https://scholar.dominican.edu/cgi/viewcontent.cgi?article=1002&context=psychology-faculty-conference-presentations on May 19, 2024.

Mattos, M., DuFour R., DuFour R., Eaker, R., & Many, T. W. (2016). *Concise answers to frequently asked questions about Professional Learning Communities at Work.* Bloomington, IN: Solution Tree Press.

Maxwell, J. C. (2011). *The five levels of leadership.* New York: Hatchette Book Group.

Mayo Clinic. (n.d.). *Mayo Clinic mission and values.* Accessed at www.mayoclinic.org/about-mayo-clinic/mission-values on January 31, 2024.

McChesney, C., Covey, S., & Huling, J. (2012). *The 4 disciplines of execution: Achieving your wildly important goals.* New York: Free Press.

Miller, J. M., & Youngs, P. (2021). Person-organization fit and first-year teacher retention in the United States. *Teaching and Teacher Education, 97,* 103226. Accessed at https://doi.org/10.1016/j.tate.2020.103226 on May 28, 2024.

Mone, E., & London, M. (2018). *Employee engagement through Effective Performance Management: A practical guide for managers* (2nd ed.). New York: Routledge.

Motto. (n.d.a). In *Cambridge dictionary.* Accessed at https://dictionary.cambridge.org/us/dictionary/english/motto on January 31, 2024.

Motto. (n.d.b). In *Merriam-Webster's online dictionary.* Accessed at www.merriam-webster.com/dictionary/motto on January 31, 2024.

Muhammad, A. (2018). *Transforming school culture: How to overcome staff division* (2nd ed.). Bloomington, IN: Solution Tree Press.

National Blue Ribbon Schools. (n.d.). *About National Blue Ribbon Schools.* Accessed at https://nationalblueribbonschools.ed.gov/background/ on September 22, 2024.

Nohria, N., & Beer, M. (2000). *Cracking the code of change.* Accessed at https://hbr.org/2000/05/cracking-the-code-of-change on September 22, 2024.

Peek, S. (2023, June 22). *Management theory of Stephen Covey.* Accessed at www.business.com/articles/management-theory-of-stephen-covey/ on September 22, 2024.

Peiper, H. (2023, April 24). *A new mission for Starbucks.* Accessed at https://stories.starbucks.com/stories/2023/a-new-mission-for-starbucks/ on January 31, 2024.

Pereira, D. (2023, April 7). *Apple mission and vision statement.* Accessed at https://businessmodelanalyst.com/apple-mission-and-vision-statement on January 30, 2024.

Pew Research Center. (2016, October 6). *The state of American jobs.* Accessed at www.pewresearch.org/social-trends/2016/10/06/the-state-of-american-jobs on May 26, 2024.

Pink, D. H. (2011). *Drive: The surprising truth about what motivates us.* New York: Riverhead Books.

Robbins, P., & Alvy, H. (2004). *The new principal's fieldbook: Strategies for success.* Alexandria, VA: ASCD.

Rogala, A. (2011, January 20–22). *The influence of internal communication on different aspects of company functioning* [Conference paper]. International Marketing Trends Conference, Paris. Accessed at https://archives.marketing-trends-congress.com/2011/Materiali/Paper/Communication/Rogala.pdf on January 30, 2024.

Rotenberry, P. F., & Moberg, P. J. (2007). Assessing the impact of job involvement on performance. *Management Research News, 30*(3), 203–215.

Ryba, K. (2023, August 22). *Unpacking organizational culture.* Accessed at www.quantumworkplace.com/future-of-work/importance-of-organizational-culture-research on September 22, 2024.

Schmitt, J., & deCourcy, K. (2022). *The pandemic has exacerbated a long-standing national shortage of teachers*. Economic Policy Institute. Accessed at www.epi.org/publication/shortage-of-teachers/ on February 26, 2024.

Shavelson, R., & Borko, H. (1979). Research on teachers' decisions in planning instruction. *Educational Horizons, 57*, 183–189.

Shreim, S. (2020). *Vision, mission, values, aspirations, do they matter?* Cambridge, MA: Business Model Hackers.

Sinek, S. (2009). *Start with the why: How great leaders inspire everyone to take action*. New York: Portfolio.

Sinek, S. (2017). *Find your why: A practical guide to discovering purpose for you or your team*. New York: Portfolio.

Slåtten, T., Lien, G., Mutonyi, B. R. (2022). Promoting organizational vision integration among hospital employees. *BMC Health Services Research, 22*, 26.

Slåtten, T., Mutonyi, B. R., & Lien, G. (2021). Does organizational vision really matter? An empirical examination of factors related to organizational vision integration among hospital employees. *BMC Health Services Research, 21*, 1–17.

Stiggins, R. (2008). *An introduction to student-involved assessment for learning* (5th ed.). Upper Saddle River, NJ: Pearson.

Tony's Chocolonely. (n.d.a). *Frequently asked questions*. Accessed at https://tonyschocolonely.com/us/en/our-mission on May 17, 2024.

Tony's Chocolonely. (n.d.b). *What is Tony Chocolonely's mission?* Accessed at https://tonyschocolonely.com/us/en/frequently-asked-questions on May 17, 2024.

Tsipursky, G. (2023, July 11). *A guide to onboarding new hires (for first-time managers)*. Accessed at https://hbr.org/2023/07/a-guide-to-onboarding-new-hires-for-first-time-managers on January 30, 2024.

U.S. Embassy and Consulate in the Republic of Korea. (2017, February 21). *Martin Luther King, Jr.: I Have a Dream speech (1963)*. Accessed at https://kr.usembassy.gov/martin-luther-king-jr-dream-speech-1963 on January 30, 2024.

Wickham, N. (2023, July 6). *The importance of employee recognition: Statistics and research*. Accessed at www.quantumworkplace.com/future-of-work/importance-of-employee-recognition on October 31, 2023.

Williams, K. C., & Hierck, T. (2015). *Starting a movement: Building culture from the inside out in professional learning communities*. Bloomington, IN: Solution Tree Press.

Wright, B. E., & Pandey, S. K. (2011). Public organizations and mission valence: When does mission matter? *Administration & Society, 43*(1), 22–24.

INDEX

B
Brown, B., 122
Buffum, A., 15

C
celebrations
  celebrating the collective commitments, 133–134
  celebrating the goals, 183–184
  celebrating the mission, 31–32
  celebrating the motto, 225
  celebrating the shared vision, 92
  committing to celebrate, 8
  importance of, 246
  reproducibles for, 50, 51–53, 109–110, 157, 206, 207, 236, 237
Coker, D., 24
collective commitments
  about, 121–122
  anchors away, 134–135
  celebrating, 133–134
  common challenges to development of, 132–133
  examining the evidence of successful collective commitments, 123–126
  if-then charts, 132–133
  knowing the ropes for development of, 133
  navigating, 122–123
  professional learning communities and, xxi–xxii
  reproducibles for, 137–171
  research for developing, deep dive into, 126–127
  stages of development for, 127–132
  staying the course, 134
common language, 7
communication
  collective commitments and, 123, 127
  mission statements and, 23
  why and, 16
Covey, S., 174
Coyle, D., 244
Culture Playbook, The (Coyle), 244

D
decision making, 83–84
developing common language, 7
developing stage
  about, 3
  developing collective commitments, 131–132
  developing goals, 180–181
  developing mission statements, 28–29
  developing mottoes 223–224
  developing the shared vision, 88–89
  hiring and connecting the work, 248–249
  maintaining the work, 250
Disney, 220
Doten-Snitker, K., 83
DuFour, R., 220
DuFour, R.
  on collective commitments, 122, 123, 134
  on goals, 174
  on leadership, 255
  on mission statements, 1, 24
  on mottoes, 220
  on purpose of schools, 15
  on recognition, 246
  on vision, 81

E
Eaker, R., 220

F
foundational first steps
  clarifying loose and tight structures, 7–8
  committing to celebrate, 8
  creating guiding coalitions, 6–7
  developing common language, 7
Friziellie, H., 16
Fullan, M., 255

G
goals. *See also* SMART goals
  about, 173–174
  anchors away, 184
  celebrating, 183–184
  common challenges to development of, 182
  examining the evidence of successful goals, 176
  if-then charts, 182
  knowing the ropes for development of, 182–183
  mission statements and, 21
  navigating, 174–175
  reproducibles for, 186–216
  research for developing, deep dive into, 176–177
  stages of development for, 177–182
  staying the course, 184
Golden Circle, 16
Gordon, J., 16
Gruenert, S., 122
guiding coalitions
  creating your guiding coalition, 6–7
  reproducibles for, 47, 62–63, 67–68, 74–75, 276

H
Hall, B., 6
Heart! (Kanold), 8
hiring, connecting, and maintaining the work
  about, 241–243
  anchors away, 255
  celebrating, 253–254
  common challenges to, 251
  examining the evidence of successful hiring,

connecting, and maintaining the work, 244–245
if-then charts, 251
knowing the ropes for, 252–253
navigating, 243–244
reproducibles for, 257–277
research for, deep dive into, 245–246
stages of for hiring and connecting, 246–249
stages of for maintaining the work, 249–251
staying the course, 254–255

I
if-then charts
common challenges to developing collective commitments, 132–133
common challenges to developing goals, 182
common challenges to developing the mission, 30
common challenges to developing mottoes, 224–225
common challenges to developing the shared vision, 91
common challenges to hiring, connecting, and maintaining the work, 251
implementing stage
about, 3
developing collective commitments, 130–131
developing goals, 179–180
developing mission statements, 27–28
developing mottoes, 222–223
developing the shared vision, 87–88
hiring and connecting the work, 247–248
maintaining the work, 250
In Praise of American Educators: And How They Can Become Even Better (DuFour), 134
Ingram, E., 83
initiating stage
about, 3
developing collective commitments, 129–130
developing goals, 178–179
developing mission statements, 26–27
developing mottoes, 222
developing the shared vision, 87
hiring and connecting the work, 247
maintaining the work, 249–250
introduction
foundational first steps, 6–8
how to navigate this book, 5–6
impact of the PLC process, 1–2
reproducibles for, 9–11
in this book, 3–5
who this book is for, 2–3

K
Kanold, T., 8
Kotter, J., 6–7
Kotter International, 15
Kullar, J., 38, 41

L
Learning by Doing (DuFour), 24, 246
Lencioni, P., 259
Litzler, E., 83
loose and tight structures, clarifying, 7–8

M
Many, T., 220
Margherio, C., 83
Marzano, R., 15, 174
Mattos, M., 220
Mayo Clinic, 124–125
mission. *See also* collective commitments
about, 19–20
anchors away, 32
celebrating, 31–32
common challenges to development of, 30
examining the evidence of a successful mission, 22–23
if-then charts, 30
knowing the ropes for development of, 31
navigating, 20–21
reproducibles for, 34–76
research for developing, deep dive into, 23–24
stages of development for, 24–30
staying the course, 32
mottoes
about, 219–220
anchors away, 226
celebrating, 225
common challenges to development of, 224–225
definition of, 230, 231, 238
examining the evidence of successful mottoes, 220–221
if-then charts, 224–225
knowing the ropes for development of, 225
navigating, 220
our why, 14
reproducibles for, 228–239
research for developing, deep dive into, 221
stages of development for, 221–224
staying the course, 226

P
PLC lite, 6
preinitiating stage
about, 3
developing collective commitments, 128–129
developing goals, 178
developing mission statements, 25–26
developing mottoes, 221
developing the shared vision, 86–87
hiring and connecting the work, 247
maintaining the work, 249
professional learning communities (PLCs)
clarifying loose and tight structures and, 7–8
collective commitments and, xxi–xxii
creating your guiding coalition and, 6–7
developing a common language and, 7
foundation of, xxi
impact of the PLC process, 1–2
PLC lite, 6
why we can't skip this step, 15

R
Rains, C., 15
reproducibles for
acknowledgement survey, 170
action plan for our next steps, 277
analyzing the power of a motto, 232, 233, 239
applicant interview rubric, 266
beliefs and collective commitments sort, 146
beliefs to commitments, 147, 148
celebration jot, 171
celebration planning, 50, 157, 237
celebrations survey, 236
collective commitments continuum, 137
collective commitments violations, 156
collective commitments wishlists, 144, 145
creating rituals and celebrations, 206
criteria-based interview questions, 264–265
data analysis to identify department goals, 208
data analysis to identify teacher goals, 210
data analysis to identify team goals, 209
data picture of our district, 192–193

data picture of our school, 194–195
drafting collective commitments, 150–152
evidence of action, 163
evidence of impact, 117, 118
example beliefs to commitments, 149
foundation of our district or school—example, 269
foundation of _____, 270, 271
fulfilling our collective commitments, 164, 165
goals continuum, 186, 187
goals surveys, 202–203, 204–205
goals to impact student learning, 188–189, 190–191
guiding coalition analysis—developing stage, 67–68
guiding coalition analysis—implementing stage, 62–63
guiding coalition analysis—sustaining stage, 74–75
guiding coalition mission formalization, 47
guiding coalition synthesis, 276
hiring and connecting new staff continuum, 257, 258
hiring committee application, 259
hiring committee professional commitments and norms, 260
investigating and creating the mission statement, 45–46
maintaining the work continuum, 272, 273
maintaining the work planning sheets, 274, 275
mission continuum, 34, 35–36
mission in action and parent celebration certificates, 51–53
mission proposal and adoption (step 1), 48
mission proposal and adoption (step 2), 49
mission sort, 44
mission survey analysis, 58, 59
mission surveys, 54–55, 56–57
motto continuum, 228
motto sort, 229
my dreams for you, 142–143
new hire onboarding, 261–262
one word, 234
planning to celebrate, 109–110, 207
power of a mission statement, 38–40, 41–43
power of a motto, 230, 231, 238
power of collective commitments, 138–139, 140–141

power of a shared vision, 96–97, 98–99
proposal and adoption (step 1), 107
proposal and adoption (step 2), 108
ratification survey, 153–155
recognition nomination, 158
reference question examples, 267, 268
school action plan—developing stage, 69
school action plan—implementing stage, 64
school action plan—sustaining stage, 76
screening criteria for a vacancy, 263
setting our district department or school team goals, 216
staff feedback, 159, 160
staff reflections—developing stage, 65, 66
staff reflections—implementing stage, 60, 61
staff reflections—sustaining stage, 70–71, 72–73
status surveys, 166–167, 168–169
student SMART goals, 213–214
synthesizing the "one word," 235
taking ownership, 161–162
teacher SMART goals, 211–212
team accountability partners, 215
tool: key vocabulary sort, 9–11
trending stories, 100–101, 102–103
trending stories analysis, 104–106
using our data part 1: studying our data, 196, 197
using our data part 2: setting our goals, 198, 199
using our data part 3: goals action plan, 200, 201
vision continuum, 94
vision sort, 95
vision survey analysis, 115, 116
vision surveys, 111–112, 113–114
what's my why, 37
Revisiting Professional Learning Communities at Work: Proven Insights for Sustained, Substantive School Improvement (DuFour), 122
Ryba, K., 8

S
Schmidt, J., 16
School Culture Rewired: How to Define, Assess, and Transform It (Gruenert and Whitaker), 122
Sinek, S., 2, 15, 16
SMART goals. *See also* goals
  about, 175

examining the evidence of successful goals, 176
reproducibles for, 211–212, 213–214
Spiller, J., 16
Starbucks, 123–124
Start With Why (Sinek), 16
sustaining stage
  about, 3
  developing collective commitments, 132
  developing goals, 181–182
  developing mission statements, 29–30
  developing mottoes, 224
  developing the shared vision, 89–90
  hiring and connecting the work, 249
  maintaining the work, 250–251

T
Taking Action (Buffum), 15
Tony's Chocolonely, 81–82

U
ultimate why, 16
universal why, 14–15

V
values. *See* collective commitments
vision. *See also* collective commitments
  about, 79–80
  anchors away, 92
  celebrating, 92
  common challenges to development of, 90–91
  examining the evidence of a successful vision, 81–82
  examples of, 85
  if-then charts, 91
  knowing the ropes for development of, 91
  navigating, 80–81
  reproducibles for, 94–118
  research for developing, deep dive into, 82–84
  stages of development for, 84–90
  staying the course, 92

W
Warrick, P., 15
Whitaker, T., 122
why
  about, 13
  anchors away, 16–17
  our why, 13–14
  ultimate why, 16
  universal why, 14–15
  why we can't skip this step, 15–16
Wickham, N., 8
Williams, J., 83

Z
Zach Elementary, 126

Learning By Doing, Fourth Edition
Richard DuFour, Rebecca DuFour, Robert Eaker, Thomas W. Many, Mike Mattos, and Anthony Muhammad
In this fourth edition of the bestseller *Learning by Doing*, the authors use updated research and time-tested knowledge to address current education challenges, from learning gaps exacerbated by the COVID-19 pandemic to the need to drive a highly effective multitiered system of supports.
BKG169

Training Teacher Leaders in a PLC at Work®
Jasmine K. Kullar
In this book, author Jasmine K. Kullar empowers teacher leadership teams with the knowledge to implement the PLC process successfully while developing ten essential leadership skills that will help influence their colleagues to advance student achievement.
BKG201

The Teacher Team Leader Handbook
Chad M. V. Dumas
Education expert and award-winning researcher Chad M. V. Dumas provides teacher team leaders with clarity on their role and approach, accompanied by actions that help teams get going, gain momentum, overcome obstacles, and refine skills that maximize their effectiveness in professional learning communities.
BKG210

The 15-Day Challenge
Maria Nielsen
The 15-Day Challenge offers a step-by-step process for collaborative teams that builds on the three big ideas and four critical questions of a PLC at Work®. In each chapter, you'll find practical actions for how to support all students in mastering essential learning standards.
BKF969

Beyond PLC Lite
Anthony R. Reibel, Troy Gobble, Mark Onuscheck, and Eric Twadell
Move your school teams beyond "PLC Lite" with ten evidence-based actions that will center student agency and efficacy in curriculum, assessment, instruction, and intervention practices. Gain access to rubrics, protocols, and templates designed to build a culture of continuous improvement.
BKF913

Solution Tree | Press *a division of* Solution Tree

Visit SolutionTree.com or call 800.733.6786 to order.

Wait! Your professional development journey doesn't have to end with the last pages of this book.

We realize improving student learning doesn't happen overnight. And your school or district shouldn't be left to puzzle out all the details of this process alone.

No matter where you are on the journey, we're committed to helping you get to the next stage.

Take advantage of everything from **custom workshops** to **keynote presentations** and **interactive web and video conferencing**. We can even help you develop an action plan tailored to fit your specific needs.

Let's get the conversation started.

Call 888.763.9045 today.

solution-tree.com